# KAISER WILHELM II
## *Germany's Last Emperor*

*John Van der Kiste*

SUTTON PUBLISHING

First published in the United Kingdom in 1999 by
Sutton Publishing Limited · Phoenix Mill · Thrupp · Stroud
Gloucestershire

Paperback edition first published 2001

British Library Cataloguing-in-Publication Data

A catalogue record for this book is available from the British Library.

ISBN 0 7509 2736 4

Typeset in 10/12pt New Baskerville.
Typesetting and origination by
Sutton Publishing Limited.
Printed and bound in Great Britain by
J.H. Haynes & Co. Ltd, Sparkford.

# Contents

# *Preface*

Some twenty years ago I wrote my first full-length book, a biography of Kaiser Friedrich III. For several years I had been fascinated by the personality of this enigmatic, little-known, tragic ruler and his wife, Queen Victoria's eldest daughter. I was equally intrigued by the personality of their eldest son Wilhelm, Friedrich's successor, and just as much by the different, even contradictory, perceptions of him in almost every book I read. During his reign Wilhelm was spoken of indulgently as the man who wanted to be the bride at every wedding and the corpse at every funeral. One of the shrewdest judges of character of the time, his uncle King Edward VII called him 'the most brilliant failure in history'.

After Wilhelm's abdication, the most hated man in Europe, he was later rehabilitated; alongside the demon Hitler, he seemed mild indeed. Nobody, Winston Churchill wrote in an admirably understanding essay in the 1930s, should judge the Kaiser's career without asking the question, 'What should I have done in his position?' The future prime minister – who was to offer Wilhelm a safe haven in England a few years later – saw him as a solitary human figure raised by an accident of birth to be the ruler of a mighty nation, placed far above the status of ordinary mortals.[1] When he died in June 1941, the historian G.P. Gooch paid tribute in the *Contemporary Review* to 'an unsubstantial ghost', whose patriotism was beyond challenge and intentions excellent, 'but he never realised his unfitness to rule'. He called the Kaiser one of the vainest of men, but a good husband and to whose name no scandals clung; he also said Wilhelm was 'entirely free from the virus of anti-Semitism'.[2] This judgment, verging on the hagiographical, presented the image his surviving relatives wished to perpetuate. Broadly in line with Churchill's verdict, it stood more or less unchallenged for about another four decades. In June 1974 the Monarchist League placed an announcement in the In Memoriam column of *The Times*: 'His deposition made Nazism inevitable.'[3]

Was this the full truth about the Kaiser, the ruler who was partly English by birth, sometimes ardently pro-English in his sympathies, yet a personification of Prussian militarism at its worst? Was he just the handicapped child who became an expert shot and horseman, the grandson who adored and revered Queen Victoria though he occasionally made fun of her, the virtuous, God-fearing, faithful husband and devoted father? Or was he the cruel and disloyal son who alternately mocked his mother and accused her of treason; the bisexual philanderer who indulged in illicit liaisons behind his doting wife's back and terrified his sons when he was at home; the warlord who spoke of cutting down his enemies without mercy in speech after speech while seen by his entourage and family as a weak and cowardly figure behind the bombast and bluster?

As a subject for biography he has been well, even indulgently, served by the sympathetic scholarship of Michael Balfour in *The Kaiser and his Times* (1964). Balfour saw in him a sovereign who claimed to be a leader while 'in fact he followed others and allowed himself to be moulded by his environment instead of impressing his personality upon it'. Instead of blaming him for the catastrophe of 'the Kaiser's war', he asks, 'should not one blame instead the system which could assign so onerous a post to someone who had so little chance of filling it with credit?'[4] Tyler Whittle's similarly impartial *The Last Kaiser* (1977) was hailed by some authorities in Germany, alongside J. Daniel Chamier's *Fabulous Monster* (1934), as evidence that only English writers had the necessary imagination and freedom from prejudice to recognize him as the 'tragic hero' that he was.[5] The Kaiser was lucky to have such faithful guardians of his reputation, but since then a darker picture has emerged.

By this time the 'Fischer controversy' of 1961 had broken the patriotic self-censorship policy by accepting the significance of the *Kriegsrat* of December 1912 and thus established beyond reasonable doubt that Germany's aims in the First World War had been broadly similar to those pursued under Hitler, and that she bore a major share of responsibility for causing that earlier conflict.* It followed that the central figure at the apex of Wilhelmine Germany, while not the autocrat he fondly imagined himself to be, was himself therefore somewhat responsible. The pendulum of condemnation that pointed the finger at him for being at least partly to blame for starting 'the Kaiser's war', which had moved away from him in a period of impartial reflection, was swinging back. By the 1970s the tougher, more penetrating scholarship of John Röhl, whose recent discovery of other papers, notably the original diaries of three of the Kaiser's confidantes, helped to pave the way for a more honest if less kindly portrait of the Kaiser. Count Robert von Zedlitz-Trütschler, the Kaiser's court marshal from 1900 to 1912, had published selections from his diary as long ago as 1923. Though the full version has never been discovered, these edited extracts were so damning that one commentator referred to them as the vengeful courtier's 'spitoon', thus leading one to

* See p. 156.

wonder what had been withheld. The Kaiser's head of the naval cabinet, Admiral Georg von Müller, left journals published posthumously in two volumes in 1959 and 1965, but he had doctored them carefully himself in the 1920s and the editor had also prudently removed certain passages from the final edition. Finally Captain Sigurd von Ilsemann, the Kaiser's adjutant in exile, left two similar volumes published in German a little later, from which several damning paragraphs were omitted at the request of the Hohenzollern family immediately prior to publication. 'It always makes me quite ill to hear the Kaiser speak in this manner. What would the judgment of history be if the public were to learn of such talk?'[6] read one such entry, referring to an anti-Semitic tirade, for July 1927.

The turning point came in 1977 when Professor Röhl and Nicolaus Sombart jointly directed a seminar at the University of Freiburg on 'Kaiser Wilhelm II as a Cultural Phenomenon'. Two years later Röhl and Sombart and a group of other historians gathered at Corfu to debate and present papers on the Kaiser, his influence on Germany's policies, and his relationship to contemporary German society. No biographer of the Kaiser can fail to acknowledge the great debt to their pioneering studies which resulted from these. As well as Röhl's researches, mention must also be made of the magisterial two-volume work by Lamar Cecil of the character whom he calls 'an exceedingly foolish man, so that to explain – and sometimes merely to relate – what he did or said reduces a biographer to the greatest perplexity,'[7] and of Hannah Pakula's biography of the Empress Frederick, the most detailed and penetrating account yet of this much misunderstood, tragic figure. Significantly, the new primary material in these books, while adding much to our understanding of the Kaiser, reinforces the impression that Balfour's and Whittle's assessments erred on the side of generosity.

Strangely, some contemporary German historians took it upon themselves to argue that 'everything worth knowing' about the Kaiser and his Court had been discovered long ago, that a preoccupation with such matters was dangerously retrogressive and 'personalistic', and to emphasize the monarchical aspects of Wilhelmine political culture was to be 'historicist' and to weaken the relevance of historical study to an understanding of contemporary politics.[8] Such arguments may be the natural corollary of Marxist historians who dispute the effect of monarchs on the events and society of their time, but not of those who would rather accept Thomas Carlyle's verdicts that 'history is the essence of innumerable biographies', and that 'the history of the world is but the biography of great men' (and also men whose greatness is disputed).

By any standards the contradictory, baffling, larger-than-life personality of Kaiser Wilhelm II is one that cries out for continued study. The eldest grandchild of Queen Victoria and the Prince Consort was one in a succession of modern German figures who sought to raise Prussia to pre-eminence in, if not total domination of, Europe, in a line that began with Bismarck and could be followed through Wilhelm II to Hitler and Köhl. On the threshold of the millennium, one would do well to remember the former Kaiser's words in a letter to his last surviving sister (3 November 1940), looking forward to 'the *U.S. of Europe* under German leadership, a united European Continent',* and compare them with the writings (May 1940) of Herr Clodius, Deputy Director of the German Foreign Ministry, of a vision for a new Europe which he called 'a Greater Germany', and those of German Chancellor Helmut Köhl (September 1995) in a speech to the Council of Europe, calling for 'the political union of Europe' and affirming in his view that 'if there is no monetary union then there cannot be political union, and vice versa'.[9]

With regard to the use of English and German names, I have followed the modern style of reader recognition rather than consistency. Therefore the subject of this book is Wilhelm rather than William, and his father Friedrich rather than Frederick, while his mother is referred to by her English rather than German names. To avoid confusion between the German and Austrian sovereigns, Wilhelm and his predecessors are 'Kaiser' throughout, while Franz Josef and his successor Karl are 'Emperor'.

I wish to acknowledge the gracious permission of Her Majesty The Queen to publish certain material of which she owns the copyright; and the kind permission of Ian Shapiro, at Argyll Etkin Ltd, and of Dale Headington, at Regal Reader, for the use of previously unpublished manuscript material. My friends Karen Roth, Shirley Stapley, Theo Aronson, Roman Golicz, Robert Hopkins and Robin Piguet have been unstinting in their advice, encouragement and supply or loan of various materials for research. The staff of Kensington & Chelsea Borough Public Library have again been kind enough to allow me the run of their incomparable reserve biography collection. Last but not least, thanks are due to my mother, Kate Van der Kiste, for reading through the draft manuscript and recommending countless improvements in both content and clarity, and to my editors, Jaqueline Mitchell and Alison Flowers, for helping to see the finished work through to publication.

* See p. 223.

# List of Plates

The plates are between pp. 116 and 117.

1. Prince and Princess Friedrich Wilhelm
2. Prince Wilhelm
3. Kaiser Wilhelm I
4. Queen Victoria and Queen Augusta
5. Prince Otto von Bismarck
6. Crown Prince Friedrich Wilhelm
7. Kaiser Wilhelm II
8. Empress Augusta Victoria
9. Charlotte, Hereditary Princess of Saxe-Meiningen
10. King Edward VII
11. Count Philipp von Eulenburg
12. Prince Bernhard von Bülow
13. The children of Kaiser Wilhelm II
14. The Empress Frederick
15. Crown Prince Wilhelm
16. Crown Princess Wilhelm
17. Empress Augusta Victoria
18. Kaiser Wilhelm II
19. Princess Victoria Louise
20. Prince and Princess Henry of Prussia
21. Kaiser Wilhelm II
22. Admiral Alfred von Tirpitz
23. Kaiser Wilhelm II and King George V
24. 'Swollen-headed William'
25. General Paul von Hindenburg
26. General Erich von Ludendorff
27. Kaiser Wilhelm II with an aide-de-camp at Doorn
28. Kaiser Wilhelm II with an aide-de-camp at Doorn
29. Kaiser Wilhelm II in old age
30. Empress Hermine

xi

CHAPTER ONE

# The Young Prince

Prince Friedrich Wilhelm of Prussia was born on 18 October 1831 in the Neue Palais, Potsdam. He was the first child of Wilhelm, second in line to the throne of Prussia after his father, King Friedrich Wilhelm III, and eldest brother, Crown Prince Friedrich Wilhelm, and Augusta, daughter of the Grand Duke of Saxe-Weimar.

Wilhelm and Augusta had been married in June 1829. For some time he had been in love with Princess Elise Radziwill, a member of the Polish aristocracy deemed of insufficiently noble birth to marry a Hohenzollern of Prussia. Having declared solemnly that he would never give his heart to another, the Prince obediently proposed to Augusta, who accepted him with a dutiful lack of enthusiasm that matched his own. He was a Prussian soldier through and through, while she had been brought up at the liberal court of Weimar, devoted to music, literature and art. Those who knew her well predicted, all too accurately, that her life in philistine Prussia would not be happy.

Husband and wife had little in common, and by the time of their son's birth they had developed such a mutual aversion that they were leading almost separate lives. It was impossible for them to stay in the same room for long without quarrelling. Though the heir apparent, Wilhelm's elder brother and his wife Elizabeth, had not managed to produce a child, Wilhelm and Augusta showed no undue concern with ensuring the succession. Seven years later, in December 1838, a daughter named Louise was born, and Augusta declared that she had fulfilled her marital duty. In June 1840 King Friedrich Wilhelm III died after a reign of forty-three years. His eldest son succeeded him, taking the title of Friedrich Wilhelm IV. As heir apparent, Wilhelm assumed the title of Prince of Prussia and his eight-year-old son became heir presumptive.

Prince Friedrich Wilhelm, or 'Fritz', as the family called him throughout his life, was a lonely child. His unimaginative father only took a perfunctory interest in him, adamant that he should grow up to be a good soldier but little more. A conventional upbringing was supervised by nurses and governesses until the age of seven, when he was entrusted to a military governor and tutor. Always closer to his mother, he took after her in many ways, particularly in his love of reading and later a liberal outlook on the issues of the day. When he was eighteen he

1

astonished the reactionary General Leopold von Gerlach, who had told him how he envied the young man his youth 'for he would no doubt survive the end of the absurd Constitutionalism. He was of opinion that a representation of the people would become a necessity, and I endeavoured to make it clear to him that Constitutionalism did not necessarily follow upon the absence of Absolutism.'[1]

In August 1845 Queen Victoria of England and Prince Albert visited the Prussian royal family at Aachen and were guests of honour at a special banquet. Thirteen months later Augusta was invited to stay with them for a week at Windsor. Acquaintance soon ripened into mutual friendship, and with it Albert's vision, inspired largely by his Uncle Leopold, King of the Belgians, and mentor Baron Christian von Stockmar, of a Prussia allied to Britain, at the head of a united, constitutional Germany. Who better to reign over this Greater Germany than their friend's son Friedrich, as King or even Kaiser, and his consort – their beloved eldest child 'Vicky', Victoria, Princess Royal?

In May 1851 Prince Albert's Great Exhibition, a tribute to the industrial and artistic skills of peacetime Britain and her empire, opened in London. Taking their pride of place as guests were the Prince of Prussia, who had come with great reluctance, his wife and son. The ten-year-old Princess Royal was something of a child prodigy. Almost as soon as she could read she was fluent in French and German as well as English, and she shared her father's intellectual, artistic and political interests. She acted as a very knowledgeable guide as she showed Friedrich around the exhibits. By the time he and his parents were back in Berlin, he was as firm in his Anglophile inclinations as his mother. While he could hardly have been in love with the vivacious youngster who had escorted him around with such enthusiasm, he must have realized that a tentative future was being planned for him by the elder generation.

In September 1855 Friedrich was invited to Britain again, this time without his parents, to stay with Queen Victoria and the family at Balmoral, their Scottish Highland home. He had parental permission to propose to the princess, now a very forward fourteen year old, and probably did not dare to return home without having done so. On 29 September they all went out riding with the young couple lagging behind. Friedrich picked a sprig of white heather as an emblem of good luck, telling Victoria nervously as he presented it to her that he hoped she would come to stay with him in Prussia – always. On the day after his departure, Albert wrote to tell Baron Stockmar of the week's events, adding that the young people were 'ardently in love with one another, and the purity, innocence, and unselfishness of the young man have been on his part equally touching'.[2]

As the bride-to-be was still so young, there was no question of an immediate official announcement of the engagement, though disapproving tongues wagged in Berlin and the news leaked out within a few days. In a leading article (3 October) *The Times* attacked the engagement as 'unfortunate', calling Prussia a 'wretched German state', and the Hohenzollerns 'a paltry German dynasty'. When the betrothal was announced to the courts of Europe in April 1856 a rising young conservative politician, Otto Bismarck, then Prussian representative at the German *Bundestag* in Frankfurt, summed up the prevailing view in Berlin in a letter to General Gerlach: 'If the Princess can leave the Englishwoman at home and become a Prussian, then she may be a blessing to the country. If our future Queen on the Prussian throne remains the least bit English, then I see our Court surrounded by English influence. . . . What will it be like when the first lady in the land is an Englishwoman?'[3]

The wedding was scheduled to take place in January 1858, two months after the bride's seventeenth birthday. In Berlin the Court had taken it for granted that their future King would lead his consort up the aisle there. Queen Victoria had decided otherwise, as she informed Lord Clarendon, her Secretary of State for Foreign Affairs (25 October 1857): 'Whatever may be the usual practice of Prussian princes, it is not *every* day that one marries the eldest daughter of the Queen of England. The question therefore must be considered as settled and closed.'[4] Three months later to the day, Monday 25 January 1858, families and guests gathered in the chapel at St James's Palace where Prince Friedrich Wilhelm, just promoted to the rank of major-general of the Prussian First Infantry Regiment of Guards, led his trembling bride, radiant in a dress of white silk trimmed with Honiton lace, to the altar. After a two-day honeymoon at Windsor Castle for the couple, 'two young innocent things – almost too shy to talk to one another'[5] in the bride's words, they returned to Buckingham Palace to join the family again, and then to Gravesend for their departure on the yacht *Victoria and Albert* to Prussia.

They entered Berlin on 8 February, a bitterly cold day. Wearing a low-cut dress without any wrap or coat for extra warmth, the quietly shivering Princess immediately disarmed Queen Elizabeth of Prussia, who had had no enthusiasm for her nephew's 'English marriage'. She asked the girl if she was not frozen. 'Completely, except for my heart, which is warm,' was the tactful answer. They settled in the Berlin Schloss, a shock for a young woman so used to English standards of comfort and cleanliness. There was a constant stench of bad drains, no bathrooms or running water, the beds were infested with bugs and long-disused rooms were knee-deep with dead bats. The Princess's in-laws were an unwelcoming, unprepossessing crowd, from the prematurely senile King, the embittered Anglophobe Queen Elizabeth, the ever-bickering regent and his wife, to the loud-mouthed, heel-clicking princes who unashamedly regarded their wives as second-class citizens, brood mares and nothing more.

By early summer the Princess was expecting a child. Neither of the prospective grandmothers seemed to be pleased, Queen Victoria rather ungraciously calling it 'horrid news' which made her 'feel certain almost it will all end in nothing'.[6] The Princess was unwell throughout autumn and winter, but her physician Dr Wegner refused to believe there were grounds for concern, as did Queen Victoria's own physician, Dr James Clark, when he was sent to examine her. He insisted blandly that everything would revert to normal once the baby was born. Only her experienced midwife, Mrs Innocent, had any idea of the horrors in store. Arriving in Berlin soon after Christmas 1858, she took one look at the expectant princess and feared that they were 'in for trouble.'[7]

Precisely what happened at Unter den Linden at the childbed of Princess Friedrich Wilhelm of Prussia will probably never be known. Amid all the conflicting accounts of events, only one thing can be said with certainty – that the doctors and physicians were retrospectively involved to a considerable degree in covering up a mismanaged birth which nearly cost the lives of mother and child. The assertion that Queen Victoria distrusted most of the German doctors and sent Dr Eduard Martin, a German accoucheur who had however proved his ability by attending her own last pregnancy in 1857, is less likely than the theory that Prince Wilhelm took Baron Stockmar's advice and engaged the services of Dr Martin, at that time chief of obstetrics at the University of Berlin, as the man best qualified to assist. There was evidently some professional jealousy between both men, and Wegner, more courtier than physician, hesitated to jeopardize the sensibilities of his royal patient by conducting the necessary examination[8] – even at the risk of letting nature take its course by allowing her and her child to die. Mortality in childbirth was not uncommon, and it was unlikely that his professional reputation in Berlin would have been damaged if this had been the outcome.*

When the Princess's labour began shortly before midnight on 26 January, Dr Wegner, Dr Clark, at least one other German doctor

---

* Queen Victoria owed her place on the British throne, if not indeed her entire existence, to such a tragedy. In November 1817 Princess Charlotte of Wales, wife of Prince Leopold of Saxe-Coburg (now King Leopold of the Belgians), had died in giving birth to a stillborn son.

(though no names have been mentioned in subsequent reports and accounts), the midwife, Countess Blücher and Countess Perponcher, a lady of the bedchamber, were on hand, and the father-to-be was also present. Countess Blücher, an Englishwoman married to a German, was a confidante of Queen Victoria, Princess Augusta, and one of the few women in Berlin whom Princess Friedrich Wilhelm could trust implicitly. It was evidently thanks to the Countess that the mother-to-be had a badly needed crash course in the 'intimacies' of childbirth that Queen Victoria, with her disgust for anatomical details, had never been able to bring herself to impart to her daughter. Wegner scribbled a note summoning Dr Martin at once, but it was given to a servant who posted it instead of delivering it by hand – whether out of carelessness or for more sinister reasons was never established.[9] As a result it did not reach Dr Martin's residence until 8 a.m. the next day, after he had already left on his rounds. Two hours later he was getting into his carriage for the university lecture hall when he received the note with the rest of his morning mail. Simultaneously another footman appeared, summoning him to the palace at once.

To his horror Dr Martin found Dr Wegner and his German colleague or colleagues in a corner of the room while the distraught Prince Friedrich Wilhelm held his semi-conscious wife in his arms, having put a handkerchief into her mouth several times to prevent her from grinding her teeth and biting herself.[10] One of the doctors told him resignedly, in English, that it was no use, 'the Princess and her child are dying'.[11] At the sound of voices the Princess opened her eyes, and from her expression Dr Martin was convinced that she had understood. It was thanks to his grim determination that the mother lived, as did the son to whom she gave birth minutes later. Statistically the odds had been heavily against him. That same year, 98 per cent of German babies born in the breech position, as this one was, were stillborn.[12]

'In truth I could not go through such another',[13] Dr Clark wrote to Queen Victoria later that week. The young mother wrote to Queen Victoria that Dr Wegner had showed 'a great deal of tact, discretion, feeling during the whole time . . . but I do not know what I should have done without Sir James', while as for Dr Martin, to whom she had initially taken a violent dislike, he was 'an excellent man & I feel the greatest confidence in his skill', but she could never absolve him completely from blame for the 'bungling way' in which she was treated.[14] Wegner claimed the credit for bringing her and her son through the whole business, which he hardly deserved. Exhausted by her ordeal, she was confined to bed for a month. By the time she had recovered, it was too long after the event for her to realize who had genuinely saved her life. Some sixty years later, a war-weary continent might have had good reason to rue the doctors' devotion to duty, at least where their part in saving the baby was concerned.

At 3 p.m. 101 salutes were fired to announce the arrival of a new prince, third in line to the throne of Prussia. Newspaper editors in their offices had been alerted to the potential tragedy nearby by a messenger sent by the despairing doctors. Only as the echoes died away did they realize that Her Royal Highness Princess Friedrich Wilhelm's obituary could be put on hold. Meanwhile, crowds stood around in the falling snow, patiently awaiting the news. In his excitement the war veteran Field-Marshal Wrangel strode out on to the palace balcony to tell them optimistically that the infant was 'as sturdy a little recruit as heart could wish to see!'.[15]

Dr Martin's grim report, written a fortnight later, was closer to the truth when he called the baby 'seemingly dead to a high degree'.[16] All the doctors concentrated on trying to save the mother. Her child was handed to a German midwife, Fraulein Stahl, who repeatedly smacked the tiny bundle until his lungs began to function and he started crying. Wrapped carefully in his layette, he was then presented to his paternal grandparents and a circle of courtiers who admired him and congratulated the shattered father on having ensured the succession for another generation.

Three or four days after the birth Mrs Innocent drew Dr Martin's attention to the baby's left arm, hanging lifelessly from the shoulder socket. The father was told at once. When he asked the German doctors, they reassured him that the damage was only temporary paralysis which would improve with a little gentle massage at first, followed by exercises at a later stage.

What was the effect of the child's disability on his subsequent character? In his own memoirs, written and published sixty-seven years hence, he noted with admirable sang-froid that his arm 'had received an injury unnoticed at the time, which proved permanent and impeded its free movement'.[17] Even when he was an adult it remained about 6 in shorter than the right. Adorned with heavy rings, the hand was perfectly formed and looked healthy apart from an ugly brown mole, but it was too weak to grip or hold anything heavier than a piece of paper. It would just go into his coat pocket, where he could keep it out of sight. Throughout his life few photographs showed his left arm clearly, let alone the hand; from an early age, the art of concealing it from the camera lens became second nature to him. At meals he could not manage an ordinary knife and fork, but his bodyguard always carried a special combined one, while the person sitting next to him discreetly cut up his food. As if to compensate, his right hand had an iron grip, something he would often exploit as an adult when greeting people for the first time with a vice-like handshake, sadistically turning the rings on his fingers inwards first so as to add to the other person's discomfort. If these men or women were English, he laughed heartily at their winces as he made jibes about 'the mailed fist'.

The injuries were not confined to an undeveloped hand. His neck had also been damaged at birth – as the arm and hand muscles and nerves were all torn from the vertebral column in the neck during the final stages of delivery, his head was tilted abnormally to the left, and the cervical nerve plexus was subsequently damaged. The hearing labyrinth of the left ear was defective, resulting in partial deafness from childhood and lifelong problems with balance, probably as a result of damage to part of the brain closest to the inner ear. Throughout adolescence and early manhood he suffered from alarming growths and inflammations of the inner ear, and at the age of forty-seven he underwent a major operation which left him deaf in the right ear as well.[18]

A theory that lack of oxygen in the first few minutes of life caused some degree of irreversible brain damage can neither be proved nor ruled out. In the case of a child whose closest antecedents numbered at least two cases of severe mental instability, it was a worrying possibility. Perhaps one can attach undue importance to the fact that the boy's great-great grandfathers, Tsar Paul of Russia on his father's side, and King George III of England on that of his mother, had been considered insane in their latter years, as well as the fact that the then King of Prussia, the boy's childless great-uncle, King Friedrich Wilhelm IV, was likewise so mentally enfeebled by this time that he had little perception of events around him. Nevertheless the theory of brain damage, or insanity, if not a disquieting combination of both, cannot be disregarded. Not for many years was King George III's 'madness' more correctly ascribed to a combination of senile dementia and porphyria, an inherited constitutional metabolic disorder which, recent evidence suggests, may have been passed down to the Princess, and in turn to her eldest daughter and possibly this eldest son as well. When Prince Friedrich Wilhelm and his father were told of the baby's disability, the unsympathetic grandfather remarked coldly that he was not sure whether congratulations on the birth of a defective Prince were in order.[19]

'What epithet history will attach to his name is in the lap of the gods,' the Prince Consort wrote rather ponderously to his daughter in March; 'not Rufus if your wishes come true, not The Conqueror, perhaps "the Great"? There is none with this designation . . . we have had "the Silent", but that should not mean that your son will be a chatterbox.'[20] As an adult Wilhelm would have surely felt 'the Great' was an appropriate designation, but as Kaiser of Europe's most aggressive military power he would never be able to lay claim to that of 'the Conqueror', and rarely would a monarch be less deserving of 'the Silent'. 'Chatterbox' proved more prophetic.

With the resilience of youth, the Princess put a brave face on her son's deformity, emphasizing his positive qualities in a letter to Queen Victoria (28 February); 'Your grandson is exceedingly lively and when awake will not be satisfied unless kept dancing about continually. He scratches his face and tears his caps and makes every sort of extraordinary little noise, I am so thankful, so happy, he is a boy. I longed for one more than I can describe, my whole heart was set upon a boy and therefore I did not expect one.'[21] Some weeks later she ruefully mentioned to her mother what she thought was the cause of the child's disabilities – a severe fall on a slippery parquet floor in the Schloss the previous September, when she caught her foot in a chair, 'to which I attribute all my misfortunes and baby's false position'.[22]

Christenings of royal Prussian children generally took place when the baby was three weeks old, but in this case it was delayed because of the mother's delicate state of health. Prince Friedrich Wilhelm Victor Albert, the last two names in honour of his grandparents in England, was baptized on 5 March. To their disappointment they were unable to attend, and the Queen was represented by Lord Raglan, the Crimean war commander. Proud as she was of her son, the Princess felt anguish 'to see him half covered up to hide his arm which dangled without use or power by his side'.[23] For a time she was much preoccupied with the best course of action for his arm. His English nurse Mrs Hobbs rubbed massage oil on it faithfully, telling the sceptical mother that she was sure it was working, although neither really believed it. Another British doctor, Sir Benjamin Brodie, was asked by Queen Victoria to examine the child and discuss the matter with Sir James Clark. He recommended that the right arm should be tied up occasionally in order to force the Prince to use his left, but managed to convince everyone except the Princess that it was gradually improving and would eventually reach normal length. The suggestion, she pointed out patiently to Queen Victoria, was nothing new, as the arm had been tied down to his side and leg for an hour a day. He did not mind it in the least, but lay on his back on the floor or the sofa kicking his legs in the air, 'laughing and crowing to the ceiling as happy and contented as possible'. To her he seemed unaware that he had another arm as there was evidently so little feeling in it.[24]

The Princess doted on babies, and within a few days of his birth she had started breast-feeding him, to the revulsion of her mother-in-law. Knowing Queen Victoria's views on the subject were at one with hers, she wrote to the Queen asking for her approval in putting an end to 'this odious habit'. Much to the young mother's disappointment her baby was promptly handed over to a wet nurse, whose milk irritated his bowels and caused regular stomach upsets. Some years later Augusta, by then Empress, told her grandson – by this time only too eager to hear anything against his mother – the cruel lie that she could not face feeding him herself because she found his injured arm repugnant.[25] The parents adored their firstborn child, and Prince Friedrich Wilhelm carried him proudly around the palace, showing him off to anybody who was around. To an aunt he wrote that 'in his clear blue eyes we can already see signs of sparkling intelligence'.[26] The Princess wrote to her mother that he was 'really a dear little child, he is so intelligent and lively & cries so little, but as he is so forward, great care must be taken not to excite him'.[27]

Not until September 1860, by which time he was twenty months old, did Queen Victoria and the Prince Consort have an opportunity to see him. Now he was not alone in the nursery, for in July after an easy labour Vicky had given birth to a daughter, whom they named Charlotte.

On 2 January 1861 the prematurely senile King Friedrich Wilhelm IV died, and the regent became King Wilhelm I. Aged sixty-three, he was sure that his reign would not last long. That August Wilhelm, now second in succession to the throne, made his first trip abroad when he and his parents spent a few weeks at Osborne on the Isle of Wight. This, he would later write, was the scene of his earliest distinct recollections, especially the Prince Consort dandling him in a table napkin.[28] As the only one of Queen Victoria's grandsons whom 'Grandpapa Albert' ever saw, he would always have a special place in the indulgent, ever-forgiving Queen's affections. Within four months the tired, careworn Prince Consort was dead. His grief-stricken eldest daughter had only just recovered from a serious attack of influenza and she was unable to join her widowed mother. Her husband left for England immediately and was one of the chief mourners at the funeral.

Wilhelm's next journey to England was in March 1863 for the wedding of his 'uncle Bertie', Prince of Wales, to Princess Alexandra of Denmark. Clad in Highland costume, Wilhelm – now 'Willy' *en famille* – cheerfully made an exhibition of himself. On his way to St George's Chapel, Windsor, he threw his Aunt Beatrice's muff out of the carriage window. Beatrice was only five years old at the time, and in no position to exercise any authority over him. Queen Victoria's youngest child, she was and always remained her mother's 'Baby', a name her nephew soon picked up. When she told him petulantly that he must address her as aunt, he snapped back, 'Aunt Baby, then!' Bored during the long marriage service, while most of his relations were shedding emotional tears, he pulled the dirk from his stocking and threw it noisily across the chapel floor. When his young uncles Arthur and Leopold remonstrated with him, he bit them in the legs.

Such high-spirited mischief was seen again eight months later, when the family were back at Windsor and the artist William Powell Frith was engaged on an official group portrait of the wedding. Willy was fascinated to watch the picture taking shape, but could not resist teasing the painter. 'Mr Fiff, you are a nice man, but your whiskers ——'. His Aunt Helena came and put a hand over his mouth, but he struggled free and repeated himself more loudly than ever. She stopped him again, blushing but unable to suppress her laughter as she led him to another corner of the studio and lectured him on good manners. As he could hardly order 'the royal imp' out, to keep him quiet Frith let him paint his own daubs on one very small part of the vast canvas. All was well until his nurse came in, saw his face and cried out in horror. He had been wiping his brushes on it, richly decorating himself with uneven streaks of bright colour. Assuring her that he could fix it at once, Frith grabbed the child firmly with one hand and rubbed turpentine into his face with the other. Some got into a scratch on his skin, and he screamed as he struck the artist as hard as his good fist would allow, before hiding under the table and howled until he was exhausted. Thereafter he proved such an uncooperative sitter for his appearance in the picture that the artist never captured more than a vague likeness.[29]

Little did Prince Wilhelm know that his nursery years were unsettling times for his parents. They had both been shocked, and his mother temporarily shattered, by the unexpected death of the Prince Consort in December 1861 at a time when they sorely needed his advice and moral support. King Wilhelm I intended to reform the Prussian army, and his *Landtag*, the Prussian parliament, would not accept his proposals for strengthening the regular forces and weakening the reserve *Landwehr*, or land army. Asserting his prerogative, the King dismissed his ministers and dissolved the *Landtag*. New elections strengthened liberal representation at the strength of the conservatives, and the new assembly refused to vote additional funds for the King's reforms. By the summer of 1862 the matter had reached constitutional deadlock, with neither sovereign nor ministers and elected representatives prepared to compromise. In September the King told Crown Prince Friedrich Wilhelm with regret that he was going to abdicate; God and his conscience, he solemnly averred, would not allow him to do anything else. Totally unprepared, not to say deceived by the actor in his father, the Prince begged him to reconsider. In fact the offer was sheer bluff, for the King's trusted admirer and confidant, General Albrecht von Roon, had telegraphed

Otto von Bismarck, the Prussian ambassador in Paris, recalling him to Berlin immediately to head a new government, as the only man ruthless enough to take on the *Landtag*, defy the constitution and carry the King's reforms through. Bismarck duly obeyed the call and was appointed minister-president of Prussia.

Neither the Crown Prince nor Princess had any illusions about the man who was just beginning nearly thirty years of rule over Prussia. The Crown Prince's distrust had been awakened by the minister's own report of a meeting in London with the Prime Minister Lord Palmerston and his Secretary of State for Foreign Affairs, Lord John Russell, and Bismarck's statement that he found the English constitution alien to his philosophy as it allowed for 'great and permanent encroachments on the prerogatives of the Crown, especially in military matters'. This despatch, he told his wife, 'foretells what might be in store for us if that man were sooner or later to control the destinies of Prussia'.[30] To the Crown Princess he was 'a most unprincipled and unrespectable character – a brouillon and an adventurer'.[31] Bismarck's statement in a speech to the chamber of deputies made his philosophy clear: 'Germany does not look to Prussia's liberalism, but to Prussia's might. The great questions of the times will not be solved by speeches and majority decisions, but by iron and blood.'[32]

By the time they came to England for the wedding of the Prince of Wales in March 1863, they were seriously considering asking Queen Victoria if she could persuade King Wilhelm to allow them to live for half of every year in England.[33] Returning to Prussia, they realized that such a gesture would look like running away. They struck a blow against the forces of reaction when the Crown Prince made a speech at Danzig in June 1863 publicly disassociating himself from a measure announced by Bismarck and endorsed by the King curtailing the freedom of the Prussian press. The King was beside himself with rage, and when the Crown Prince refused to apologize or retract his statement he threatened to have his son imprisoned in a fortress, but Bismarck knew that martyrdom would be counter-productive. 'Deal gently with the young man Absalom' he advised, choosing to give the heir a severe reprimand and ordering him not to make any similar pronouncements in future. The matter was dropped – but neither forgiven nor forgotten.

Wilhelm was aged four at the time of the 'Danzig incident'. Though much too young to know what his parents were going through, the tense atmosphere doubtless communicated itself to him. Within a few years he would be taking sides himself in what almost amounted to civil war within the family, and it would not be on the same side as that of his parents.

At the time he had other problems on his mind, none greater than that of the machine supposed to rectify the damage done to him at birth. First used in April 1863 when he was aged four, it comprised a belt round the waist to which was affixed an iron bar passing up the back, with an object looking like a horse bridle attached. Into this the head was strapped and turned as required, the iron being moved by a screw. When the head was held firmly in the leather straps it was forced to turn to the left in order to stretch muscles on the right side of the neck, and prevent his head from being drawn down to the right. This was to be worn for an hour a day, and if there was no discernible improvement within a month or so, the doctors would recommend an operation which involved cutting some of the sinews of the neck. Dr Wegner assured the Crown Princess that it did not matter if her son walked around while wearing the machine, thinking there was no need to keep it secret, and the man who made the instrument was sure to talk about it throughout Berlin. Horrified at such insensitivity, the Crown Prince and Princess told him firmly that they would forbid anybody else from seeing him wearing it.[34]

In the end the neck operation was not carried out, probably because it was such a risky procedure and the doctors thought twice about experimenting on such an illustrious patient. To risk turning their slightly handicapped future King into a complete invalid or even worse was something to be avoided at all costs. Even so, it is doubtful whether the machine had any positive effect, other than making the boy more determined than ever to overcome his disability. The very sight of it caused tantrums and made him difficult to control. More useful were the exercises prescribed to make him hold himself upright and try to use his left arm more. A sergeant would arrive every morning to take charge of him, and if he did not feel in the mood to do his exercises he would announce that he was about to say his prayers or recite poetry instead.[35]

Despite this, Wilhelm and the other children had relatively happy childhoods. By the time he reached his fifth birthday he and his sister Charlotte, or 'Ditta', after his attempts to call her 'sister', had a brother Henry, born in August 1862. During the next ten years the Crown Princess would have five more children, of whom three survived to maturity. By the standards of the day it was not perhaps a large family, but that she should have had seven more after being extremely fortunate to come through her first experience of childbirth was little short of remarkable. In an age when the dictum that 'children should be seen and not heard' ruled, and that they should spend little time with their parents, the Prussian royal children were fortunate in belonging to such a close-knit family. Among Wilhelm's happiest memories of these early years was being allowed to sit with his mother while she painted in her studio. A gifted artist, she was equally adept at sketching, and painting in oils and watercolours, and she liked him to read aloud as she worked on her art or embroidery.

The Crown Prince saw much more of his children than he had seen of his own father at a similar age. Though he was a war hero to his sons and daughters after he returned from fighting in the short and victorious Prusso-Danish War of 1864 – a war which brought him into collision with his brother-in-law the Prince of Wales, furious at Prussia's cavalier treatment of his wife's country – his military duties, parades, manoeuvres and inspections were not so intensive that he was denied time to be with his family while they were growing up. Part of the reason was that Bismarck and the King deprived him of responsibility as a result of his speech at Danzig. Therefore, the Crown Prince had every opportunity to pass on his great interest in ancient and medieval history and archaeology to his sons. Wilhelm was spellbound by a massive volume, *German Treasures of the Holy Roman Empire*, so vast that his father had to place it on the floor as he turned its pages, explaining the illustrations to his son, and conveying his hopes of restoring the German Empire which had existed in medieval Europe.

At other times he would take the children on visits to relatives, to museums and galleries, or on long walks in the countryside. He taught them to swim, row and sail on the River Havel, and when they were older he took them hunting. That Wilhelm became a good swimmer and proficient at rowing despite his weak arm says much for his determination. He could be forgiven for showing signs of pride, something Queen Victoria frequently counselled against, warning the Crown Princess to 'bring him up simply, plainly, not with that terrible Prussian pride and ambition which grieved dear Papa so much and which he always said would stand in the way of Prussia taking that lead in Germany which he ever wished her to do'.[36]

In January 1866, at the age of seven, Wilhelm left the nursery and moved into the schoolroom. Captain von Schrotter of the guards artillery, later a military attaché in London, was appointed his governor. A sergeant was engaged to teach him to play the drum, and a schoolmaster from Potsdam to teach him reading and writing. Six months later Georg Hinzpeter was chosen as his civil tutor. Nobody had a greater influence on the boy's character than this severe bachelor of thirty-eight with a doctor's degree in philosophy and classical philology, and not always for the good. His educational system, comprising twelve hours a day of study and physical exercise, was 'based exclusively on a stern sense of duty and the idea of service; the character was to be fortified by perpetual "renunciation", the life of the prince to be moulded on lines of "old Prussian simplicity" – the ideal being the harsh discipline of the Spartans'.[37] The Crown Prince and Princess were so impressed with him that Henry was also committed to his charge two years later.

It was part of Hinzpeter's policy never to give the boys any praise, approval or encouragement. For breakfast they ate dry bread, and at tea they were only allowed bread and butter. When their cousins were invited to join them for tea, they had to be perfect hosts and offer them appetising-looking cakes without eating any themselves. As Wilhelm recognized, in retrospect if not at the time, this regime was easily explained: 'The impossible was expected of the pupil in order to force him to the nearest degree of perfection. Naturally, the impossible goal could never be achieved; logically, therefore, the praise which registers approval was also excluded.'[38] Hinzpeter did his work well, but with brutal efficiency. Humourless, with no understanding of a child's nature, he incurred the distrust of Ernst von Stockmar, son of the Prince of Wales's former tutor and former secretary to the Crown Prince and Princess. Fearful of being accused of interference if he spoke his mind too strongly, Stockmar had had his doubts about Hinzpeter on first sight and was tempted to warn them prior to appointing him that 'he wants heart and is a hard Spartan idealist'.[39]

Hinzpeter's supervision extended beyond the schoolroom. Every Wednesday and Saturday they visited museums, galleries, factories, foundries, workshops, farms or mines, so they could see what was involved in the work and manual labour and talk to the workmen. It was part of his idea to teach the children something about social inequalities and the conditions of the working class. At the end of every such excursion Wilhelm had to go up to the man in charge, remove his hat and make a small speech of thanks. When they visited mines and factories he was fascinated to see at first hand the nation's growing industrial strength, and in later years he claimed that this had given him some insight into social and labour problems. On the other hand, museums and art galleries bored him, despite his feeling for history, and as an adult he veered between the philistinism of his paternal grandfather and a half-hearted attempt to play the dilettante.

On their walks Hinzpeter encouraged Wilhelm to express an opinion about everybody they met. He should never be afraid of expressing his views, the tutor told him, and he should not allow himself to be dominated by anybody, even his most responsible advisers. Such motivation did not prove helpful in the long run. When he was almost eight, his mother wrote to Queen Victoria of her son's failings: 'he is inclined to be selfish, domineering and proud, but I must say they too are not his own faults, as they have been hitherto more encouraged than checked'.[40]

Hinzpeter also helped Wilhelm to overcome his fear of riding. When he watched a groom lifting the Prince gently on to the back on a pony and leading it on the rein, it looked like an admission of defeat. Ignoring the weeping boy's protests, he made him sit on the pony without stirrups, and told him to take the reins in his right hand. When he repeatedly fell off the tutor patiently put him back, and after several weeks Wilhelm found he could keep his balance. Soon he was developing horsemanship skills which would have been praiseworthy even in a boy with two good arms. He wore a golden bracelet on his left wrist through which the rein could be passed,[41] as his hand appeared to hold the reins but had no control over the horse, which was specially trained to respond to knee pressure. For a future sovereign to be afraid of horses was not necessarily a disgrace, as his near-contemporary, the Tsarevich of Russia, later Tsar Alexander III, was a bear-like individual whose physical strength and vast frame belied a terror of riding long before he became too heavy to mount anything other than a carthorse. Yet as second in line to the throne of the most military minded state in Europe, Prince Wilhelm needed to learn equestrian skills. But if Hinzpeter had refrained from forcing him to master what had seemed impossible, his charge might have grown up a more balanced character.

The prince had already begun to overcome his disability in another way, while at Balmoral with his parents in August 1866. Walking into the ghillies' room one afternoon where they were cleaning their guns, he tried to pick up a weapon but it proved too heavy for his good arm. As he was about to throw a tantrum one of the men, without saying a word, gently put a small light rifle that had been the Prince of Wales' first gun into his hand, and showed him how to use it. This was the kind of encouragement to which he responded best.

On 27 January 1869 Wilhelm celebrated his tenth birthday. He was invested with the Order of the Black Eagle, and allowed to wear the uniform of the first infantry regiment of the guards. Apart from his brother Henry, he had few childhood companions. One of the exceptions was Poulteney Bigelow, fifteen-year-old son of the American minister in Berlin, who was invited to play with the princes at Potsdam in the summer of 1870. He found them good company, especially when they were freed from their tutor's watchful eye. It was fun to kick footballs along the roof of the Neue Palais, until too many broken panes of glass attracted Hinzpeter's attention, or playing by the river and sailing a model frigate presented to one of their great-uncles by their mother's great-uncle, King William IV of England. With hindsight, Bigelow believed that this vessel was 'the parent ship' of the future Kaiser Wilhelm's navy.[42] They corresponded with each other until the latter's death. The American 'was an uncommonly amiable fellow; amongst us boys he held a place of high esteem because, coming as he did from the "Wild West", he was able to tell us tales of murder about trappers and Red Indians, and acted as experts in our games of Red Indians'.[43]

Real life war games would soon intrude on the boys' consciousness. In July 1870 France and Germany were at war. Within weeks Emperor Napoleon of the French was defeated and abdicated, his empire in ruins, and out of the ashes the new German empire was proclaimed at Versailles in January 1871. It was a promotion which gave no pleasure to the newly elevated but intensely touchy King Wilhelm of Prussia, now German Kaiser, who did not hide his irritation at having to exchange his splendid time-honoured crown for another. Crown Prince Friedrich Wilhelm sent home captured colours and eagles from the front, and the keys of surrendered cities to his sons. Hinzpeter pinned a large map up on their wall, and together they placed flags on pins to show troop movements and advances as news came back of each triumph. The princes were at Homburg when they heard of the great German victory at Sedan. Cheers in the street and a torchlight procession by the excited townspeople woke them from their sleep, and they got up excitedly in their nightshirts to watch, not realizing that everybody could see them on the balcony. When Hinzpeter gave them an angry lecture the next day for such undignified behaviour they were astonished.

In June 1871 victorious troops from Potsdam made a spectacular entry into Berlin through the Brandenburg Gate. Wilhelm was allowed to take part, riding on a small dappled horse between his father and Uncle Friedrich, Grand Duke of Baden. A few weeks later the Crown Princess took her children for a long holiday in England, leaving her husband to recuperate from a viral infection contracted partly through feeling run-down after the war.

There were now six children in the family, the three youngest being five-year-old Victoria, three-year-old Waldemar and baby Sophie, just a year old. With the birth of a fourth daughter, Margrethe, in April 1872, the family was complete. Unlike their Hohenzollern cousins, the children were small and rather weak. In the nineteenth century parents, royal and otherwise, were proud of fat children as they believed that when their infants were sick, the more weight they had 'to draw on' the better. At about 5 ft 2 in the Crown Princess was hardly taller than her own mother, though the Crown Prince stood almost a foot above her. Always sensitive to criticism of the children from her in-laws, the Crown Princess was furious with her husband's cousin Prince Friedrich Karl, who did not hesitate to voice his unsolicited personal opinion that a one-armed man should never be allowed to become King of Prussia.[44] The boorish Friedrich Karl and his equally unpleasant father Karl, the Kaiser's brother, had always viewed with contempt the Crown Prince, firstly because of his bouts of ill-health in childhood and their belief that they would provide more robust monarchs of Prussia, and secondly because of his more liberal, artistic leanings. At Court they were among the most outspoken opponents of the Anglo-German connection, and an unfriendly rivalry between both lines of the family would always simmer just below the surface.

Crown Prince and Princess Friedrich Wilhelm and their children spent every winter in Berlin, the summer in Potsdam and a holiday in July or August, if possible, in England or occasionally perhaps in Holland, where the bracing sea air was considered healthy for them. At home the children took breakfast with their mother and father, and the younger ones came to their parents' room at 7 a.m. while they had their cup of tea and toast in bed before getting up. Though she was always busy, recalled her second daughter Victoria, the princess never neglected the family. 'Every moment that she could spare away from the various duties which devolved upon her was spent with us.'[45]

The Crown Princess was keen to remove her eldest son for a while from the martial, celebratory atmosphere of post-war Berlin, as she feared it might have the wrong effect on him. In January 1871 she had written to Queen Victoria that her son had the Prince of Wales's 'pleasant, amiable ways – and can be very winning. He is not possessed of brilliant abilities, nor any strength of character or talents, but he is a dear boy and I hope and trust will grow up a good and useful man.'[46] It was considered that something of the more comfortable, less martial milieu of England would benefit him. At Windsor the elder children were allowed to make butter and cream cheese in the royal dairy at Frogmore, while at Osborne Wilhelm and Henry enjoyed firing off brass cannons in the model fort built for their uncles. On a visit to Portsmouth Wilhelm was very excited at being allowed to go down in a diving bell, and he and Henry were shown over Nelson's *Victory* and the cadet training ship *St Vincent.*

In April 1873 Wilhelm sat and passed his qualifying examination for admission to a *Gymnasium*, the equivalent of a German grammar school, taking papers in Latin, Greek and mathematics. Later that month the Crown Prince and Princess were invited to represent Prussia at the universal exhibition in Vienna, and Wilhelm went with them. He was much taller than and twice as broad as Crown Prince Rudolf of Austria, the Habsburg heir, who was five months older. The Crown Princess thought the latter 'a light graceful boy with very nice manners',[47] but Wilhelm was less impressed by the contemporary with whom he had little in common, than with the boy's mother, Empress Elizabeth, whom his mother had described to him as the most beautiful woman in Europe. On meeting her he was so overcome that it was only when admonished by his mother that he remembered to kiss the Empress's hand: 'I was completely carried away with the beautiful vision which had fully justified my mother's verdict.'[48]

In September 1874 Wilhelm was confirmed in the Friedenskirche at Potsdam, with his parents, the Kaiser and Empress, and the Prince and Princess of Wales among those present. According to his mother he 'was not at all either shy or upset and showed the greatest sangfroid. He read his confession of faith in a loud and steady voice – and answered the forty questions that the clergyman put to him without hesitation or embarrassment! I do not think he was touched or much impressed!'[49] Perhaps she did him an injustice, for in his words the ceremony moved him 'very deeply'.

Later that month Wilhelm went to school at Cassel, an idea suggested by Hinzpeter, who believed that if he had to compete with his peers a degree of humiliation would spur the Prince on to develop a fitting sense of superiority. Where the education of Prussian princes was concerned it was a revolutionary move, as at this stage of their life they generally went for military training instead, and the Kaiser looked coldly on this departure from precedent. Such a school, he thought, was inappropriate for his grandson as he might be exposed to dangerous influences from some of the teachers, and it led to heated scenes with his son and daughter-in-law for approving Hinzpeter's proposal. People said that his parents were trying to frustrate his grandfather's wish for him to appear in public as much as possible. At the same time Henry was going to the Cassel Polytechnic School to prepare for his naval career, and the brothers saw each other from time to time.

At school Wilhelm rose daily at 5 a.m. every day and was working at his preparation an hour later. From 8 a.m. to midday he was at lessons, with exercise from midday to 2 p.m. From 2 to 4 p.m. he was at school again, then there was a private lesson with Hinzpeter. Dinner was from 5 to 6 p.m., followed by work from 6 to 8 p.m., then extra tuition in French and English from 8 to 9 p.m. He enjoyed reading and history, but had little fondness or aptitude for mathematics. Modern languages came easily to him, while Latin and Greek gave him a lifelong interest in ancient history and archaeology, even though he later thought that too much emphasis was placed on classical languages. Ancient history was 'confined mainly to a recital of facts, while the character of rulers and statesmen, and the description of customs, manners, and the intellectual life was treated in a very step-motherly fashion'. German history, which stopped at the year 1648, was taught in a very general, superficial way, 'without any attempt to arouse enthusiasm for the national idea'.[50] Even at this early age he was conscious of a sense of pride in Prussia and Germany under Bismarck, the pride which his grandfather applauded but his parents deprecated.

Significantly, in the light of later prejudices, Prince Wilhelm's best friend at Cassel was a Jew, Siegfried Sommer. An academically bright pupil who was always top of the class, Sommer later became a senior and highly respected judge with a little assistance from his old friend, by then Kaiser; and his grandson Professor Sir Geoffrey Elton, the eminent Tudor historian, later upheld the family tradition of scholarship. Hinzpeter arranged monthly 'conciliation dinners' to which local notables were invited to meet their future sovereign and his brother. They were strained, even glum affairs, as the princes and their guests were at their most formal, artificial best. At other times there were occasional visits to the opera and theatre, swimming, fencing and riding.

In Wilhelm's view the Cassel experiment, if it was to be viewed as such, achieved mixed results. Too little emphasis, he thought, had been placed on the formation of character and needs of practical life. Later he blamed his parents for exposing him to the humiliation of lower class marks than mere commoners, and in this his grandfather supported him. Even so there is no evidence that he resented their decision at the time. On the contrary, he still enjoyed a very close, if a little bizarre, relationship with his mother. Several of his letters to her while he was at school had dwelt on his 'little secret' for her and her alone, dreams that he described in embarrassing detail of rituals in which they embraced each other tenderly and he watched her remove her gloves, then kissed her 'dear, soft warm hands'. His descriptions of 'the soft insides of your hand' were the first indications of a lifelong obsession. She treated his remarks with self-deprecating good humour, telling him her 'poor hands' were 'very clumsy and mostly concerned with paint or ink when they are not on the piano, or spinning or scrubbing the little ones!'[51]

In January 1877 Wilhelm and sixteen other sixth-formers passed their final exams at Cassel and received their leaving certificates. Two days later, on his eighteenth birthday, he officially came of age. The Kaiser invested him with the Order of the Black Eagle and Queen Victoria asked the British ambassador to confer on him the Order of the Bath. However, he wanted the Garter, and the Crown Princess tactfully wrote to her mother that Tsar Alexander II of Russia and Emperor Franz Josef of Austria had already conferred on him the highest Orders within their power, and not only the Prince of Wales but also the Dukes of Edinburgh and Connaught had the Black Eagle. Wilhelm, she said, 'would be satisfied with the Bath, but the nation would not'. Queen Victoria saw through the little white lie, but magnanimously conceded and the Garter was his. Now he had much more than just another order of chivalry. He also had his army commission, and was to put in a nominal six months' service; he now had his own set of apartments in the Neue Palais, Potsdam. Hinzpeter no longer had direct responsibility for him, or indeed for any of the princes, and at the age of fifty he was permitted to retire. He and Wilhelm remained friends and they continued to correspond until the tutor died in 1907; his former pupil, by then Kaiser, attended his funeral.

The Crown Princess had hoped her son would spend a few terms at Oxford University, but no one else at Court welcomed the idea. Instead, Wilhelm followed in his father's footsteps and that of his English Uncle Alfred, now Duke of Edinburgh. In October 1877 he went to Bonn University and read political science and jurisprudence. The Villa Frank in the Coblenzstrasse had been set aside for him and his household. Theoretically the prince was a free and private individual at the university, though in practice as the Kaiser's grandson he was subject to obligations and limitations. He had to be available at any time should the Kaiser, his family, or the army need him for state or military duties. To Wilhelm's curriculum of political science and jurisprudence were added history, German literature, history of art, philosophy, physics and chemistry. He was taught privately at his home by carefully chosen tutors, and it was only for chemistry experiments that he attended a demonstration theatre at the Poppelsdorfer Palace with other students.

Wilhelm was also required to entertain notables from time to time, as he had done at Cassel. He joined one of the student societies, the Borussia corps, although its members' behaviour repelled him with their love of duelling, gambling and heavy drinking. From them he picked up the rather affected Potsdam accent, or *Potsdamer Ton*,[52] a nasal, coarse bark less suited to normal conversation than the parade ground. The prince's favourite leisure pursuits were amateur theatricals, playing croquet with the daughters of a neighbour, the local magistrate, and dancing with them in the evenings. He enjoyed boating, and sometimes he and his companions would take a night steamer to Coblenz and row back to Bonn the following day. Wilhelm's grandmother, Empress Augusta, spent much of her time at Coblenz Castle, using her deteriorating health as an excuse for absenting herself from the Court where she had never felt at home, and she always enjoyed having him to call on her.

Travels further afield were rare, but sometimes Wilhelm visited his maternal grandmother at Osborne, Balmoral or Windsor. Queen Victoria, he recalled, 'was always particularly kind to me from the very first, she was a *real* grandmother, and our relations to one another were never changed or dimmed to the end of her life'.[53] She treated him almost as the youngest of her own children, and he nearly always personally showed her the respect that she often wished he would towards his own mother. In the autumn of 1878 Wilhelm went to Paris for a fortnight, where he was received with coldness. As the Franco-Prussian War was still a recent memory he could hardly have expected anything else, but it was a shock for him not to be fawned on everywhere he went. He had no desire to see the city again – 'the feverish haste and restlessness of Parisian life repelled me'[54] – and never set foot there again.

Nowhere did the prince enjoy himself more than with his Hessian cousins at the homely court of Darmstadt. As he had no lectures on Saturdays he would leave Bonn on Friday afternoon to travel there, returning on Monday morning. His mother encouraged these visits, hoping that the more homely *Gemütlich* atmosphere there would round off some of the angularity he had acquired at Berlin. Wilhelm would stay with his Aunt Alice and her husband Louis, Grand Duke and Duchess of Hesse and the Rhine, and their family. With the children – Princesses Victoria, Elizabeth ('Ella'), Irene and Alix, and Prince Ernest ('Ernie') – he would go riding or rowing, play tennis or croquet, then rein in his horse, or throw down his racquet in the middle of a game and order them to come and sit down to listen to him as he read passages from the Bible. The eldest, Victoria, a rather self-assertive tomboy, was a good companion, and he taught her to smoke. However he seemed fondest of Ella, seventeen months her junior, and at this time much the prettiest of the sisters. Whenever she spoke he was silent, as if hanging on her every word. All the cousins found him likeable enough, but too mercurial, volatile and restless, full of energy one moment, morose and brooding the next. They nicknamed him 'Wilhelm the Sudden' and 'Gondola Billy'. Maybe his behaviour was partly because of his determination to show them that his deformed arm was no handicap; maybe it was just his way of demonstrating that Prussia was and always would be the leader in Germany.

Ironically in the light of subsequent events, Wilhelm was still devoted to his mother. To her friend Marie Dönhoff he wrote (12 December 1878) that he would have to spend Christmas at 'that dreadful Berlin! Where society are so bad towards my poor Mama and where I don't know and don't care for anybody in the least!'[55]

That winter double tragedy darkened the lives of the family at Darmstadt for ever. The Grand Duchess lacked the strong constitution of her mother and sisters. She had already lost an infant son, a haemophiliac who fell from a window and bled to death at the age of two. In November Victoria caught diphtheria and the infection spread to all the others except for Ella, who was hurriedly sent to stay with other relatives. The youngest child, four-year-old May, succumbed to the disease and just as the rest were recovering, the exhausted Grand Duchess fell ill and on 14 December, the anniversary of the Prince Consort's death, she too passed away. Wilhelm had been greatly attached to his aunt, and was deeply moved by sympathy for the motherless children. He wrote several sentimental verses for Ella at about this time, none of which survive; he may have destroyed them in one of his more worldly moments.

Within the family there was some talk of marriage between the cousins, but even in the autumn, before Alice's illness and death, Queen Victoria had advised the Crown Princess that her son's suit had been gently declined. Mother and daughter both regretted it, Queen Victoria commenting in April 1880, some eighteen months later, that she 'could not but think with regret of what *might* have been'.[56] Ella's heart had already been promised to the handsome but cold-hearted Grand Duke Serge of Russia, younger brother of Tsar Alexander III. It is tempting to speculate on the possible course of history if she had agreed to become the consort of her restless Hohenzollern cousin instead. Fate had marked her out for twenty years of childless if not loveless marriage to a homosexual who treated her increasingly as a child instead of a wife. Ella was only released from this existence by her husband's assassination at the hands of a terrorist; after becoming Mother Superior in a Convent, she too was murdered by the Bolsheviks. Never the most outspoken of women, but a personality of singular purpose and compassion for others, would she have had the force of character required to bring to heel, if not actually influence, her husband in his more excitable moods? Wilhelm never forgot Ella, and for years he could not bear to meet her except on ceremonial occasions when it was unavoidable, but her picture always remained on his desk.

On 27 March 1879, six weeks after his eleventh birthday, Waldemar, Wilhelm's youngest brother, also succumbed to diphtheria. If Wilhelm had been a little jealous of his parents' undoubted affection for their youngest son, he put his feelings aside as he held an all-night vigil in the Friedenskirche beside the coffin: 'our pain (was) deep and cruel beyond words'.[57] The grief-stricken parents were shattered; the Crown Princess was racked for months with rheumatism, neuralgia and intense depression which came close to breaking her spirit. Her misery deepened when she was told, or read in the papers, of an Orthodox Protestant minister who publicly declared that the Prince's death was a trial sent by God to humiliate her hardened heart.

Like his parents, Prince Wilhelm had his own personal crisis. Rejected by his cousin Ella, he told Hinzpeter that he thought his withered arm made him unattractive to women. This confession and its implicit lack of self-confidence overlooked the fact that there were several Protestant princesses in Europe eager to marry the next German Kaiser but one. Soon after Waldemar's death he went blackcock shooting at Görlitz in Lower Silesia, near Primkenau, the principal residence of his distant kinsman Friedrich, Duke of Schleswig-Holstein-Sonderburg-Augustenburg. The Duke was an old friend of his parents, and to their abiding shame he had been dispossessed and much of his inheritance confiscated by Bismarck after his abortive claim to the duchies of Schleswig and Holstein and defeat in the war of 1864. Wilhelm began paying court to the eldest daughter of the house, Augusta Victoria ('Dona'), a plain, pious but even-tempered young woman three months older than him, who knew him a little following a brief meeting ten years earlier. Wilhelm had not recovered from his disappointment over Ella, but Dona was available and seemed well disposed towards him. The Augustenburgs were regarded as of rather lowly rank among German princely families, and he was prepared for opposition to the idea of such a marriage. The Crown Prince and Princess cared less for considerations of rank than the rest of the family, and they were delighted by their son's choice. They liked the Princess; they also saw such a marriage as a kind of atonement for the events of 1864. Above all they hoped that the influence of a wife would soften Wilhelm's increasingly arrogant manner.

The Duke had suffered from cancer for some months and died in January 1880, though his sister-in-law Helena, the Crown Princess's sister, told her that uncertainty about his daughter's future had been the cause of his death. With him went the last lingering objections of the Kaiser and Bismarck to Wilhelm's marriage. However, they had not created any major obstacles to the marriage because it suited their purpose very well to see the young man set up his own household away from the pro-English influences of his parents. The Crown Prince attended his old friend's funeral, and was unpleasantly surprised when Wilhelm neither showed any emotion over his death, nor sent his condolences to his future wife over the loss of her father. As she was still in mourning the engagement took place quietly on St Valentine's day the following month.

To his mother Wilhelm wrote 'most touching letters (in his own funny style) about his great happiness'.[58] She sensed it would be an unpopular match with the more hidebound elements at Berlin, 'because the poor Holsteins are *mal vu*, and there is a widespread, though very false, idea that they are not *ebenbürtig* [sufficiently aristocratic]. But I am sure this prejudice will wear off very quickly.'[59] A month later she could tell Queen Victoria that the bride-to-be had made an excellent impression at Berlin: 'Her smile and manners and expression must disarm even the bristly, thorny people of Berlin with their sharp tongues, their cutting sarcasms about everybody and everything. The announcement has been much better taken than I had dared to hope.'[60] Bismarck told his cronies that the 'Holstein cow' would introduce a fresh strain into the Hohenzollern breed, as she was neither English nor endowed with the personality or cleverness of the Empress or Crown Princess, while Hinzpeter was pleased that his 'dearly beloved problem child' would be marrying 'someone who understands him and sympathizes with him in his weaknesses'.[61]

# CHAPTER TWO

# *Marriage and Responsibility*

Wilhelm's engagement was publicly proclaimed by the Kaiser on 2 June 1880. He was promoted to the rank of captain and given command of a company in the first regiment of foot guards. If the Crown Prince and Princess hoped that his impending marriage would change Wilhelm for the better, they would soon be disillusioned. Under Dona's unquestioning worship, he became more insufferable than ever. One distasteful incident that summer revealed an unpleasant aspect of his character. Like their mother, Waldemar had adored animals, and after his death she doted on one of his cats, which they had owned since she was a kitten, and allowed the animal to lie on her bed every morning. Such devotion was no proof against a heartless keeper who shot the cat, hung her against a tree and cut off her nose. The distress of his horrified mother and sisters meant nothing to Wilhelm, who callously told them 'it was laudable zeal in pursuance of his duty on the part of the keeper, as cats might harm pheasants'.[1]

In the autumn Wilhelm accepted an invitation to Sandringham as part of a family gathering to celebrate the birthday of his Uncle 'Bertie', Prince of Wales. Two days before the birthday he left without warning, to spend the next fortnight at Cumberland Lodge, Windsor, the home of his uncle and aunt, Prince and Princess Christian. As the Prince was the younger brother of the late Duke Friedrich and the Princess, Helena, was his mother's younger sister, they were equally close family, but this display of bad manners did nothing to make them feel any more comfortable about entertaining him. The Prince of Wales diplomatically turned a blind eye, but his wife's everlasting dislike of everything and everyone Prussian (the Crown Prince and Princess excepted) was rekindled and she refused to accompany her husband to the wedding.

Wilhelm's next birthday, his twenty-second, was the last he celebrated under his parents' roof, but deep in her heart his mother felt she was not really losing him. This son had never really been hers, she wrote sadly to Queen Victoria, 'he has never been so devoted to me as the one who died'.[2] As a young man on the threshold of marriage, he seemed to be a disappointment to both parents. The Crown Princess had told her mother that it was the dream of her life to have a son who would resemble her own father in soul and mind. She had seen for herself that for all his positive qualities her eldest brother the Prince of Wales, to whom she was devoted, had fallen far short of the standards set for him by the Prince Consort. Though she knew that to expect perfection in her own son and heir was asking the impossible, she was saddened to find in him a product of the Berlin military milieu of the type she had viewed with dread on her arrival in Prussia as an eager young bride of seventeen. Again, just as Queen Victoria recognized that Bertie was her 'caricature', Vicky saw how her eldest son resembled her in many ways. This fact did not escape Wilhelm either; as he would tell the British ambassador in Berlin, Sir Edward Malet, a few months after his accession, he and his mother had the same characters, and consequently 'if we do not happen to agree, the situation becomes difficult'.[3]

The Crown Prince had likewise hoped to find in his successor a balanced young man with something of his own liberal outlook and interest in the arts. Instead, thanks to the combined influence of Kaiser Wilhelm, Bismarck and Hinzpeter, he was confronted with an arrogant, priggish youth who worshipped Bismarck's authoritarian methods and appeared to accept unquestioningly the policy of 'blood and iron' as not merely the answer to everything, but the principle that had made a Greater Germany out of the kingdom of Prussia. It was left to a historian writing some eighty years later to summarize the problem – the prince was the product of two cultures, torn between the ideals of the Prussian Junker and the Liberal English gentleman,[4] and at the same time alternately filled with admiration for Britain's mid-nineteenth-century achievements and envy of British 'arrogance'.

On Saturday 26 February Dona made her formal entry into Berlin in a carriage drawn by eight black horses wearing heavy red, brass-studded harness. Attired in evening dress with a long train, she was uncomfortable and nearly froze in her slow progress along the gravelled road. Leading the procession was a contingent of the master butchers of Berlin, dressed smartly in top hats and frock coats. A flock of white doves was released as her carriage reached the Brandenburg Gate and passed between crowds lining the streets, while the burgomaster greeted her with an inaudible speech of welcome and she thanked him with an equally inaudible reply. At the palace the Crown Prince greeted her and presented her to the grenadiers, all lined up and standing to attention, as he told her she would henceforth be 'mother of the company'.[5] The bridegroom stood at their head. Recently promoted to honorary major and captain of the bodyguard, he had led a detachment of guards along the Unter den Linden to the royal palace, where they formed a guard of honour to welcome the bride. Her attendants thought Wilhelm seemed more preoccupied with their smart turnout than with that of his future wife.

The festivities in the palace that night lasted for six and a half hours. Despite her chilly entrance to Berlin the bride, according to the crown princess, 'looked charming and everyone was taken with her sweetness and grace'.[6]

The wedding took place on the evening of Sunday 27 February. Two ceremonies were held. The first, the civil contract, was held in comparative privacy with close relations, lawyers and scribes at the Kürfursten Hall present to sign the marriage contract. Next a bevy of Court chamberlains in gold-braided uniforms, accompanied by heralds and silver sticks, marched from the Electors' Chamber in the Schloss to the royal chapel. The cavaliers of the bride followed, and then the bride was led to the communion table by the bridegroom. She was dressed in white damask, a veil covering her from head to foot. Over the myrtle in her hair she wore the crown under which Prussian princesses were traditionally married. Resplendent in his uniform as captain of the 1st foot guards, the groom walked with her to the communion table. Behind them, carrying the bride's train, came four bridesmaids, accompanied by Countess Brockdorff, Dona's mistress of the robes, while the groom was followed by his adjutants. As the procession approached the chapel, the cathedral choir inside intoned a psalm. Preceded by his court functionaries, the Kaiser passed through the folding doors, between the Queen of Saxony and the bride's mother, followed by the Kaiser's civil and military staff, and ladies and gentlemen of the Queen and the Duchess. Next were the German Empress, between the King of Saxony and the Prince of Wales; the German Crown Princess, between Gustav, Crown Prince of Sweden and Prince Christian of Schleswig-Holstein; and the German Crown Prince, between his sister the Grand Duchess of Baden and Princess Christian, each trio attended by their ladies and gentlemen in waiting. Bismarck was present as well, though he generally absented himself from what he found tedious royal functions on grounds of ill-health. The bridal couple placed themselves in front of the communion table before their relatives, and the Revd Herr Kögel, the Kaiser's chaplain, delivered a brief address and exchanged the rings, as thirty-six salvoes of artillery announced the precise moment of marriage.

The wedding service, the Crown Princess wrote afterwards, was 'exhausting, suffocating and interminable as all the Berlin state weddings are', and 'a harangue which the young couple listened to standing, and which is so cold and so funereal that one has not the impression of attending a wedding! Service it cannot be called.'[7] Next all guests filed past the Kaiser, Empress and bridal couple, bowing to each in turn. For dinner the chief royalties sat at a large table, the rest at small round tables. Shortly before 10 p.m. the whole party returned to the White Hall for the final ceremony of the evening, the *Fackeltanz* or torchlight dance, a wedding ceremony unique to Prussia. The Kaiser and Empress were seated on thrones, the bride and groom on gilded chairs slightly above floor level, the other princesses seated and the princes standing. When everyone was ready the lights were extinguished, the band of the *garde de corps* began to play solemn marches, the doors were thrown open and the marshal of the court carrying his wand of office led into the room twenty-four pages, each with a resin torch. Keeping in step with the music, they walked sedately around the hall before bowing to the bridal couple. The latter then stepped down from their chairs and, hand in hand, proceeded round the hall in a similarly dignified fashion. Next they walked back to the Kaiser and Empress, the bride taking the hand of her grandfather-in-law and her brother, the Duke of Holstein, the groom took the hands of his mother and mother-in-law, and all six circled the hall. In similar fashion the couple took the hands of each royal guest in turn. Throughout the tedious ceremony, the bride acquitted herself well, looking 'most graceful and dignified', while the groom revelled in being the centre of attention. A formal banquet was held on Monday, followed by a gala performance of Gluck's *Armide* at the Opera House.

The Marble Palace at Potsdam, a large building on the Heiligensee, had been set aside by the Kaiser for Wilhelm and Dona. Uninhabited for years, alterations had to be made before it was in a fit state for them to move in, and until then they stayed in the nearby town palace.

As personalities they had less in common than the Crown Prince and Princess. Wilhelm was fortunate to have found a wife with little desire for independence and, it must be said, not much of a mind of her own. With her inferior education she was overawed by his apparent cleverness, his dilettantism and restlessness. A placid, God-fearing woman brought up to believe that her destination in life was to make and keep her husband's home comfortable, she asked little more. Rigidly evangelical and with an ardent detestation of Catholics, she chose her ladies-in-waiting with such care that they were known irreverently as the 'Hallelujah Aunts'. Even Wilhelm, no friend of Catholics himself, found their passionate Protestantism and religious bigotry excessive.

For much of their first few years of married life he was greatly preoccupied with learning statecraft under Bismarck's protégés, representing his grandfather on missions to other European courts, and at army manoeuvres. They did not see a great deal of each other, and if she privately resented his being away so much, she submitted meekly to it as part of her royal duty. She and her 'Hallelujah Aunts' presumably remained in blissful ignorance of some of his activities, for within a year of their marriage he was already seeking some of his pleasures outside the wedding ring. Through a letter to Frau Wolf, a notorious Viennese procuress, he made the acquaintance of an attractive Austrian girl, Ella Somsics, who had settled in the Linkstrasse in Berlin. She was happy to become the mistress of a future German Kaiser and entertain him on his regular, highly secret visits to her rooms. There was no likelihood of his wife being tempted to err while he was away. At first he was jealous even if a manservant took undue interest in her décolletage, but soon he learned to trust her implicitly; flirtation with servants, let alone mild infidelity, would never enter her head.

Those around Prince and Princess Wilhelm thought he made it plain to the point of rudeness that he was bored with his clinging, cloying wife and found her excessive domesticity stifling. At any rate he appeared determined to show everyone that he would not be dominated at home and hearth like the gossips had said his father was. Count Waldersee and others considered her 'an excellent woman', thus implying that a princess who kept her mouth closed because she presumably had nothing interesting to say would never give the Berlin military and political establishment any trouble. More to the point, perhaps, were the less charitable but hardly exaggerated views of the socialite Daisy, Princess of Pless, an acute judge of character. Clothes and children, she said, were the main subjects of Princess Wilhelm's conversation, and the only things she thoroughly understood: 'For a woman in that position I have never met *anyone* so devoid of any individual thought or agility of brain and understanding. She is just like a good, quiet, soft cow that has calves and eats grass slowly and then lies down and ruminates.'[8] Dona's cousin by marriage Princess Marie of Edinburgh, later Queen of Roumania, admitted that she was a good mother and wife, 'but her amiability had something condescending about it which never rose to the height of cordiality or ease; there was effort in it. Somehow her smile seemed glued on; it was an official smile.'[9] However, Dona fulfilled her obligations to the dynasty with becoming regularity. Within the first eleven years of marriage she bore Wilhelm six sons and a daughter.

Their first son was born on 6 May 1882 and named Wilhelm after his father. Friction ensued with the family when the Crown Princess bought her daughter-in-law some prettier clothes, telling her she owed it to Wilhelm and herself to look more attractive, but the kind if slightly tactless gesture was not appreciated. Dona said resignedly that there was no point in getting her figure back as she was certain to lose it again soon, because her husband intended to make the succession safe. It was hardly a kind remark to make to a mother-in-law who had almost died while giving birth to her first son, and who had never fully recovered from the deaths of her third and fourth sons in infancy. The Crown Princess had staked much on persuading the Kaiser to allow his grandson to marry a young woman who had been looked down on by most of the Hohenzollerns, and this was the kind of gratitude she received in return.

Dona's mother-in-law was not the only member of the family to find her a disappointment. As children Wilhelm and the mischievous Charlotte had always been close. Now married to Prince Bernhard of Saxe-Meiningen, Charlotte was an elegant, sophisticated young woman, the unofficial leader of the smart set in Berlin. She made it clear that she did not care for her brother's plain, slow-witted wife. Brother and sister would never be on such harmonious terms again. Bernhard endorsed his wife's opinion, bemoaning Dona's 'stupidity, lack of education, and tactlessness'.[10]

In January 1883 the Crown Prince and Princess celebrated their silver wedding anniversary. The Crown Princess had decided to revive the old Windsor custom of *tableaux vivants*, in which all the children could take part. Rehearsals were marred by quarrels, and the performance itself was ruined partly by Dona, who wore a close-fitting costume that made her second pregnancy too obvious and missed a vital cue, as well as by Charlotte, who was determined to upstage everyone else. The Crown Princess was furious, and soon Dona was reduced to tears. Wilhelm, already angry because the Prince of Wales had come to the celebrations while the Princess of Wales refused to accompany him, came to his wife's defence and exchanged sharp words with his mother.

The Crown Prince and Princess had hoped that marriage might have a positive effect on Wilhelm's character, but instead he became more and more insufferable. It was evident that beneath Dona's meek, submissive mask lay an influential, reactionary bigot whose small-minded views only reinforced his own. She hated the English, who in her eyes personified the worst excesses of liberal politics and immorality. She treated her parents-in-law with icy formality and her husband supported her without question. Wilhelm disdainfully called his parents and three younger sisters 'the English colony'. He complained that his father ignored him, or treated him like a *dummer Junge* (dumb child), and with deliberate rudeness, and blamed his mother for making her husband her 'creature', as well as never leaving father and son alone for more than five minutes whenever they met, so that his father's friendly demeanour instantly turned to one of sullen suspicion as soon as she entered the room.[11] On the rare occasions Wilhelm visited them, they said, he travelled with such a large suite that it was impossible for them to get near him for a private talk. They asked the Prince of Wales if he could have a friendly word with his nephew on his visit to attend their silver wedding celebrations, but whether the talk took place or not, there was no perceptible difference in Wilhelm's attitude. Later that year the Prince of Wales sent him a complete Highland outfit. He had himself photographed attired thus, with the inscription 'I bide my time' printed beneath, and had copies distributed liberally among family and friends.

Bismarck did not hesitate to exploit these family divisions for his own ends, in this case using the next Kaiser but one as a standard bearer against the forces of liberalism which looked to the Crown Prince and Princess. In the spring of 1884 he encouraged the aged Kaiser to delegate certain diplomatic missions, which should have been offered to the Crown Prince by right, to his son instead. In May Wilhelm went proudly to St Petersburg as Germany's representative at the coming of age celebrations of sixteen-year-old Grand Duke Nicholas, Tsarevich of Russia. While there he made the acquaintance of Bismarck's son Count Herbert, who was counsellor at the German embassy in St Petersburg. He relished the attention paid to him as chief envoy of the German empire, and he was deeply impressed with the bearing of the young infantry recruits on parade at the Winter Palace. Nevertheless, he betrayed rather more than he intended when he wrote in detail about the physical appearance of the soldiers; 'a very nice-looking lot, though the fact that hardly any of them had any hips made their white capes look as though they had been poured into their slim bodies'.[12] He also got on well with Tsar Alexander III, a family loving man who had revered his late cuckolded mother and initially viewed Wilhelm with distaste after hearing of family differences at the German Court, until assured by Count Herbert von Bismarck that the Crown Princess was to blame. After Wilhelm's departure the Tsar told the German ambassador that he had been very gratified by their conversation, and everything the Prince told him pleased him enormously; 'he grasps things exactly right and understands everything'.[13] On his return home the Prince wrote to the Tsar that he would always do what he could to guard Russian interests in Germany, especially against the 'false and intriguing character' of his uncle the Prince of Wales. This unsolicited slur on the brother-in-law of the Tsar's wife was not forgotten.

Family loyalties were strained even further by the arrival in the European royal marriage market of the Battenberg family. In 1851 Prince Alexander of Hesse had contracted a morganatic marriage with Countess Julie von Hauke, lady-in-waiting to his sister Marie, then wife of the Tsarevich of Russia. Of their four sons the eldest, Louis, married Princess Victoria of Hesse, elder sister of the Ella to whom Wilhelm had lost his heart. Another, Henry, became betrothed in 1885 to Queen Victoria's youngest daughter, Beatrice, an alliance which brought about strong criticism of the Battenbergs' less than royal birth, and outright condemnation of the Queen's partisanship of the family, from her eldest daughter's family at Berlin. The Queen was particularly angered by Empress Augusta's caustic comments, and even more by the 'extraordinary impertinence and insolence and, I must add, great unkindness of Willie and the foolish Dona'. As she remarked, Dona, 'poor, little insignificant princess',[14] was of hardly more noble birth herself than the Battenbergs.

Such dissension was significant as yet another Battenberg brother, Alexander ('Sandro'), hoped to marry into the Hohenzollern family. Appointed sovereign prince of the new Balkan state of Bulgaria in 1879, he paid a series of visits to the courts of Europe two years later, during which he was presented to the Crown Prince and Princess at Potsdam. He was seeking an eligible princess in the hope that marriage would strengthen his hold on the none too secure Balkan throne, and thought he had found a suitable consort in his hosts' eldest unmarried daughter Victoria. The Crown Princess found Sandro charming, and enthusiastically supported the match. The Crown Prince disagreed, partly because of the young man's morganatic parentage, partly as he dreaded the idea of his daughter ending up as the wife of a dethroned exile, but mostly because he knew his parents would never consent and did not wish to stir up yet more family strife.

Wilhelm firmly opposed any such marriage for his sister and did not hesitate to voice his opinion that the Battenbergs' lowly birth made them ineligible as prospective husbands for Hohenzollern princesses. For a while the exchanges between him and his mother on the subject were so heated that his friends advised him to keep his distance from his parents until matters had cooled. His champions in Prussian public life at the time watched the family differences with interest. Count Alfred von Waldersee, quartermaster-general of the general staff, recalling the fate that some felt might have befallen the heir in 1863 after his speech at Danzig, said that if the Crown Prince was suddenly to become Kaiser, 'there would be nothing for it but to transfer the Prince to a distant garrison'.[15] while Wilhelm said openly that Germany could never tolerate a foreigner like his mother on the throne, and on his grandfather's death it might be necessary to 'separate' his father from her.[16]

Wilhelm never had an 'inner circle' of friends, for the demands made on his time and strength by military service and diplomatic missions left him with little opportunity to enjoy simple companionship. In the autumn of 1881 he was promoted to major; in the following year he was transferred from the foot guards to the hussars, rising to the rank of colonel in October 1883 and general in January 1888. Of the select circle around him at this time, Count Waldersee was one of the most important figures. Twenty-seven years older than Wilhelm, he was married to the widow of Dona's uncle. The Countess did her best to exert a good influence on him; fiercely evangelical, like Dona herself, she attempted to steer him away from unbecoming habits such as heavy smoking and enjoying pornography. The Count's effect on the impressionable young Prince was less benign. With his remarkable memory and sense of orientation, studying maps intently before manoeuvres or rides so that his brain absorbed every detail, as well as a convivial soul, 'he was always the leading spirit in our friendly merrymakings'.[17] Nevertheless, he hated and despised the Crown Prince and Princess, and had no scruples about undermining any sense of loyalty in their eldest son.

Another significant figure, albeit briefly, was Count Herbert von Bismarck, who was being groomed as a future foreign minister. Like his father, Herbert Bismarck was a conscientious worker with his father's passion for political knowledge and intrigue, but without his insight or judgment of character, and with even less consideration for the feelings of others. Knowing that Wilhelm was less than totally devoted to his boring wife, and unaware that provision had already been made for such diversions, Herbert volunteered to find him a mistress. His offer came to Dona's attention, and from then he was no friend of hers. 'Beyond a certain comradeship such as readily arises between young men', Wilhelm recalled, 'given similarity of interests and good will on both sides, our relations did not progress; we were never united by sentiments of real friendship.'[18] The feeling was reciprocated, as Herbert Bismarck did not take long to see the future Kaiser's faults. He complained to Baron Holstein that Prince Wilhelm had no staying power, no interest in army life beyond wearing a handsome uniform and marching through the streets to the accompaniment of music and, most damning of all, was 'as cold as a block of ice', convinced that other people were only there to be used, 'after which they may be cast aside'.[19]

The third, one of the few real friends he ever had, and the one who would prove to be the most controversial, was Count Philipp von Eulenburg. A former guards officer who had won the Iron Cross for service in the Franco-Prussian War, he had never liked army life and transferred to the diplomatic corps with relief. He was attached to the embassy in Munich when Wilhelm and Dona first met him. While he disliked England and did nothing to counteract the Prince's anti-English prejudices, he had much of the enlightened, artistic outlook of the Crown Prince and Princess, and even the late Albert, Prince

Consort. Unlike the average heel-clicking Prussian of his generation, he hated practical jokes, and Wilhelm respected his feelings to the extent of never playing one on him. Sensitive and creative, he wrote novels and short stories, loved paintings and painted himself, encouraging Wilhelm to paint seascapes; he had a fine singing voice, and composed several songs. He and his wife held musical *soirées* where he played the piano and sang his own compositions with such expression that Wilhelm, turning the pages of his music, would be driven 'into almost feverish raptures'. Wilhelm, recalled Eulenburg, 'loved to greet me, when we met on shooting-mornings in the forest, with turns and phrases from my verses. I have had many a ravished listener to my performances, but hardly ever have I inspired such ravishment as in Prince Wilhelm.'[20]

In August 1886 they took a brief holiday together in Bavaria. The relationship, described by one recent historian as 'heliotrope-scented',[21] did not pass unseen by anxious contemporaries. Bismarck detected an apparently sincere 'attitude of adoration' and each time the Prince looked up, noticed he could be certain of 'seeing those worshipping eyes fixed upon him'.[22] Wilhelm made no secret of the fact to close and trusted acquaintances, among them Hinzpeter, to whom he introduced Eulenburg as 'my bosom friend – the only one I have', that there was an extraordinary bond between them.

In those days when homosexuality was frowned on in some countries and a punishable offence in others, few dared to speculate openly on a more intimate relationship between them. One who did some years later, albeit in veiled terms, was the frequently outspoken Princess Daisy of Pless: 'there is, in the good sense, quite a lot of the woman in the Emperor; he never forgot a slight and he could be feminine in his malice when anyone humiliated him'.[23] Only respect prevented her from committing further thoughts to paper on the 'feminine' aspect. Eulenburg was married with a wife and six children (a further two had died in infancy). Yet in the light of allegations made in court twenty years later, coupled with the discreet observations of contemporaries, a deliberate avoidance of the obvious conclusions would savour of whitewash. The reputations of the notorious homosexual King Ludwig II of Bavaria, remembered best for his extravagant castles and patronage of Wagner, and of the similarly inclined King Karl of Württemberg, were protected at the time, though in a less prudish moral climate a hundred years later it was no longer felt necessary to suppress facts. However there were married contemporaries of Wilhelm's whose orientation was definitely not heterosexual – among them Ferdinand, Prince of Bulgaria, Oscar Wilde (both of whom had children), and Grand Duke Serge of Russia (who did not). Whether Wilhelm sought gratification of this kind outside his marriage or not, one can only speculate, but it was possible. Forty years later Emil Ludwig wrote in his biography of the former Kaiser that Eulenburg 'was the first to open the gates of the garden of Romance to the young man who had been forced into the part of hard-bitten Prussian Prince, and now was taking leave of an adolescent poor alike in love and in the dreams of youth'.[24] Axel von Varnbüler, a civil servant and diplomat, wrote to Kuno von Moltke, a mutual friend, of 'your individuality', 'these pure heights', or other similar, less pejorative terms. Significantly Wilhelm had written to Eulenburg that he never really felt happy at Berlin, only at Potsdam with his regiment; before that, 'I had lived through such horrible years when no one understood my individuality.'[25] Either he had chosen his words with astonishing carelessness, or he had admitted his inclinations in the customary veiled terms of the day. Nevertheless, historian Isobel Hull, who examined the question in considerable depth, concluded that despite the suspicions of journalist Maximilian Harden,* it was unlikely that Wilhelm and Eulenburg had a physical relationship,[26] while John Röhl maintained that Wilhelm 'went through life neither realizing nor accepting his own homosexuality'.[27]

   The Prince, his mother wrote in a letter to his father (13 November 1884), was 'somewhat narrow-minded and hard-hearted – only time can help him do away with these evils! He only associates with hard-core officers, Junkers and Berlin society'.[28] It was an assessment with which Major-General Leopold Swaine, British military attaché in Berlin, broadly agreed in a letter to Queen Victoria's private secretary Sir Henry Ponsonby (16 March 1885), though he expressed more positive hopes for the future. The Prince, he admitted, was narrow-minded, 'like most of his countrymen', and his early marriage as well as the great age of his grandfather had prevented him from being allowed to travel more widely before settling down. 'His military surroundings flatter him, and the life he leads between Potsdam and Berlin, and Berlin and Potsdam, is not calculated to increase his knowledge of the world or to induce him to understand either his own nation, or that some good may be got out of seeing other countries and other peoples otherwise than out of books'. Despite these shortcomings he was 'a right good young fellow, and he is the making of everything deserving the great future he has before him. He works hard, he reads everything that he thinks will instruct him, he is self-willed, but he has great determination. *He requires very careful leading.*'[29]

---

*See below, p. 128ff.

At the time Wilhelm was in one of his bitterly Anglophobic moods. Three years earlier, in May 1882, when Lord Frederick Cavendish was appointed chief secretary to the lord lieutenant of Ireland and assassinated in broad daylight soon after his arrival in Dublin, he tastelessly said it was 'the best news that I have received today'.[30] Now Queen Victoria was angry with him because of his hostility towards the Battenbergs, refused to let him visit London that year and refrained from acknowledging a military plan he had sent her for the relief of General Gordon, besieged and killed by the Mahdi at Khartoum. Wilhelm said angrily that the Queen was an 'old hag',[31] the senile captive of her German-hating children, and had plainly lived too long. Despite his dislike of England, Eulenburg looked askance at the Prince's 'blind fury' against England, which might prove to be a diplomatic liability for Germany one day.[32]

Prince Wilhelm's first visit to Russia had been successful enough, but the second was a failure. After his first trip he had taken it upon himself to write regularly to Tsar Alexander III and the Tsarevich, and some of his letters clumsily tried to turn the Tsar against his English relations. In one he allegedly advised the Tsar not to trust anything he might hear from his father, the Crown Prince, as he was 'under my mother's thumb and she, in turn, is guided by the Queen of England and makes him see everything through English eyes'. Another poured scorn on the Prince of Wales: 'we are not at all pleased at this appearance – pardon, he is your brother-in-law – with his duplicity and love of intrigue he will doubtless try either to encourage the cause of the Bulgarian [Alexander von Battenberg] . . . or discuss politics with the ladies behind the scenes'.[33] Some doubt has been cast on the authenticity of these and similar documents, which may have been forged by the Russians, but the Tsar's deceptively friendly initial reception turned Wilhelm's head and made him overestimate his own importance. In private Tsar Alexander III was inclined to defer to the views of his consort Marie, younger sister of the Princess of Wales, and to some extent his more assertive brother Grand Duke Vladimir, whom he disliked and never trusted but whose powerful Germanophile, anti-English views were echoed by others in imperial and government circles at St Petersburg. Wilhelm felt he had a powerful ally in Vladimir.

The visit during the autumn of 1886 came at a difficult time, for that summer he had suffered severely from pain in his left ear and spent two months convalescencing. He was still recovering when the Kaiser informed him that he was about to be sent to Russia as part of a new German–Russian *rapprochement,* to advertise abroad the continued existence of the *Dreikaiserbund,* or alliance of the three Emperors

(German, Russian and Austrian); and to express to the Tsar German approval for a free hand in the Balkans and the Dardanelles. When Wilhelm loyally pointed out that for him to undertake the mission would offend his father, he was told that Bismarck was opposed to sending the Crown Prince, who was manifestly pro-English, anti-Russian and a close friend of the Prince of Bulgaria, the Tsar's sworn enemy. Reluctantly Wilhelm went to Brest-Litovsk, where he dutifully told the Tsar as he was bidden. Having formed an unfavourable opinion of the Prince, the Tsar told him brusquely that if he wished to take possession of Constantinople he would do so, and did not require the permission or consent of Prince Bismarck, but promised to continue supporting the *Dreikaiserbund* and thus safeguard the peace of Europe.

At about the same time Bismarck appointed him to an unofficial position at the foreign office in Berlin, 'to receive tuition in the management of the Office and the distribution of duties among the officials of the various departments, and to become conversant with the trend of policy through the examination and explanation of individual despatches'.[34] Such apprenticeship should have been the preserve of the Crown Prince by right, and the latter had every reason to object, as he did. 'In view of the immaturity as well as the inexperience of my eldest son, together with his tendency towards overbearingness and self-conceit, I cannot but frankly regard it as dangerous to allow him at present to take any part in foreign affairs',[35] he wrote to Bismarck, who threw the letter aside without bothering to reply. It was galling for the parents to see their son being treated by the chancellor as though he was Crown Prince if not Kaiser already. Such humiliation, however, was nothing in comparison with the tragedy about to unfold at Court.

In March 1887 royalties from throughout Europe came to Berlin for the ninetieth birthday celebrations of Kaiser Wilhelm. His grandson had long revered the imposing old gentleman with extravagant moustache and sidewhiskers, and a few strands of hair waxed to the dome of his head every morning. He slept for five hours each night, rising at 6 a.m. and standing on the pavement outside the palace an hour later in all weathers to take the salute as his guard marched past. Invariably courteous at receptions, he was almost stone deaf, and thanks to shoddy dentistry he talked so indistinctly that it was hard to tell whether he was speaking in German or French. He still argued fiercely if incoherently with his wife, now a wheelchair-bound invalid whose life had briefly hung in the balance until a major operation for breast cancer in 1881. Any illness of hers made him anxious; having been married for nearly sixty years to a woman with whom he quarrelled almost daily while they were under the same roof, he could hardly bear to face a future without what had become a way of life. Having narrowly escaped after an attempt on his life in his eighty-second year, he seemed almost indestructible. Eight years later he was becoming ever more feeble after a succession of mild strokes, but each time he was ostensibly on his deathbed, the sight of sorrowing relatives seemed to rouse him to defiance and hasten recovery. Even so one of the dinner guests, Crown Prince Rudolf, reported that he looked so terrible that he could not live much longer.

Crown Prince Friedrich Wilhelm, now aged fifty-five, lacked his father's iron constitution. He suffered from severe colds every winter; years of frustration had resulted in a sad lack of self-confidence. Moods of depression and what he called *Weltschmerz* (world-weariness) were taking their toll. He seemed to have a foreboding of future events, and in the 1870s he had told Hinzpeter – who confided the words to Wilhelm many years later – that he would never rule; the succession would skip a generation.[36] The Crown Princess saw it as her duty to spur him on to look to the future with optimism in which she too had rather less faith than she might admit. Since the death of their son Waldemar something had died in her, and in its place there was a steely, sometimes single-minded tenacity. Increasing ill-health, particularly attacks of neuralgia, sciatica and rheumatism, may have been a result of porphyria passed down by her great-grandfather, and perhaps affected her judgment.[37]

At the birthday banquet the Crown Prince made a speech proposing his father's health, and then announcing the betrothal of his second son Henry to his cousin, Irene of Hesse, one of Ella's younger sisters. His generally resonant voice sounded unusually hoarse. For the last few months he had been unwell with one ailment after another. Measles caught from his younger daughters the previous spring was followed by a few weeks of recuperation at Homburg before a round of visits to exhibitions, attendance at the funeral of King Ludwig of Bavaria, who had been deposed and drowned in June 1886, followed by festivals and military manoeuvres. On an autumn holiday in Italy he caught a severe cold; at the end of the year his voice was still hoarse, and when symptoms persisted for weeks Dr Wegner decided to seek specialist advice from Professor Gerhardt. A small swelling on the lower portion of the left vocal cord was diagnosed, and proved resistant to initial attempts to remove it firstly with a wire snare, then a circular knife, then cauterization with red-hot platinum wire.

It was evident that the patient had more than a simple tumour, as had been supposed, and some suspected that the growth might be cancerous. In April Dr Wegner sent him to convalesce at Ems. When he returned on 13 May he thought he was cured, apart from persistent hoarseness. It was a shock when diagnosis confirmed that a swelling on the vocal cord was still present, and larger than before. Another opinion was required and Wegner consulted Professor Bergmann, a surgeon who had to rely on Gerhardt's diagnosis. He recommended an immediate external operation on the growth, which he was convinced was malignant; for this to be successful he would need to split the larynx in order to remove the swelling permanently.

The alarmed Crown Prince now began to fear his father might outlive him. As he was heir to the throne the Kaiser had to be informed, as did Bismarck and Wilhelm, second in succession to the throne. Bismarck summoned three more doctors, who confirmed their colleagues' diagnosis. An operation was planned for 21 May, and it was agreed that the patient should be kept in complete ignorance until the last moment. Aware of the risk in such an operation, Bismarck and Dr Wegner wanted to seek yet another specialist opinion from outside Germany. For political reasons it was deemed inadvisable to consult anyone from Austria or France, and Wegner recommended Dr Morell Mackenzie, an eminent Scottish laryngologist practising in London. His colleagues agreed with Bismarck that Mackenzie was the right man. In the light of their fervent denials after the event, and their assertions that the Crown Princess had insisted on sending for a British doctor as she (or, as one German newspaper stated baldly, the 'interfering' Queen Victoria) did not trust German medicine, the fact that they made the decision was crucial. Mackenzie duly arrived, examined the Crown Prince's throat and cut a small section from the growth, which he sent to the renowned pathologist Professor Virchow. The latter found the sample to be too small for conclusive examination and requested another. Three further portions were removed, and after examining each he stated that no trace of cancer could be found in any of them.[38] Despite this the other German doctors insisted that the growth was malign and carcinomatous, and that the Crown Prince would die if not operated upon, whereas Mackenzie maintained just as firmly that such an operation would kill him at once.*

The Crown Prince and Princess had been invited to represent the Kaiser at Queen Victoria's jubilee celebrations in London the following month. They were loath to turn down such an invitation, especially as the Crown Princess had every right to be there as the Queen's eldest child. Despite concern for his father's health, Wilhelm took it for granted that

---

*Dr Bergmann performed the operation on two patients with the same symptoms in 1890 and 1896, and in both instances the patient died on the operating table.

he would be representing the Kaiser instead. When he heard that Dr Mackenzie had said the Crown Prince could take part after all, and be treated in his London surgery at the same time, he was indignant. Perhaps he felt that unjustifiable risks were being taken with his father's life, but at the same time he believed he was being upstaged. Queen Victoria was not inclined to invite him, partly because of accommodation and lodging problems, but especially as he and Dona had been so rude to her about the Battenberg marriages, and behaved so badly towards his parents. Knowing that he would be more insufferable still if not invited, the Crown Princess and the Prince of Wales asked her to reconsider and she gave in reluctantly.

The reactions of those close to Wilhelm were crucial. Rumours were circulated, possibly by Count and Countess Waldersee – if not, they certainly did nothing to dispel them – that the Prussian constitution forbade the accession of an heir unable to speak, or suffering from a fatal disease. Perhaps it was fortunate for Wilhelm that Prince Friedrich Karl, the Crown Prince's cousin, had died two years previously – ironically, of a cancerous tumour in the face and at the same age – so that no more was heard of the unsuitability of a one-armed man becoming Kaiser. Such rumours were false and Bismarck, now beginning to realize that Prince Wilhelm was not the pliant, malleable pupil he had once seemed, lost no time in telling him not to believe such nonsense.

As the Crown Prince was a grown man, the Kaiser (too senile by now to understand the situation) and Bismarck stipulated that they could not oppose his decision to go to London for the jubilee. The only condition they could make was that two of the Prussian doctors should be included in his suite so that they could have some say as to how much he should be allowed to exert himself in the programme. Dr Wegner and Dr Landgraf, Gerhardt's assistant, were chosen.

On 29 May Wilhelm visited his mother to tell her that the Kaiser had personally told him that he and no other should represent him in London, and that he himself had written to Queen Victoria to tell her this was his grandfather's express wish. The Crown Prince and Princess were angry, and afterwards the latter wrote to convey a truer picture of events to her mother. Wilhelm, she said, thought her 'very *leichtsinnig* [irresponsible] in not putting a more serious construction on his Papa's ailment, and that Dr Mackenzie held out false hopes to me. As William understands nothing whatever about it, what he says is quite indifferent to me . . . he has a perfect system – of considering himself answerable to the Emperor alone and arranging everything with him as if we did not exist.'[39]

In order to flatter him it was agreed that Wilhelm could take part in all ceremonial functions, while his parents would attend as family. He would be representing his grandfather at the jubilee in a sense, while Queen Victoria made it clear to him that he was not the 'official representative'. To avoid undue exertion the Crown Prince did not attend the state banquet at Windsor Castle which followed their arrival in England. However, there was never any doubt as to who would be more warmly received – father or son. Riding beside the Queen's carriage in the white uniform of the Pomeranian cuirassiers, with silver breastplate, eagle-crested helmet and Garter star glistening in the June sunshine during their procession *en route* from Buckingham Palace to Westminster Abbey for the thanksgiving service on 21 June, the Crown Prince towered above them all. Nobody had yet uttered the forbidden word 'cancer' to him, though in his darker moods he suspected as much. Likewise, the Londoners who watched and cheered knew that his health was giving cause for anxiety, and their sympathies and good wishes were unquestioningly with him. Wilhelm, Dona and their eldest son Wilhelm had their own place in the procession, albeit less prominently.

After the festivities Wilhelm and his family returned to Germany, while the Crown Prince and Princess relaxed at Osborne and Balmoral. Queen Victoria had her doubts about Mackenzie, who for all his knowledge and skill tended to make enemies too easily and was somewhat rash in promising a complete cure, albeit with favourable conditions. Reluctantly she acceded to the Crown Princess's request to confer a knighthood on him, but when she asked him searching questions afterwards about her son-in-law's case she was disturbed that he could tell her so little.

By October the Scottish air was too cold for them and they moved first to Toblach in the Austrian Tyrol, then to Venice and then Baveno. Here on 18 October all the children except for Charlotte gathered to celebrate their father's fifty-sixth birthday. Wilhelm was encouraged to find him looking comparatively well, but when he told his mother he could not share 'the fateful optimism' about his condition, she became angry with him. Already public opinion in Germany was demanding his return. It was obvious that the Kaiser could not last for much longer, and for his heir to be abroad at such a time was inexpedient. Inspired probably by Bismarck, they did not hesitate to say openly that they knew he was suffering from cancer but that he refused to admit it as he did not want to be pronounced incurable and therefore debarred from ascending the throne.

Early in November they moved south to Villa Zirio, San Remo, on the Mediterranean. Within twenty-four hours there was an alarming deterioration in the Crown Prince's condition. Mackenzie's assistant, Dr Hovell, sent for his senior colleague, who examined him and had to admit to the patient when asked bluntly if it was cancer that 'it looks very much like it, but it is impossible to be certain'.[40] Immediate family and ministers were informed, and on 12 November the *Reichsanzeiger* (German Official Gazette) announced in an unsigned bulletin that the Crown Prince's disease was 'due to the existence of a malignant new growth' which was of a 'carcinomatous' character.[41]

Wilhelm's intervention a few days later was singularly ill-timed. The most sympathetic judgment is that he accepted without question the verdict of his flatterers that his father was being mishandled by Mackenzie and, excited by the prospect of premature power, tried to exert his influence in what he considered to be the right direction.[42] The distraught Crown Princess believed that their eldest son did not care for his father, while he himself was convinced that had the operation taken place in May his father would have recovered by now. More alarmed than he cared to admit by Wilhelm's new sense of self-importance, Bismarck might have been able to act as conciliator if only the Crown Prince and Princess had been able to trust him. Needless to say, he had only himself and his behaviour for the last twenty-five years to blame for the fact that they could not. Maybe Bismarck realized too late that his flattery of Prince Wilhelm and the wilful campaign of denigration against the young man's parents had reaped a greater harvest than he had expected. The next generation of politicians did not shrink from spiteful comment. Typical of their spleen were the words of Baron Friedrich von Holstein, at that time first counsellor of the German foreign ministry, who called the Crown Princess 'a degenerate or corrupt character'. She came to Prussia, he went on, 'her father's spoiled darling, convinced she was a political prodigy. Far from acquiring influence here, she saw herself obliged to renounce any kind of political activity and to conform to the restraint of the Prussian court which she hated. She has always despised her husband. She will greet his death as the moment of deliverance.'[43]

The only mediator on the horizon was Queen Victoria, who could see the faults on all sides from a distance and tried to ease the situation by letter. She was well aware that her daughter had inadvertently made enemies in Germany, if unwilling to acknowledge that she had done so largely by carrying out her parental instructions never to forget her position as the Queen of England's eldest daughter; but at the same time she was ready to make allowances for her grandson's behaviour.

Two more doctors, Professor von Schrotter and Dr Krause, had recently been sent to San Remo to replace Gerhardt and Bergmann. At a consultation with Mackenzie they agreed unanimously that as the disease was undoubtedly cancer of the larynx, the only alternatives were either tracheotomy, an incision in the windpipe, which would avoid danger of suffocation, or total removal of the larynx, resulting in permanent loss of voice and maybe of life as well. Even the former operation would only prolong his life by weeks or possibly months. When given the stark choice, the Crown Prince and Princess agreed that he would submit to tracheotomy if and when it became necessary.

Shortly after this Wilhelm arrived, bringing Dr Schmidt, who he said had been sent to examine his father and take a report back to Berlin with him. There are two separate, contradictory accounts of what happened next. Whatever the truth of the matter, he had not made allowances for the Crown Princess's frantic state of mind. According to her letter to Queen Victoria (15 November), he told his father to get up and dressed to return to Berlin for an operation. Struggling to hold her temper, she suggested that they should go for a quiet walk together. Wilhelm retorted that he had no time as he would be too busy speaking to the doctors. When she told him firmly that they had instructions to report to her and not to him, he maintained that he was acting on his grandfather's orders, and that he was to see the doctors were not interfered with in any way. The manner in which he was addressing her before others, and with his back half turned towards her, she found intolerable. The Crown Princess said she would tell his father how he had behaved and, ask that he be forbidden to visit them in future – and with that she walked away. 'He was as rude, as disagreeable and as impertinent to me as possible when he arrived, but I pitched into him with, I am afraid, considerable violence.'[44]

Realizing he had gone too far, she went on, he sent the chamberlain Count Radolinski after her, to say he had not meant to be rude, and begging her not to tell his father anything, but it was his duty to see that the Kaiser's commands were carried out. She said she bore him no malice, but she would suffer no interference. They went for a walk together, and he was pleasant to everybody, including Mackenzie. 'When he has not his head stuffed with rubbish at Berlin he is quite nice and *traitable*, and then we are very pleased to have him,' she continued, 'but I will not have him dictate to me – the head on my shoulders is every bit as good as his.'[45]

Nearly forty years later, Wilhelm recalled in his memoirs that he 'had to allow the flood of her reproaches to pass over me, and to hear her decided refusal to allow me to see my father' until he heard a rustling at the top of the stairs, and looked up to see his father smiling as he welcomed him. He ran up the stairs, 'and with infinite emotion we held each other embraced, while in low whispers he expressed his joy at my visit'.[46] His letter to Queen Victoria at the time (11 November) mentioned nothing of this, but underlined that despite the impression he often gave to the contrary, he was genuinely moved by the situation.

The final descision [*sic*] of the Doctors has been taken this morning, & the fearful hour has at last after all arrived! They told Papa everything & he received the news like a Hohenzollern & a soldier, upright, looking the doctors straight in the face. He knows that he is irretrievably lost and doomed! And yet he did not move an inch or a muscle, they were immensely moved by this splendid display of character. His great & noble heart did not flinch & he is serene, composed & calm, like a brave captain, who knows that in leading his forlorne [sic] hope he will fall with his brave men, he holds up his head & even tries to cheer us up when we all of us broke down after the doctors had left. It is quite horrible this confounded word 'hopeless'! Poor Mama is doing wonders, she is perpetually on the verge of completely breaking down, & yet she keeps on that gigantic struggle against her feelings only not to distress Papa, & not to let the household see her grief; the poor gentlemen are distracted & can scarcely speak & our doctor is in tears. Besides Grandmama is seriously ill & not fit to hear any bad news & the Emperor very deeply affected by the bad news, so that one is nearly off one's head with anxiety.[47]

Six days later Bismarck published a proclamation creating Wilhelm *Stellvertreter des Kaisers*, or deputy Kaiser, and in effect virtually regent, with the authority, to sign state papers on the Kaiser's behalf should he himself become incapacitated. While the idea was reasonable, it was tactless of Bismarck not to consult the Crown Prince first, and allow him only to hear about it once the decision had been taken. A notification of the duties, signed by Bismarck, arrived at the Villa Zirio, and the Crown Princess awaited a suitable moment to show it to her husband. A couple of days later their second son Henry arrived, taking from his pocket a letter from Wilhelm describing his position in rather self-satisfied tones. The Crown Prince had not been so angry for a long time, declaring that he would not have his son, father and the chancellor act as though he was already dead; he would return to Berlin and confront every one of them. He and his wife were at length pacified by Bismarck's assurance that, contrary to their fears, the order had nothing to do with attempting to alter the succession and would automatically lapse with the accession of the Crown Prince on his father's death.

Despite his new responsibilities, Wilhelm somehow found time to indulge in a few private liaisons. During this fateful autumn, while eyes were focused anxiously on his father at San Remo, his eldest son ostensibly went hunting in Austria. Ella Somsics secretly followed him by train from Berlin with a friend, Anna Homolatsch. He met them in an inn at the village of Mürzsteg, but refused to reimburse them their travelling costs. They stormed out in anger, Ella having thoughtfully taken his monogrammed cufflinks marked with the Prussian crown, to display as a souvenir around Vienna. Realizing his mistake, he begged them to return, and presumably offered to pay their expenses after all, as they joined him later at *Gasthaus zum König von Sachsen*, at Eisenerz. A policeman was about to order Ella and Anna away when one of the Prince's suite intervened to explain that the ladies were 'for his master'. The three of them took a room for the night and made so much noise that all the other guests were awakened.

Word of Wilhelm's pillow talk during this escapade reached the ears of Crown Prince Rudolf, who informed an Austrian military attaché of Wilhelm's 'enchanting conversation with these two unclean females'. The Prussian heir presumptive spoke with unconcealed cynicism about his parents and his wife, reserving the greatest scorn for his seriously ill father, who could be likened to his fellow Crown Prince of the Habsburg empire as a 'conceited popularity-seeker under Jewish influence'; Austria was 'rotten, close to dissolution', and on the verge of collapse, to the extent that her Emperor could, if he liked, 'eke out his life as an insignificant monarch in Hungary'; and that as a nation the Austrians were pleasant people, 'but useless pansies and gourmands, no longer fit for life'.[48]

Even bearing in mind Crown Prince Rudolf's hatred and contempt for Wilhelm, there is no reason to suppose that he was exaggerating. The imperial heirs had long had a mutual antipathy. Wilhelm was pained 'to see how little friendship the Crown Prince [of Austria] felt for the new German Empire and the Dual Alliance, and how his soul revolted from the Prussian idea', and considered these as the main reasons for their relations chilling to the point where 'they were reduced to what political necessity demanded'.[49] This smacks of pomposity when one realizes why Rudolf disliked Wilhelm so much. Rudolf was appalled that a future Kaiser, five months younger than him, should be a 'dyed-in-the-wool Junker and reactionary' who called the *Reichstag* 'this pig-sty', and who announced his intention of having the Liberal parliamentarian Eugen Richter, a leading voice against anti-Semitism, beaten up by six NCOs.[50]

Quite apart from this distasteful little interlude, Wilhelm's public behaviour left much to be desired in the eyes of Bismarck as well as his parents. At about this time he was introduced to the Court chaplain, Adolf von Stöcker, and his anti-Semitic Christian Socialist Movement, a narrow-minded circle devoted to baiting and thwarting Jews and Roman Catholics. The Crown Prince, Princess and Empress found discrimination utterly abhorrent and had always kept their distance from this bigoted ensemble, but the Prussian officer corps, Kaiser Wilhelm himself, and several at Court shared some if not all of their views and policies, namely keeping the German race 'pure', prohibiting Jewish immigration into Germany, excluding Jews from public office, and removing them from all teaching posts in public schools. After the Crown Prince had attended a service at a Berlin synagogue as a demonstration of solidarity against recent attacks on Jews, the notoriously anti-Semitic Count and Countess Waldersee tried to canvass support for expelling the Crown Princess in disgrace from the country, and for an army coup to capture her husband, remove him from the succession, and place the anti-Semite Wilhelm on the throne after his grandfather instead.

Prince Wilhelm had long been an admirer of Stöcker, whom he called 'a second Luther',[51] and had defended him two years earlier when he was found guilty in a libel case brought by a Jewish newspaper editor. Feeling the Court could be damaged by publicity surrounding the proceedings, the Kaiser had demanded his resignation, until the Prince had written him a lengthy and passionate but very articulate letter – inspired and probably drafted partly if not wholly by Waldersee – defending the man who, he said, was the Hohenzollern monarchy's most powerful pillar and bravest protector against the slanders of the Jewish press and law courts.

In November 1887 Wilhelm presided over a meeting in Berlin for the 'development of evangelistic church life and Christian charity', praising national splendour, military glory and German purity. Bismarck, who distrusted Stöcker, reproached the Prince for uttering such nonsense and meddling in matters beyond him, only to be told that the power of the present chancellor would not last; he must not be allowed to forget that the Kaiser was master. When Bismarck had articles published in the official press taking the religious conservatives to task for using the Prince, the latter wrote petulantly to Hinzpeter that he did not deserve such treatment, as for the chancellor's sake he had 'for years locked myself out of my parents' house'.[52]

At about the same time Wilhelm drafted a proclamation to the German princes which was to be published in the event of his accession. Bismarck told him to burn it. Sulking, Wilhelm replied that when he came to the throne he would have all Jewish influence over the press stopped. Told that this would be a violation of the constitution, Wilhelm said grandly that they would have to get rid of the constitution as well.

Adding to his grievances at the time was a sense that his relatives in England were ignoring him. After dining and shooting with him in December his friend Colonel Swaine told Sir Henry Ponsonby of his bitterness. When he went to San Remo, he had told Swaine, Queen Victoria had asked him for an account of how he found his father. He wrote a long letter on the subject but neither received a letter in return, nor any acknowledgement. Such action, Wilhelm felt bitterly, 'leaves him out in the cold and will never tend to bring him nearer to his English Relations'. He was equally upset at rumours outside Germany that he was 'very anti-English and most warlike'. England and Germany, he said, 'should go hand in hand in all political questions and that we two being strong and powerful should uphold the Peace of Europe. You [England] with a good fleet and we with our great Army can do this and if my English Relatives will only give me the opportunity I would tell them this myself. But if they don't write to me and don't speak to me when the opportunity presents itself how can they ever know what my feelings really are.' Queen Victoria wrote indignantly to Ponsonby (13 December) that Colonel Swaine flattered Prince Wilhelm far too much. His English relations, she made clear, had been 'shocked and pained at his behaviour towards his Parents for some time past – passing them over and settling things behind their backs with the Emperor'. At San Remo he had shown so little feeling and respect towards his mother in front of strangers: 'Let him be a dutiful and affectionate son trying to help and support his Mother in her terrible anxiety instead of opposing and annoying her and his Father who should in no way be annoyed or irritated and she should be most happy to be on friendly and affectionate terms as when he was a child.'[53]

The Crown Princess was grateful not to have been in Berlin at the time to see her son make such a fool of himself. Though she saw reports in the papers – which she kept from her husband as far as possible, in order that he should not see falsehoods about his illness which would only make him more depressed than he was already – she was too preoccupied with trying to keep his spirits up to bother unduly about matters beyond their control. In any case she and her husband realized that their long apprenticeship was drawing to a close, even though in circumstances sadly different from those they had envisaged.

The Crown Prince appeared to rally over Christmas and the new year of 1888, but in January his condition deteriorated. On 8 February the tracheotomy became necessary to avoid any danger of suffocation. The operation was successful though the patient would have to breathe through a canula in future. Meanwhile, at the end of the previous month Wilhelm had celebrated his twenty-ninth birthday with promotion to general commanding the second infantry brigade of guards. The promotion was a swift one, his father felt, as he had 'never commanded an infantry regiment, much less one of the line, as I have been most anxious for him to do for years'.[54]

Yet even Wilhelm was less preoccupied for the moment with military matters than with a sudden obsession with an Anglo-Jewish plot. One can only assume that Waldersee and Stöcker were behind this nonsense. On 19 February he wrote to Eulenburg describing the doctors in attendance on his father as *Judenlümmel* (Jewish filth) and various other derogatory terms, as well as being filled with racial hatred and 'anti-Germanism to the very edge of the grave'. It was bad enough, he averred, to have a deformed arm thanks to the incompetence of an English doctor, without having an Anglo-Jewish doctor, Moritz Markowitz, masquerading under the name of Morell Mackenzie, now killing his father.[55]

The Kaiser knew he was dying, and at the end of February he sent his grandson to San Remo to bring his son back to Berlin at once so he could see him one last time. But nothing could alter the Crown Princess's conviction that the most important thing was for her husband to stay in the mild climate of San Remo as long as possible, especially as the Kaiser had been ill so often during the last few years and always recovered. For him to leave at once, she wrote to Queen Victoria, would be 'utter madness'.[56]

However, Wilhelm was on his best behaviour, making an effort to appear friendly and considerate for once. He could sympathize with his father's wishes to stay where he was, for he had come to San Remo after representing the Kaiser at the funeral of his cousin Ludwig, second son of the Grand Duke and Duchess of Baden, who had died suddenly on 23 February. The bitter cold had caused a recurrence of his old ear trouble. Not having seen his father for several weeks, he was horrified at the change in his appearance. The yellow colour of the Crown Prince's face, he noticed, testified to the rapid progress of his disease. He was perpetually tormented by a severe cough, and he had to rely on scribbling notes every time he wanted to say something, as his hoarse whisper of a voice had gone for good. Despite Wilhelm's differences with his mother, he was moved by the sight of the devotion with which she nursed her evidently dying husband, 'and how nothing in the world would persuade her to believe the awful truth'.[57]

Prince Wilhelm returned to Berlin with the doctors' considered opinion that his father had no more than six months left. On 7 March he telegraphed his parents to report that the Emperor was very weak after a bad night, and two days later the Crown Prince was about to take his morning walk in the park of Villa Zirio when he was handed a telegram addressed 'To His Majesty The German Emperor and King Friedrich Wilhelm'.

The new sovereign had wanted to reign as Kaiser Friedrich IV, thereby implying a line of continuity from the medieval Hohenstaufen rulers. However, his wife, eldest son and Bismarck pointed out that as he was King Friedrich III of Prussia it would be advisable to use the same form for his imperial title. Arrangements were made for their return to Berlin, and for them to move into Charlottenburg Palace, in apartments belonging to their daughter and son-in-law Prince and Princess Bernhard of Saxe-Meiningen. These had been well-heated in preparation, and as the palace was surrounded by parkland, some distance from the city of Berlin, there was less risk of dust, a vital consideration for a patient who had just undergone a tracheotomy.

The Kaiser's first meeting as ruler with his eldest son and heir, now Crown Prince Wilhelm, was on the evening of 11 March. Father and son embraced each other emotionally, but as for the reunion between mother and son, there is only the dubious account of a pseudonymous Count Axel von Schwering who alleged that the Empress Victoria 'turned her head aside, and seemed to busy herself with the Emperor, without making any sign that she noticed her son'.[58] The Kaiser was dissuaded from attending his father's funeral on 16 March, a day of bitter wind and snow, and could only watch the procession from his window. Crown Prince Wilhelm took his place as chief mourner, following the coffin and leading other members of royalty present, among them the Prince of Wales, the Tsarevich and the Crown Prince of Austria.

In England there was uncertainty as to how ill the new sovereign really was. Speculating on the outlook for Anglo-German relations if he should recover, the *Graphic* in London thought it unlikely that any major constitutional changes would be made during his reign. 'Surrounded by watchful and jealous rivals, Germany cannot afford to waste her strength in making hazardous experiments in the art of government. But the Emperor Frederick will at least do nothing to hinder legitimate constitutional development, and it may be in his power to prepare the way for important reforms which new conditions will render necessary. We in England have every reason to wish that he may have a long and prosperous reign, for it is known that he shares his wife's desire for the establishment of the most intimate and cordial relations between Germany and Great Britain.'[59]

This was the last desire of certain people in Berlin. Bismarck had asked Bergmann how long the Kaiser could be expected to live. On being told that he could barely last through the summer, the chancellor knew he could be patient. This was more than could be said for his son Herbert, who told Count von Bülow, a future chancellor, that he would regard their sovereign's 'political departure' as a good thing. In view of his wife's influence over him and her very English attitude of mind, 'a long reign of the Emperor Frederick would make us dependent on England, and that would be our greatest misfortune. It could affect us politically at home as well as abroad.'[60]

A new bond between father and son was evident at the start of the new reign. On the first Sunday on which Crown Prince Wilhelm, his brother and sisters went to Charlottenburg to attend service in the palace chapel, the Kaiser showed him plans and elevations for a projected rebuilding of Berlin cathedral. The architect Herr Raschdorff had completed these after consultation with him and his wife when they were Crown Prince and Princess, and as he would not live to see completion of the work, he wanted his son to ensure that they would be carried out after his death.

Wilhelm also received an order authorizing him to act as the Kaiser's representative in signing certain state documents, a similar appointment to that which he had held since November in lieu of his grandfather. It was rumoured that the Kaiser wanted to make his wife regent. Everyone knew that the chancellor would oppose such a step and the Crown Prince, as well as his brother Henry, asserted at once that 'the Hohenzollerns, Prussia and the German Empire would not let a woman rule them'.[61] As the Kaiser knew that such a reaction was inevitable, and as he did not have the physical strength to press for any such policies, it was unlikely that he would have planned such a move which he knew would be fiercely contested.

Nevertheless, Wilhelm felt that difficulties were being put in his way when he tried to visit his father, with attempts being made to cut them off or prevent contact altogether. He claimed that spies were posted to give notice of his arrival at the palace, in order that he would be greeted at the door with the news that the Kaiser was asleep and that his mother had gone out for a walk. The purpose, he believed, was to prevent him from speaking with his father without witnesses being present. One day he successfully slipped in by the back stairs into his father's bedroom with the aid of a valet, and his father was delighted to see him, wanting to know why he had not visited more often. Wilhelm said he had tried several times to visit, but was never admitted; the Kaiser confirmed that his presence was welcome at any time. Next time Wilhelm saw various unknown faces watching from the doctors' room, and he locked the door. On leaving the palace he expressed his displeasure at the presence of these men, only to be told that they were in no position to get rid of journalists protected by Mackenzie.

Wilhelm's behaviour and bearing during his father's reign are difficult to interpret. Biographers and historians are obliged to rely largely on his own account and on the surviving letters of his mother, as well as Queen Victoria's letters to some extent, all written from a highly defensive point of view. Examining the combined evidence impartially, and more than a century after the event, it is possible to be certain of only one thing. At such a tense time he was torn between the desire to be a loyal son, between apprehension and excitement at being about to enter the inheritance to which he had been born, and between the toadying of those, such as Waldersee, who did their best to turn his mind against his parents in the hope of gaining promotion in the next reign.

While it is easy to level a charge (as many biographers have done) at the Empress that she was exaggerating her by no means inconsiderable problems in letters to Queen Victoria, her mother probably understood her better than anybody else and would never have been taken in. 'I have no words to express my indignation and astonishment about the conduct of your three [eldest] children', the Queen wrote (31 March). 'This must not be allowed – and if it is not exaggerated by repetition I think you ought to send for them and threaten them with strong measures if it goes on!'[62] Quite what measures the Empress could impose on a son who could become Kaiser at any time it is difficult to imagine, but the Queen's words made it clear that her grandson's attitude left much to be desired.

At the same time the Queen tried to act as mediator, even suggesting give and take where necessary. The Empress was almost alone in hoping that her second daughter Victoria would soon be married to Alexander von Battenberg, who had been forced to abdicate from the throne of Bulgaria in September 1886 and was now living as a private citizen in Austria. His nerves and health undermined by his experiences, unknown to almost everyone but his immediate family, he had lost his heart to an opera singer, Joanna von Loisinger. Meanwhile, the Queen had implored her daughter not to contemplate such a marriage without Wilhelm's acquiescence, as it would 'simply bring misery on your daughter and Sandro, besides placing her in an impossible and humiliating position'.[63] Wilhelm's solution to the matter savoured strongly of another century. The previous year, he had twice alternately threatened to 'put a bullet through the head' of Prince Alexander or to 'club the Battenberger to death'.[64]

The Queen had apparently failed to mention Sandro's romance with Joanna to her daughter. Had she done so instead of laying less emphasis on Wilhelm's attitude, she would have saved her much anguish. Bismarck, who had threatened to resign if the engagement took place, had informed her of the liaison but she dismissed his reports as malicious gossip. Determined to do what she could for Princess Victoria while she was first lady of the German empire, a position she knew she would not occupy for long, the Empress tried to hasten the betrothal, even if it meant a secret marriage, flight from Germany for her daughter and new son-in-law, and a commission for the latter in the Austro-Hungarian army. She asked Radolinski to assist with the necessary arrangements, he told Wilhelm, and all plans were halted. The Empress agreed to postpone the issue and compromise by asking her husband to add a clause to his will instructing Kaiser Wilhelm, on accession, to acquiesce in his sister's marriage to Alexander. It was a forlorn hope.

On Bismarck's seventy-third birthday, 1 April 1888, the Crown Prince made a speech referring to the 'severely wounded Emperor', and praising 'the great Chancellor'. Deeply hurt when he read the text in the paper, the Kaiser wrote to his son expressing sorrow that his first public speech as Crown Prince showed unequivocally 'that you regard my state of health as a hindrance to the exercise of my duties, and therefore issued an appeal to rally round the "great Chancellor". You have probably not considered how disloyal it sounds to designate his Minister as the only active power in the Government over the head of the sovereign, and also how little right you especially have to make remarks on such a matter. It is for that reason that I am drawing your attention to it so that you may avoid any similar speeches in the future.'[65]

This justified reprimand, and frustration over the Battenberg marriage affair (which he must have realized would never come to pass), offended the Crown Prince deeply. He wrote sulkily to Eulenburg (12 April) that what he had had to endure within the last few days 'simply defies description and even mocks the imagination!'.[66] The worst thing, he said, was 'the feeling of deep shame for the sunken prestige of my house, which always stood so gleaming and unassailable! But yet more intolerable is that our family escutcheon should be bespotted and the Reich brought to the brink of ruin by the English princess who is my mother!'[67]

On the same morning the Kaiser had a violent fit of coughing. Dr Mackenzie decided to adjust the existing canula, and when it only brought momentary relief, he replaced it with a shorter one. When this failed to solve the problem, he chose another canula altogether. Out of professional courtesy he invited Dr Bergmann to come to Charlottenburg and watch him insert it. Wildly excited, thinking an emergency had arisen, swaying heavily from side to side and smelling strongly of alcohol, Bergmann arrived, removed the shorter canula himself rather roughly and replaced it with a new one. When it went into the patient's neck and produced a violent fit of coughing he took it out and tried again, just as clumsily and with the same result. He conceded defeat, but the damage had been done to the Kaiser, and he was left weaker than before. Mackenzie respectfully warned that he would withdraw from the case altogether if Bergmann was permitted as much as to touch the patient's throat again. The threat was unnecessary, as Bergmann had done the decent thing by writing to the Empress asking her to relieve him of the duty of working as Mackenzie's adviser. Having thus retired from the case in disgrace, Bergmann became the toast of the clique at Court. Either out of spite, or because he allowed himself to be talked into it as a gesture of defiance, Crown Prince Wilhelm ostentatiously invited him to dinner.

On 16 April Wilhelm received a message from his father's aide-de-camp, Colonel Kessel, that a mounted servant had arrived at his house from Charlottenburg to say that the Kaiser had just had another relapse. He was feverish, complaining of severe pain in his neck, and the worst was feared. An abscess was forming, noted Mackenzie, 'attributable solely to the injury done a few days before by Bergmann's random stabbing with an unguarded tube'.[68] At once he rode to the palace, and though the Kaiser's condition remained serious for several days, at length he rallied a little. It was fortunate that he did, as Queen Victoria was about to pay a private visit to Berlin in order to see her dying son-in-law for the last time.

Bismarck had mistakenly assumed that the Queen still supported her daughter and granddaughter with regard to the Battenberg marriage, and he said he would not trust her not to bring the groom and parson in her luggage to perform the wedding ceremony there and then. Rumour had it that in his worst moments he even saw Prince Alexander as a rival for the chancellorship of Germany. A virulent attack in the Berlin press accused the Queen and Empress of plotting against Germany for foreign interests. The Prime Minister Lord Salisbury was so alarmed that he tried to persuade the Queen that it would not be safe for her to go to Germany, but she knew better than him and indignantly brushed his protests aside. On her arrival at Charlottenburg on 24 April with her youngest daughter Beatrice and son-in-law Henry of Battenberg, she was received by Wilhelm, Henry and their sisters and escorted straight to the palace.

The cheers for the Queen and her daughter as they drove in an open coach through Berlin proved her point. She said farewell to her son-in-law, telling him that he must come and pay her a visit when he was better. While Victoria knew she was seeing him for the last time, she was tactful enough not to tell him what he already knew. Despite her enemies' whispers that the Empress refused to accept that her husband was dying, she admitted brokenly to Ponsonby that she knew the truth. When he told her he thought the Kaiser seemed better she told him that he was not, and her eyes filled with tears, 'but it has done him a temporary good to see mama'.[69]

While there Queen Victoria had an audience with Bismarck, who was visibly quaking at the prospect in spite of his patronizing remarks before and after the event. Though no reference is to be found in the published extracts from her journal,* it was unlikely that the Queen would have missed the chance of having a few quiet words with her grandson. He was certainly discussed in the meeting with Bismarck, when she 'spoke of William's inexperience and his not having travelled at all. Prince Bismarck replied that [William] knew nothing at all about civil affairs, that he could however say "should he be thrown into the water, he would be able to swim", for that he was certainly clever.'[70]

Rather late in the day, Queen Victoria told her daughter that she must reconcile herself to a final breaking-off of the betrothal between Princess Victoria and Prince Alexander as his personal affections were already engaged elsewhere. She saw her old friend, the wheelchair-bound Dowager Empress Augusta, 'quite crumpled up and deathly pale, really rather a ghastly sight'.[72] At the Kaiser's request Wilhelm commanded two regiments of the Prussian guard on the Charlottenburg parade ground. The Queen and the Empress came out in a carriage drawn by four horses; Wilhelm commanded the salute and accompanied the carriage as it drove down the front of the regiments.

Sir Edward Malet, British ambassador in Berlin, wrote to Lord Salisbury after the Queen's departure that Her Majesty's visit to Berlin had 'been a political success', and that Crown Prince Wilhelm had personally spoken about it to him 'in warm terms and seemed to be delighted at having had an opportunity of conversing with Her Majesty'. A truer if less charitable reflection of the Crown Prince's attitude can be gleaned from a letter he wrote to Eulenburg, saying it was high time that 'the old woman', or the 'empress of Hindustan', his grandmother, died.[73]

Any advice she gave him to make allowances for his mother's nerves at this time had no lasting effect. As early as 12 May the Empress was writing to her mother that her eldest son 'fancies himself completely the Emperor and an absolute and autocratic one. Personally we get on very well, because I avoid all subjects of any importance. If dearest Fritz pulls up again things will alter materially and he too will be more ready to listen.'[74] One week later she wrote that what she said about Wilhelm was

---

*Any allusion Victoria may have made was probably among the extracts destroyed, and not copied, years after her death by Princess Beatrice, her youngest daughter and literary executor. As Beatrice was the sister-in-law of Alexander of Battenberg, it is probable that his name would have been mentioned in any discussion between the Queen and her grandson, and even more than her brothers and sisters Beatrice was a very private person who strongly deprecated the idea of preserving private family correspondence and records – even at the loss to posterity. In his biography of his father Sir Henry, Arthur Ponsonby suggests that 'the blue pencil or even the scissors have been unwarrantably used for the excision of her natural and characteristic indiscretions'[71] in her account of the interview in her journal.

no exaggeration: 'I do not tell you one third of what passes, so that you, who are at a distance, should not fancy that I complain. He is in a "ring", a *côterie*, whose main endeavour is as it were to paralyse Fritz in every way. William is not conscious of this! This state of things must be borne until Fritz perhaps gets strong enough to put a stop to it himself.'[75]

Occasionally members of the *côterie* overreached themselves. Count Waldersee told the Crown Prince bluntly of the irritation in military and civil quarters with 'the petticoat rule which is being exercised indirectly through the sick Emperor from Charlottenburg over Prussia and Germany'. It was unnecessary for His Imperial Highness to carry out any commands sent from Charlottenburg by the Kaiser, as 'the true source which inspires them' was well known, and he could 'quietly leave them unfulfilled and set them on one side'. Astonished at such talk from a man whom he had previously considered the most reliable of friends, the Crown Prince answered coldly that he had taken the military oath of loyalty to his father. Come what may, he would adhere to it, and carry out strictly any commands coming from the Kaiser at Charlottenburg. Even if a command was to be given that the quartermaster-general, 'having attempted to seduce the brigade commander of the 2nd Infantry Brigade of Guards into disobedience to his Emperor and breach of his military oath', was to be placed in front of a sandheap and shot, he would execute the command to the letter – with pleasure.[76]

By this time it was increasingly evident that the Kaiser had only weeks left to live. On 24 May he attended the wedding of his son Henry and Princess Irene at Charlottenburg, and on 29 May the Crown Prince led his Guards Infantry Brigade in a march past his father in the palace grounds. Was the parade a rather dubious way of atoning for his previous disloyalty? According to Wilhelm, he had proposed it to his father on the morning of 28 May, and in the evening he received a letter assenting to the spectacle.[77] The Empress's version of events is rather different; according to her, 'William insisted on leading his brigade past his father in the grounds of Charlottenburg Castle, while the latter sat in cap and overcoat in a two-seated open carriage. William meant well, but it was most unfortunate, for Fritz only agreed with the utmost reluctance.'[78]

On 1 June the Court moved from Charlottenburg to Potsdam. The Kaiser had been born at the Neue Palais, and he had spent nearly every summer of his married life there. They travelled on the royal steamer *Alexandria* in brilliant sunshine, the Kaiser lying on a couch as well-wishers lined the route, cheering and throwing flowers. They knew that this was the last time they would see their Kaiser. Crown Prince Wilhelm was in command of the vessel, and the Empress tried to make friendly conversation with him on the journey, but to no effect. Each blamed their inability to get along on the entourage of the other.[79]

When the Kaiser and Empress arrived at the palace in a carriage, he wrote on his pad that he would like it to be known from then on as Friedrichskron, meaning not only 'the crown of Frederick', but also 'the crown or chief delight of him who is rich in peace'. All around him the family did their best to radiate optimism in the face of overwhelming odds. 'We have again been through days of much anxiety,' Princess Victoria wrote pathetically (5 June), 'Papa having been so ill – now, thank God, the doctors are more satisfied & we are all feeling happier with the present state of things – it is terrible to see those one loves suffer & not to be able to help – one cannot understand why just beloved Papa should have to endure such a lot – he who is goodness & kindness itself – but still I am full of hope & with heavens help there may be better times in store for us!'[80]

On 13 June Dr Mackenzie telegraphed sadly to Queen Victoria that the Kaiser was sinking, and she telegraphed to Crown Prince Wilhelm of her great distress at the news; 'and so troubled about poor dear Mama. Do all you can, as I asked you, to help her at this terrible time of dreadful trial and grief.'[81]

Next day broncho-pneumonia developed, and the doctors could no longer give the Kaiser any nourishment. Wilhelm and Dona arrived with a large suite, choosing their rooms in the palace as if they owned it already. On the morning of 15 June they took their place around the deathbed with the Empress, Henry and Irene, the Kaiser's daughters, and servants. At about 11.15 a.m., the last struggle of Kaiser Friedrich III was over.

## CHAPTER THREE

# The Young Kaiser

While an air of pathos and impending tragedy had heralded the accession of Kaiser Friedrich III, that of Kaiser Wilhelm II was marked by not only an atmosphere of brooding distrust and suspicion, but of a police state. During the previous twenty-four hours, the grounds and corridors of Friedrichskron had been filled with officers demanding quarters and rations as they whispered instructions among themselves in preparation for a virtual state of siege. Kaiser Friedrich had barely drawn his last breath before Major von Natzmer, a senior officer in charge, mounted his horse, rode around the perimeter of the palace and grounds, giving orders and inspecting guards. This was the signal for a regiment of hussars to appear, rifles at the ready, establishing divisions at every gate of the park, effectively sealing it off from the outside world. Orders were given that nobody – not even members of the imperial family or doctors – could leave without a signed permit. Every outgoing letter and telegram had to be checked and censored, each parcel carefully examined.

Only with difficulty was the new Kaiser dissuaded from issuing an order for the immediate arrest of Dr Mackenzie, or tearing his luggage and that of Dr Hovell apart. The minister of justice, Heinrich Friedberg, suddenly arrived at the palace and was aghast, warning the Kaiser that he had the power but not the right to do so – 'if you exercise the power, you will begin your reign badly'.[1] Such a draconian measure would have involved the intervention of the ambassador in Berlin, and risked a serious diplomatic rupture with England.

Nevertheless, a thorough search of the palace rooms was undertaken. Kaiser Wilhelm was determined to find his father's private letters and diaries. General von Winterfeldt, formerly a devoted servant of Kaiser Friedrich, was now equally loyal to his successor. Convinced that there must be written evidence of 'liberal plots', he searched his late master's desk thoroughly for any incriminating documents. Meanwhile, the Kaiser ransacked his mother's room, feverishly hunting through every drawer of her desk in pursuit of the same objective. His parents knew him too well, and when setting out for England to attend the jubilee the previous year their luggage had included three boxes of papers to leave there for safe keeping. Various other documents were destroyed at that time, as well as later at San Remo and at Berlin shortly after Friedrich's accession. On 14 June, when he was clearly very close to death, his wife had taken care of the rest. Inman Bernard, special correspondent of the *New York Herald*, was summoned to Friedrichskron and handed a sealed packet by Mackenzie containing the Kaiser's diaries covering the last ten years, which he was asked to deliver to the British embassy in Berlin with instructions for the ambassador to send it to Queen Victoria. The mission was accomplished successfully – and just in time – as on 17 June the Queen noted in her journal that Colonel Swaine had arrived from Berlin with the papers. Not only did the Empress intend to preserve these documents for posterity, but it was vital that she and her husband's friends and allies should be protected from any evidence which could be used against them if the new regime tried to arraign them on trumped-up charges of treason.

Frustrated by his failure, Kaiser Wilhelm II turned his attention to settling other scores. Contrary to normal practice, there was no summoning of clergy and family for prayers or any form of service inside the death chamber. Instead, and in defiance of his father's instructions and his grief-stricken mother's pleas, he allowed an autopsy to be conducted on his father's body. It was officially established that he had died of cancer of the larynx. Nevertheless, Kaiser Wilhelm was determined to uphold the name of German medicine by proving that 'his' doctors had always been right in their diagnosis of May 1887, and that Mackenzie had been at fault. The post-mortem was conducted with haste, and the final verdict pronounced on the evidence of the naked eye. It revealed that the whole of the larynx, apart from the epiglottis, had been destroyed and it now consisted of one large, flat, gangrenous ulcer, while patches of septic broncho-pneumonia were present in the lungs.[2]

Next the Kaiser opened his father's will, and read his wishes regarding the betrothal of Princess Victoria with Prince Alexander von Battenberg. Kaiser Friedrich had gone to his final rest unaware of the romance between Sandro and Johanna von Loisinger. The Empress and Queen Victoria had presumably withheld the news from him as they did not wish to upset him further, and Kaiser Wilhelm's action in sending Prince Alexander a letter forbidding the match was justifiable if unnecessary. Less reasonable and just as high-handed was his order that his father's wishes should be disregarded, and that Friedrichskron should revert to its former name of the Neue Palais. Every piece of writing paper bearing the 'incorrect' name was to be handed over and burnt.

From Friedberg the Kaiser received a sealed letter containing a request from King Friedrich Wilhelm IV that all his successors should rescind the constitution that had been wrung from him.[3] It had been placed before

Wilhelm I and Friedrich III on their respective accessions. Both had initialled it and replaced it in the royal archives. On the grounds that it 'might easily work the greatest harm if it were to come into the hands of an inexperienced heir', Wilhelm tore the letter up and burnt it, sealed and initialled the envelope, added the words 'Contents read and destroyed', and it was replaced in the archives.[4]

Within hours of his accession the Kaiser received a telegram from Queen Victoria: 'I am brokenhearted. Help and do all you can for your poor dear mother and try to follow in your best noblest and kindest of father's footsteps.'[5] Any appeal to his better nature was optimistic – her grandson was determined to stamp his own personality on his reign, and if that meant disregarding the finer considerations of family feelings, so be it.

Yet another Victoria, the Kaiser's cousin from Hesse, now married to Sandro's elder brother Prince Louis of Battenberg, was prepared to make allowances. She pitied him sincerely; she wrote to her grandmother: 'he is so young for his position, & so greatly needs a wise & honest friend to help him . . . I greatly fear, that for want of such a one, his faults rather than his good qualities will develop. When I think how warm hearted & nice he was as a boy, how greatly he changed during the last years, I cannot but think it is a great measure the fault of his surroundings.'[6] For once her grandmother was disinclined to give her grandson the benefit of the doubt. 'It is too dreadful for us all to think of Willy & Bismarck & Dona – being the supreme head of all now!' she answered a couple of weeks later; 'Two so unfit & one so wicked.'[7]

Another matter in which the Kaiser wasted no time was in his first proclamation to the people. 'Thus we belong to each other – I and the Army – we were born for each other and will cleave indissolubly to each other, whether it be the Will of God to send us calm or storm', it read in ringing tones. 'You will soon swear fealty and submission to me, and I promise ever to bear in mind that from the world above the eyes of my forefathers look down upon me, and that I shall have one day to stand accountable to them for the glory and honour of the Army.'[8] Behind these words stood a determination to compensate for his lack of military experience. Whereas his father had won his laurels on the battlefields of Königgrätz and Wörth, while his grandfather had received the surrender of Emperor Napoleon III in 1870 and also entered Paris behind the defeated Napoleon Bonaparte in 1814, their successor had no comparable history. Almost every other king, grand duke or sovereign prince in the German empire had had more experience of war. Insecurity drove him on to strut and swagger, assuming a theatrical pose that the martial atmosphere of Berlin demanded he should personify.

The funeral of Kaiser Friedrich was hastily arranged and took place on 18 June. No invitations were sent to foreign princes, though some had been sent by their heads of state to pay their respects at the obsequies. Among them were the Prince and Princess of Wales and their eldest son Albert Victor. Though Alexandra was a reluctant visitor to Germany, she had always liked and respected the late Kaiser, and she was full of sympathy for his widow. The new ruler, she declared, was 'a mad and a conceited ass'.[9] Also present were Queen Victoria's son-in-law Lord Lorne, Ernst, Duke of Saxe-Coburg, the King of Saxony, and Grand Duke Vladimir of Russia. Scant respect was paid to the departed Kaiser. While the chapel was being decorated, the coffin stood in the midst of hammering workmen like a toolchest, while again the short path to the church was guarded by troops. Deeply ashamed of his fellow countrymen's attitude, Eulenburg recalled that while the troops were dignified, 'the clergy were laughing and chattering, Field-Marshal Blumenthal, with the Standard over his shoulder, reeling about, talking – it was horrible'.[10] The Dowager Empress, henceforth known as the Empress Frederick, could not face such an insulting ceremony, and she and her three unmarried daughters had left the palace for their rural retreat at Bornstädt.

Anxious not to inflame feelings still further, the Prince of Wales wrote a tactful account of the proceedings to his mother, mentioning the 'beautiful chorales and hymns', a 'short and touching sermon' and the most moving appearance of all, that of Fritz's chestnut horse Wörth, continually neighing as two grooms led him behind the hearse. He spoke of a long conversation with Wilhelm afterwards, 'and thought him quiet and reasonable, and only anxious to do what is right (that is, if he is allowed to do so)'.[11] Nine days after the funeral he wrote to the Empress Frederick that he knew of the difficulties with her son, but begged her not to be disheartened; 'above all if possible try and have some influence with him, so that he may not be entirely at the mercy of those in whose political opinions you cannot agree'.[12]

The Kaiser made it clear that he was not going to be intimidated by the Queen of England. Either out of tactlessness or defiance, he sent General Winterfeldt as special envoy to make the official announcement of Kaiser Wilhelm's accession to the throne at Windsor, and was given a cold reception. The Kaiser angrily told Colonel Swaine, the British military attaché in Berlin, that he felt he was still being treated as a grandson and not as German Kaiser. When Swaine passed these comments on to Sir Henry Ponsonby, the Queen replied bluntly that she had intended the reception to be cold. Winterfeldt 'never uttered one word of sorrow for [Kaiser Friedrich's] death, and rejoiced in the accession of his new master'.[13]

All state and Court appointments had lapsed at the end of the previous reign. The Kaiser accordingly set about confirming the appropriate men in office or choosing their successors. Prince and Count Bismarck were reappointed to their previous posts. Field-Marshal Moltke, now nearing his ninetieth year, resigned as chief of general staff, to be succeeded by the obsequious Waldersee, though he remained president of the defence committee. There were many household offices to be appointed or confirmed, among them the great chamberlain, the head marshal, the great cupbearer, great and second masters of ceremonies and master of the horse.

Though the Kaiser revelled in pageantry, he dispensed with a coronation. When asked about the matter by Bismarck, he declined to have one on the grounds that there was no constitutional necessity for it, and that his grandfather had 'laid special emphasis in his coronation on the principle of monarchy by divine right'.[14] Bismarck told him it was a judicious gesture, as he would thus be saving the exchequer 10 million marks. In fact Article XI of the German constitution of 1871, devised by Bismarck himself 'to perpetuate the partnership he had achieved with Wilhelm I' in his previous eight years in office, affirmed that the presidency of the union belonged to the King of Prussia 'who shall, in this capacity, be termed German Kaiser'.[15] As there was therefore no German imperial crown, there could be no sacred ritual of coronation for the Kaiser as there was for the Tsar of All the Russias, or a King or Queen of England, so in fact the issue was academic.

More importance was attached to the opening of the first imperial parliament of the new reign on 25 June, where pomp and pageantry compensated for anything that would have been missed by the lack of a coronation. In his opening speech the Kaiser promised 'to follow the same path by which my deceased grandfather won the confidence of his allies, the love of the German people, and the goodwill of foreign countries'.[16] He hardly mentioned his father at all, and there was no reference to Britain, while he dwelt on his personal friendship with the Tsar of Russia, as well as the alliance with Austria-Hungary and Italy.

Under the imperial constitution, the German Kaiser was an autocrat with very few encroachments on his powers. Such limitations as there were on his sovereign authority pertained to the necessity for imperial decrees to carry the signature of his chancellor as well as his own, and an obligation to respect the rights of the other monarchs and princes within the empire. These only curtailed by a negligible amount, if at all, his use of the powers normally assigned to a head of state, together with the right to summon and dissolve the *Bundesrat* and the *Reichstag*, the right to propose legislation and appoint and dismiss ministers from the chancellor downwards. In addition he enjoyed authority as King of the largest German state within the imperial federation. The supremacy of the crown in Prussia had never been challenged and the *Landtag*, or Prussian representative assembly, was elected on a three-tier voting system which favoured the Junker landowning minority. Kings of Prussia traditionally sought advice from their military and civil secretariats. These were not constitutionally recognized and not part of the government, but their nominated chiefs advised the monarch in his imperial capacity as well as in his role as King, therefore exerting a major influence on policy independent of ministerial decisions.

The Kaiser was not only the most powerful man in imperial Germany, but also one of the wealthiest. In 1913 Rudolf Martin, a former official of the imperial office of the interior, wrote in *Jahrbuch des Vermögens und Einkommens der Millionäre in Berlin*, that His Imperial Majesty was the richest person in Berlin with a fortune of at least 140 million marks and an annual income of about 20 million marks, including the civil list. Only four individuals in Prussia could claim a greater fortune. His wealth increased annually, partly from additional income from his properties and capital and partly from agricultural profits from his land. He officially possessed fifty-three castles, though some were not owned by him but theoretically by the state or by other individuals and were placed at his disposal in return for the assumption of costs of upkeep by crown funds. The Kaiser owned additional buildings in Berlin which were valued at an estimated 18 million marks.[17]

In July the Kaiser consulted the director of naval construction over shipbuilding plans without first informing General Leon von Caprivi, chief of the Admiralty, who resigned in protest. He was the first of several ministers to learn that their new master would look into any aspect of government that took his fancy as he pleased. Significantly neither of his predecessors had even worn naval uniform before, but on 14 July, only nine days after Caprivi's resignation, the Kaiser went to Kiel for his first naval review in his capacity as admiral of the German fleet, watching as twenty-four vessels sailed past the imperial yacht. From boyhood he had taken almost as much interest in the navy as he had in the army. In hindsight it could be seen as the start of an obsession which would lead to the naval race with England and culminate in the events that unfolded in 1914.

Immediately afterwards he left for the first of his visits abroad, to St Petersburg, on the grounds that he was fulfilling his grandfather's mission to foster Russo-German goodwill. Queen Victoria had been disturbed by this unseemly haste. There were rumours of his going to pay visits to other sovereigns, and she had written to him (3 July): 'I hope that at least you will let some months pass before anything of this kind takes place, as it is not three weeks yet since dear beloved Papa was taken, and we are all still in such deep mourning for him.'[18] She had assumed that he would observe a full year of mourning for his father, and then pay her his first visit abroad as sovereign. He took the letter to Bismarck, who told him angrily that such 'interference' from England must cease. His answer was dismissive; at the end of this month, he informed her, he would inspect the fleet and sail to the Baltic, for a meeting with the Tsar of Russia, 'which will be of good effect for the peace of Europe, and for the rest and quiet of my Allies. I would have gone later if possible, but State interest goes before personal feelings, and the fate which sometimes hangs over nations does not wait till the etiquette of Court mournings has been fulfilled.'[19] Queen Victoria warned Lord Salisbury that 'we shall be very cool, though civil, in our communications with my grandson and Prince Bismarck, who are bent on a return to the oldest times of government'.[20]

Unbowed, the Kaiser and Herbert Bismarck went to Russia where he tried to stir up the Tsar against what he called the 'English leanings' of his mother and father. Unimpressed with his unfilial fellow sovereign, the Tsar commented coldly on the washing of dirty linen in public of the differences between Bismarck, Kaiser Friedrich and Germany's attitude towards England. In spite of this both Wilhelm and Count Bismarck deluded themselves into thinking the visit had been a great success.

Yet the aftermath of Kaiser Friedrich's death continued to haunt his son, with worsening relations between Kaiser Wilhelm on one hand and his mother and the British royal family on the other. In September 1888 a series of extracts from the then Crown Prince's diary covering the years 1870 and 1871 was published in a liberal journal, *Deutsche Rundschau*. They had been copied by one of his closest friends, Professor Heinrich Geffcken, once a student with him at Bonn who went on to become professor of political science at Strasbourg University. Geffcken was so incensed by the repeated denigration of his old friend as a nonentity that he published these extracts anonymously in order to prove that much of the credit taken by Bismarck for founding the German empire in 1871 really belonged to the then Crown Prince Friedrich Wilhelm. The Empress had not been consulted, and she was immediately accused of having instigated their publication. Bismarck declared that the précis was a forgery, while the Kaiser said that state papers had been stolen and threatened to prosecute the person or persons responsible. Geffcken admitted responsibility, and as the Dowager Empress disclosed, despite his good intentions his behaviour had been 'imprudent and indiscreet'.[21]

He was arrested and tried for treason, but no case could be brought against him and he was released.

Meanwhile, the Kaiser was preparing for the second visit abroad of his reign, one which would have considerable repercussions and inflame family relationships even further. In August Emperor Franz Josef of Austria had invited the Prince of Wales to attend army manoeuvres that autumn. As the Prince knew that Kaiser Wilhelm was due to pay an official visit to Vienna at about the same time, he wrote two friendly letters expressing pleasure at the likelihood of their meeting on that occasion. Neither was acknowledged, but the Prince still went to Vienna as planned on 10 September. Only after plans were being made for his itinerary was he informed that Kaiser Wilhelm had told Franz Josef that 'no other royal guest should dim the glory of his own stay in Vienna'. The Prince was astonished and hurt, as he had wished to avoid provoking ill-natured gossip by staying away from the capital while his nephew was present. Nevertheless, within twenty-four hours it was common knowledge throughout Vienna that the Kaiser had threatened to cancel his visit unless the Prince of Wales was asked to leave forthwith.

Crown Prince Rudolf, a good friend of the Prince of Wales but no admirer of the Kaiser, told him angrily that German agents had made mischief by spreading stories that the Prince wanted to interfere in the forthcoming dialogue between both monarchs, and embroil them with Tsar Alexander III of Russia, thereby creating trouble which could only be of advantage to England and France. Crown Prince Rudolf, who had been close to Kaiser Friedrich and his wife, wrote to friends that he would like to invite the Kaiser out on a sporting expedition 'in order to arrange a neat hunting accident which would remove him from the world'.[22] He also informed his father that he had lent Wilhelm a sum of 3,000 florins 'for an indefinite time' on a visit the latter had paid to Vienna shortly before his accession, for pleasures about which nobody else (particularly not the adoring but censorious Dona, at home in Berlin) was to know. Emperor Franz Josef was amused to hear that Wilhelm was not as self righteous as he appeared to be. At the same time the Habsburg Emperor felt confident that his young fellow sovereign would maintain the close dynastic links of friendship forged by Kaiser Wilhelm I, but he was suspicious of the enthusiasm with which Pan-Germans in Austria had greeted the new reign in Berlin. The Pan-Germans were a small but vociferous movement who sought a unified Germany under Hohenzollern rather than Habsburg hegemony, and they had alarmed Franz Josef by a demonstration in the streets of Vienna earlier that year.

In his own estimation, Kaiser Wilhelm's visit to Vienna was a complete success. Full of confidence, at a military review he did not hesitate to criticize the turn-out of Emperor Franz Josef's infantry and the effectiveness of its chief inspector – Crown Prince Rudolf.* The latter took revenge by passing an article to the journalist and editor Moritz Szeps, detailing the as-then Prince Wilhelm of Prussia's private behaviour on a visit to Austria in 1887, especially his escapades with young women, and attempts by the German ambassador to hush up the scandal when a claim for alimony was later made against him. While the Jewish Szeps was no admirer of the young German Kaiser, he knew the article was too dangerous to print even if each word was true. He forwarded it to friends of his at *Le Figaro* in Paris, where they reached the same conclusion with regret.

The sour taste that Wilhelm left behind him in the Habsburg capital on return to Berlin was nothing compared to reaction from Balmoral, where Queen Victoria was outraged by his high-handed behaviour. In a lengthy letter to Lord Salisbury, she made short work of an assertion that the Prince of Wales had not treated his nephew as an Emperor as 'really too *vulgar* and too absurd, as well as untrue, almost *to be believed* . . . to pretend that he is to be treated *in private* as well as in public as "his Imperial Majesty" is *perfect madness!* . . . *If* he has *such* notions, he [had] better *never* come *here*. The Queen will not swallow this affront.' Political relations between both governments, she agreed, should not be affected if possible 'by these miserable personal quarrels; but the Queen much *fears* that, with such a hot-headed, conceited, and wrongheaded young man, devoid of all feeling, this may at ANY moment become *impossible*'.[23]

The Prince of Wales had tried to see the best in his nephew, but now he realized he was wasting his time; they had completely different personalities. The genial, urbane prince was liked and respected throughout most of Europe. In his dealings with princes and statesmen of other nations he knew how to please and charm without appearing to try or even care; a friendly word or gesture was second nature to him. The self-conscious young Kaiser always seemed to be trying to make an impression, striving to create an effect by perpetually showing off. To complicate matters, if the Prince of Wales was not jealous of the young man who had ascended his throne before the age of thirty while he was still an heir to the throne at nearly fifty, the Kaiser resented much about the Prince of Wales – his easygoing manner, his popularity, and above all of his (or more accurately, at the time, his mother's) empire. Each was

---

*Crown Prince Rudolf's depression over the future of Europe on the accession of Kaiser Wilhelm, an event which he regarded as a disaster, was almost certainly a major factor in his taking his own life at Mayerling on 30 January 1889 – the same week as the Kaiser's thirtieth birthday was celebrated.

rude in private about the other, though they knew that their comments were bound to be repeated and reach the ears of the other. 'William the Great', the Prince of Wales said, 'needs to learn that he is living at the end of the nineteenth century and not in the Middle Ages',[24] while the Kaiser called his uncle 'an old peacock' and 'a Satan'. Baron Holstein, who had little admiration for England, admitted that Kaiser Wilhelm II was the worst diplomat in Europe – and the Prince of Wales the best.

Neither the Prince of Wales nor his brothers the Dukes of Edinburgh and Connaught cared for their nephew's overbearing manner, though as the most military minded of his family, the Duke of Connaught liked him better than the others. One of the few relations outside Prussia who got on well with him was the Russian-born Marie, Duchess of Edinburgh. She found him an interesting personality, noted her daughter Marie, 'and her own masterfulness kept him at bay. Her all-seeing eye noted the expression on every face and she was ever ready to step in when there was storm in the air.'[25]

The Kaiser made one more journey abroad that year, to Rome. With three journeys to foreign capitals within six months of his accession, wags in Berlin began to speak of *Der Greise Kaiser, der Weise Kaiser, und der Reise Kaiser* (the white-haired Kaiser, the wise Kaiser, and the travelling Kaiser). While his grandfather had been content with normal first-class railway carriages, Wilhelm commissioned a new imperial train commensurate with his status, comprising twelve pullman coaches painted in gold, blue and cream. Soon, it was joked, the royal anthem would be amended from *Heil Dir im Siegerkranz* ('Hail to thee in thy laurelled crown of victory'), to *Heil Dir im Sonderzug* ('Hail to thee in thy private railroad car').

Controversies about the brief reign of Kaiser Friedrich continued to gather pace. In October Sir Morell Mackenzie published *The Fatal Illness of Frederick the Noble*, his own account of the Kaiser's illness and death, but unwisely he did not confine himself to the discussion of the medical issues. His attacks on the German doctors' incompetence and maltreatment of their patient demonstrated how he had been provoked by their behaviour and the persistent campaign of vilification he and the Dowager Empress had endured ever since, and the British medical establishment censured him for airing his views publicly. Fortunately, the Empress was about to enjoy a brief respite from the criticism. Even for a woman of her courage, the constant barrage of attacks on her husband's memory and her own actions, and her eldest son's callous behaviour, had come close to unnerving her completely. On 29 September, the anniversary of her betrothal at Balmoral, she admitted in a letter to Queen Victoria that 'yesterday I felt very near putting an end to myself!'.[26]

On 19 November, two days before her forty-eighth birthday, the Empress Frederick and her three unmarried daughters, her *Kleeblatt* or 'trio', left Berlin to stay in England. They spent three months, including Christmas, at Windsor with Queen Victoria, returning to Berlin in February 1889. Everyone hoped that this breathing space would help to heal the family rift, and the Queen did much to impress on her daughter the importance of putting up the best she could with her son's thoughtless behaviour and that of his advisers. While they were there, in January, Bismarck proposed an Anglo-German alliance, on the understanding that it would not affect Germany's relationship with Russia. The implication was that it should be directed against France, but as Britain was under no threat Lord Salisbury advised that the matter should be allowed to rest for the moment. Meanwhile the Kaiser wrote to the Queen to say he was glad to see that she considered the 'Vienna affair' concluded, and that he would be pleased to meet 'uncle Bertie' at Osborne on his visit later that year. She told the Prince of Wales that the Kaiser could not come that year after all he had said and done, and informed Salisbury that he would have to make some form of apology to the Prince before he did make his next visit.

While the Kaiser still regularly flirted with attractive women on his journeys away from Berlin, with no Dona to keep an eye on him, he had learned the folly of becoming too involved. A few weeks after his accession, and nine months after the trysting trio had awakened the other occupants of the guesthouse that night at Eisenerz, Anna Homolatsch gave birth to a daughter and claimed that His Majesty was the father. Though she was already pregnant at the time by another man, the Kaiser was so desperate to keep the matter quiet that substantial maintenance for the child was paid by his private correspondence secretary. It was not an isolated case, for another woman, known only by the professional name of 'Miss Love', also had a daughter by him at about the same time and similarly received a generous amount of money to conceal the child's true parentage. After this he apparently behaved himself. If he could not be good, at least he was more careful. There was gossip connecting his name with various ladies from other countries, including a Mrs Gould from New York who had formerly earned her living by lying on her back in a nightclub and firing rifles with her big toe, but at most these probably did not progress beyond mild flirtation or an exchange of photographs.

Anxious to emulate his paternal grandfather in so many ways, Wilhelm drew the line at sleeping in an old camp bed. His own was heavily curtained, with quilts and blankets fastened down to keep out draughts.

His mother had inherited her own mother's passion for fresh air and proper ventilation; by contrast, her eldest son adhered to the time-honoured Prussian tradition of keeping fresh air at bay, especially as his vulnerability to colds and infection meant he dreaded lower temperatures. At first he took a hot bath every morning in an ordinary zinc painted tub, then he poured several pails of water over himself in which sea salt had been dissolved. Later he had bathrooms with fireplaces and running hot and cold water installed in all his palaces as required. In 1897 the castle at Bad Homburg was fitted with these modern conveniences in preparation for a two-day visit by the Kaiser and his wife, although he had been deaf to his mother's requests to have them installed for her when she lived there for the first four years of her widowhood. After washing he was shaved by his barber and had his moustache brushed by Herr Haby, the ends turned up in the soon to be familiar shape of a letter W. Then he would dress in the uniform he thought correct for the first activity of the day. According to his cousin Marie, Queen of Roumania, he 'changed his uniform several times a day as a smart woman changes her gown'.[27] In addition to his much-cherished foreign uniforms he had a full one for every Prussian regiment, over three hundred alone, to say nothing of those of Bavaria, Saxony and Württemberg, as well as naval and marine uniforms. All had their own individual badges, sashes, caps, helmets, epaulettes, shoulder points, belts, swords, lances and firearms. The resulting wardrobe and armoury had to be housed in a hall containing huge wardrobes, with a *Kammerdiener* on duty from morning to night to select at the shortest possible notice any outfit he might require.

According to Anne Topham, his daughter's governess, he cut a fine figure in military dress, but in civilian clothes the effect was completely lacking. Many German gentlemen lost much in appearance when out of uniform, 'but none to the extent that their Emperor did. He no longer had any shred of dignity, and, curiously enough, that charm of manner . . . was also bereft of its influence and merged into what was an offensive, wearisome buffoonery'. He was wise, she added, 'not to appear before his subjects except in uniform'.[28]

Bismarck and the Prince of Wales, to name but two contemporaries, both had a legendary capacity for fine food and, in the former's case, alcohol as well. Kaiser Wilhelm II never shared their self-indulgence; though he enjoyed smoking, he was very sparing with food and drink. At banquets he would sit through several courses without accepting anything. One could attribute this to a preference for the sound of his own voice, but in all fairness his restless, worrying character and the metabolism associated with it, coupled with the lack of a hearty appetite, made him disinclined to eat more than was necessary.[29] Dinner guests at the palace and on board his yacht often grumbled about the meagre fare. Once his aunt, Queen Alexandra, watching him sitting through one course after another without partaking himself, told him anxiously that he ought to eat more. His one gastronomic weakness, according to his cousin Princess Marie Louise, was for mince pies with flaming brandy sauce. At dinner red and white wine and champagne were served to his guests. In youth he had occasionally drunk too much, but as an adult he was more abstemious. Once he admonished Anne Topham about the 'fearful' drinking habits of the English. Imbibing 'such quantities of poisonous liquid' ruined one's constitution, and whisky and soda, which he once tried, was 'like liquid fire!'.[30] For himself and the Empress fruit juice or soda water was generally enough, though sometimes he enjoyed a glass of sparkling red wine.

As an adult he weighed just over 11 stone. With his diet and passion for exercise, including brisk walks and daily use of a rowing machine, he never put on weight. At 5 ft 8 in tall, according to his yachting friend, the Englishman Brooke Heckstall-Smith, the Kaiser appeared rather small, a fact which made him self-conscious and careful to wear uniforms which created a larger-than-life illusion with their aggressively-spiked or eagle-surmounted helmets. He was 'rather short in the neck and a little lop-sided owing to his left arm being shorter than the other. . . . He spoke English very well, with no marked or unpleasant German accent, and took pride in picking up and making use of English slang expressions and colloquial phrases.'[31] In order to conceal the Empress's superior height he generally had a large cushion placed on his chair at meals. Sensitive about his own stature, he could be callous towards short people. Later in his reign, on a state visit to Italy and the court of 5-ft-tall King Victor Emmanuel III, known throughout Europe as 'the dwarf', the Kaiser deliberately took the tallest guards regiment in his army to accompany him.

In his portraits he liked to be represented with a stern martial expression, 'the look he wore for the first thirty seconds of any interview; it was then speedily succeeded by a variety of somewhat exaggerated humorous facial changes'. Whenever he laughed he did so 'with abandon, throwing back his head, opening his mouth to the fullest possible extent, shaking his whole body, and stamping with one foot to show his excessive enjoyment of the joke'.[32]

He rose at 7.00 each morning; once washed and dressed he went for a brisk ride, often with his *Flügeladjutanten*, or aides-de-camp, for up to two hours and then had breakfast. Sometimes he would take the family for an hour's quick walk through the streets of Potsdam or Berlin, chiding his wife and children for having dawdled over their food. As the Empress had been so busy pouring out his coffee and serving his toast, the rebuke was ill-deserved. After breakfast he worked on state papers and reports, receiving brief resumés of overseas news prepared by the foreign office, granting audiences, reviewing troops, and took meals in messes or with the Empress. Lunch was served at about 1.00 p.m. For the rest of the afternoon he had audiences, went to museums and artists' ateliers, and took long walks, usually with the Empress. After dinner they would entertain a select group of people, often family, until 11.00 p.m. Soon afternoon activities extended into the morning at the expense of work, as rides, meals and walks grew longer. By 1890 Waldersee complained indignantly that his sovereign no longer had the slightest desire to work; it was 'truly scandalous how the Court Reports fool the public about Wilhelm's activity. According to them he is busy working from dawn to dusk'.[33] In the imperial German government, the Kaiser left most routine administration in the hands of his chancellor, his secretaries of state for foreign affairs and the interior and their respective staffs, and his political advisers; and he spent about two hours on paperwork himself each day, far less than most other contemporary European sovereigns. Queen Victoria devoted considerable time to her despatch boxes, and Emperor Franz Josef was at his desk for much of the day, while Tsar Alexander III also perused and signed documents conscientiously, despite well-meaning suggestions from their staffs that some of these rubber-stamp chores could be carried out by others.

Unlike them, Kaiser Wilhelm refused to be 'drowned in detail'. His attention span was very short, and he insisted on official correspondence and *Immediatvorträge*, or verbal reports, being kept to a minimum. His restlessness and love of travelling made it difficult for his ministers, officials and military entourage to keep his attention for long, even when he was not separated from them for weeks at a time. When they did have his attention, they found that with his nervous manner and butterfly mind he avoided hard, concentrated work and would not make difficult decisions. More to his style than tedious reading and signing documents of state were the public manifestations of royalty like ceremonial openings and dedications, speech-making, receiving deputations, attending military and naval reviews and manoeuvres, Court hunts and similar functions. From this point of view he was a successful monarch as he knew his subjects liked to see their sovereign. Perhaps it was not lost on him that at the height of her seclusion and unpopularity in 1871, Queen Victoria would protest that she was working just as hard at her boxes as ever, when faced with criticism from Gladstone and others that

Her Majesty was 'invisible'. Such a charge could never have been levelled at her eldest grandson.

Sometimes he attended the theatre or opera. Plays celebrating the past were his favourites, and he liked Shakespeare's historical dramas, but had nothing but contempt for the socialist dramatist Gerhardt Hauptmann, who won the Nobel Prize for Literature in 1912. His plays, which highlighted working-class deprivation and bureaucratic injustice, were to him disrespectful to the monarchy and rooted in the dreariness of the life of the poor, subject matter which he considered inappropriate for the stage.[34] Wilhelm's musical tastes embraced military music, particularly the marches of Richard Strauss, and the operas of Meyerbeer, Leoncavallo, and Gilbert and Sullivan. A youthful devotion to Wagner did not long survive his accession to the throne. In the evenings he often read newspapers and books; while he preferred technical works or military and naval history to fiction, he enjoyed novels and adventure stories by British and American writers, including Mark Twain, Bret Harte, Rudyard Kipling and Sir Walter Scott. His tastes in art reflected his literary and theatrical preferences, his favourite painters being the skilled but unimaginative historical chroniclers Hermann Knackfuss and Anton von Werner, and the seascape painter Karl Salzmann, who had taught him art while he was a young officer at Potsdam. While Wilhelm liked the eighteenth-century Rococo art of Fragonard and Watteau, modern art movements such as Impressionism and the Secessionists were imcomprehensible to him. He hated the work of Max Liebermann, a Jewish artist regarded as the most distinguished of contemporary Berlin painters, for its honest portrayal of working-class life.

At his accession Wilhelm adopted the annual routine of the Berlin season. After Easter and the traditional hunt for eggs in Bellevue Park came the *Schrippen-Fest* at Whitsun when the Potsdam garrison was given a special dinner enshrined in tradition since the days of Frederick the Great – a meal of beef, prunes and rice cooked in huge copper cauldrons, eaten at trestle tables decorated with pine and fir twigs, for soldiers and members of the diplomatic corps and special visitors as well as the whole of the royal family. In May he went to Prökelwitz for shooting with Eulenburg, and later that month the Wiesbaden festival. In June he visited large cities and the Kiel regatta, an important social occasion for yachting and also as, though most senior secretaries of state and ministers saw him at regular intervals, Kiel week was the only time in the year when the lesser-ranking ministers ever saw him. In July he took his annual cruise to the Norwegian fjords aboard *Hohenzollern*, a warship altered to function as a private yacht. At the beginning of August he and the Empress went to Cowes for the end of the English season, then the Court moved to

Wilhelmshöhe near his old school at Cassel, and on to military manoeuvres. In September they spent a few days at the Neue Palais, then went to the Kaiser's farm on the Baltic coast at Cadinen. He proceeded to his hunting lodge at Rominten near the Russian frontier, accompanied by Eulenburg and chosen companions, returning to Potsdam for the Empress's birthday on 22 October, and then going to stay with Maximilian Egon II Prince zu Fürstenburg at Donaueschingen in Baden. Christmas was spent at the Neue Palais, and the Court moved to the Schloss in Berlin on new year's day for the beginning of another season.

In order to show solidarity with his Habsburg ally, the Kaiser went to Austria-Hungary three or four times a year for manoeuvres, and Emperor Franz Josef reciprocated by joining his Hohenzollern opposite number. For the older man it was a necessary evil. Temperamentally Franz Josef had little in common with Wilhelm, disliking his swagger and bombast, and finding himself ill at ease in the *nouveau riche* atmosphere of Wilhelmine Berlin and Potsdam.

At first the Kaiser revelled in his new routine, like a child with a new toy, but after a year or so he began to tire of the treadmill. As if determined to show who was master, he soon disregarded considerations of etiquette, regardless of any offence caused. While he never lost his taste for pomp and grandeur, he made it clear that at times he preferred his own choice of company. At a dinner in 1892 Arthur von Brauer, of the Baden *Bundesrat*, noted the general disappointment after the Kaiser largely ignored the forty-two participants, never circulated and only spoke to a few individuals. At a Court ball soon afterwards, the same observer remarked with asperity that members of the diplomatic corps and their wives were unpleasantly surprised at being drawn up according to seniority because the Kaiser intended to circulate among them. They stood for more than an hour waiting for the Court to appear and then watched while Wilhelm said only a few words to the two ambassadors and their wives, ignoring everybody else.

Meanwhile a gulf was about to open up between the Kaiser and Bismarck. Wilhelm had grown to maturity during the years of Germany's most rapid industrial development. Production output doubled between his thirteenth and twenty-third birthdays, and was still accelerating at his accession. While he had little idea of living conditions in the slums and tenements of Berlin, he had visited factories and mines as part of Hinzpeter's programme of education, and he was more sympathetic than Bismarck to restricting the number of hours worked by individuals. As countryman and landowner Bismarck accepted some responsibility for industrial workers, as he did for peasants on his estate, and he proposed insurance schemes and old-age pensions far ahead of state welfare programmes in other industrial nations. But he did not believe in limiting hours of work on humanitarian grounds; people were entitled to work longer if they wanted to earn more, he thought, and he did not support legislation intended to restrain employers' rights to determine the length of a working day. In 1888 German workers averaged a 63-hour week compared with 52 hours for British industrial workers.

When the Ruhr coalfields were paralyzed by a strike in the spring of 1889 Bismarck chose not to intervene, sure that misery and hunger would soon force the men to accept the mine owners' working conditions. Moreover, a threat of more strikes among the workforce, he thought, would justify renewal of an anti-socialist law due to expire the following year. But the Kaiser professed sympathy for the working-class millions, a reaction that he owed to the social conscience of his mother and her father. Throwing constitutional convention to the winds he walked unannounced into the ministerial chamber on 14 May 1889, wearing his hussar's uniform with spurs and sword, and ordered his ministers to settle the Ruhr dispute at once. After he was gone, Bismarck told them angrily that it would soon be necessary to protect the young monarch from his own 'excessive zeal'. By the end of the week the miners had won their demands and the strike was over. Bismarck was uneasy; the idea of industrial bargaining was alien to him, and he regarded the Kaiser's intervention in such matters as ominous. Unlike his grandfather, this Wilhelm seemed to harbour ambitions to rule as well as to reign.

The Kaiser's perpetual attacks on the English in general and his mother in particular seemed to count for little among those in England who sought to appease him. To King Humbert of Italy, he ridiculed the Empress Frederick mercilessly as 'that fat, dumpy little person who seeks influence'.[35] In April 1889 he was still telling others in Germany that an English doctor killed his father, and an English doctor crippled his arm: 'this we owe to my mother who would not have Germans about her!'.[36] Nevertheless, Colonel Swaine still, somewhat cravenly, advised Sir Henry Ponsonby that it was essential for Queen Victoria to treat the grandson as Emperor and he would remain grandson. 'Treat the Emperor as grandson and he is lost as such for ever.'[37]

Despite her previously expressed reluctance to let him come to England without a full apology to the Prince of Wales, rather against her better judgment she was persuaded by her prime minister to draw a line under the situation. Lord Salisbury, the Prince wrote angrily to the Empress Frederick (8 June 1889), was consulted by the Queen, 'and he gave her the worst possible advice, making us virtually to "eat humble pie!" What a triumph for the Bismarcks, as well as for Willy!'[38] Shortly before the Kaiser's accession, Salisbury had been warned by a British specialist, Sir John Erichsen, that the future monarch 'was not, and never would be, a normal man.' Wilhelm would always be subject to 'sudden accesses of anger', incapable of forming reasonable or temperate judgments, and 'some of his actions would probably be those of a man not wholly sane'.[39] This, in retrospect, may have been a coded reference to the possibility of porphyria, and the prime minister was more willing than Victoria and her successor to make allowances for the Kaiser's instability. When Queen Victoria made him a British admiral, his letter of thanks (14 June) bubbled with gratitude: 'Fancy wearing the same uniform as St Vincent and Nelson; it is enough to make one quite giddy. I feel something like Macbeth must have felt when he was suddenly received by the witches with the cry of "All hail, who art Thane of Glamis and of Cawdor too."'[40]

Invited to England for a few days at the start of August, the Kaiser was on his best behaviour throughout. The Queen reviewed the German fleet, the Kaiser presented to her a deputation of four officers of her regiment; she bestowed on Prince Henry the Order of the Garter, and the Kaiser conferred on his cousin Prince George of Wales the Order of the Black Eagle. Matters went better than anyone had expected, and after his departure the Prince's private secretary Sir Francis Knollys told Lord Salisbury that relations between Kaiser and the Prince were excellent.

Meanwhile, it was becoming clear to certain people, if not the man himself, that the chancellor's days were numbered. Now aged seventy-four, Bismarck was spending more of his time in semi-seclusion on his estates at Friedrichsruh and Varzin. Maybe he was unaware than an anti-Bismarck faction was emerging at Berlin, including his arch-rival Waldersee, who expected to succeed him, Eulenburg, Baron Holstein, and the Kaiser's uncle by marriage, Grand Duke Friedrich of Baden. Their chief interest lay in seeing the chancellor politically isolated from other members of the government, but at the same time they were not prepared to risk national stability by making it possible for the Kaiser to dismiss him too soon. For the chancellor and his closest allies to resign *en masse* would alarm the nation, generate sympathy for him, and also dismay foreign capitals and their governments. If Bismarck knew, he was probably too weary to care. He had been in declining health for years, though nobody believed the lifelong hypochondriac when he grumbled about his numerous ailments, and they made no difference to his gargantuan appetite. Yet he was under few illusions about his young master, and had remarked philosophically to Count George Herbert von Münster, German ambassador to Paris, that the Kaiser was 'like a balloon, if one did not hold him fast on a string, he would go no one knows whither'.[41]

In October 1889 Tsar Alexander III paid a state visit to Berlin. At a private interview Tsar and chancellor talked of the Reinsurance Treaty between their respective countries which was so secret that even the Kaiser barely knew the terms. To the chancellor's surprise, the Tsar asked him whether he was sure that he would remain in office. He muttered that he hoped to enjoy many more years of good health and stay where he was as long as he lived.

Such a prize was not to be granted to one of Bismarck's old adversaries. Now aged seventy-eight, the Dowager Empress Augusta had been confined to a bathchair for a long time. Though her mind and tongue were as sharp as ever, she had become progressively weaker over the last few months, and it was evident that a serious illness would mean the end. During the harsh winter of 1889–90 she contracted influenza, and died on 7 January. The Kaiser mourned the woman who 'had become to the very core a Prussian Queen and a German Empress,' and 'the best of grandmothers to me at the same time'.[42]

By now the train of events that were to unseat Bismarck had been set in motion. The Kaiser informed the Crown Council that he would mark his thirty-first birthday on 27 January 1890 with two proclamations, one promising new laws to protect working men and women and limit their hours of labour, the other summoning an international conference at Berlin where delegates would discuss improving conditions of work throughout Europe. Bismarck had little time for measures of social reform. Elections to the *Reichstag* took place on 20 February, and the Roman Catholic Centre party emerged as the largest single party, securing more than a quarter of all seats in the chamber. The Bismarckian Conservatives had thirteen seats less than the Centre. To retain power Bismarck was prepared to reach a compromise with the Centre party and had talks with its leader, Ludwig Windthorst, who said as he left the chancellery that he had come from the political deathbed of a great man.[43]

The Kaiser told Bismarck he had no right to negotiate with party leaders without his consent, and reminded him that he was not a minister-president responsible to the *Reichstag*, but a chancellor responsible to the Kaiser. Bismarck insisted that he must be free to meet the party leaders. Not if his sovereign forbade it, the Kaiser said. The power of his sovereign, retorted the chancellor, ceased at the door of his wife's drawing room. To support his case he invoked a statute of King Friedrich Wilhelm IV, dating from 1852, which declared that all ministerial communications to the King of Prussia had to pass through the minister-president. The Kaiser told him this was out of date and ordered a fresh decree to be drawn up. How, he asked angrily, could he rule without discussing things with the ministers, if his chancellor spent so much of the year at Friedrichsruh? Sensing this was the end, Bismarck fumbled with some papers he had brought with him, making a half-hearted attempt to conceal them. The Kaiser snatched at them, his eyes alighting on an ambassadorial report containing Tsar Alexander III's indictment of his fellow Kaiser – *'Un garçon mal elevé et de mauvaise foi'* (An ill-mannered boy of bad faith). Without a word Wilhelm walked simmering to his carriage.

Three times the Kaiser sent messengers to the chancellor requesting cancellation of the 1852 statute or resignation instead, without receiving any reply. Next the Kaiser sent a note passed openly through departmental offices, angry at not being kept informed of Russian troop movements. This was the pretext Bismarck needed. The Kaiser, he said, was interfering in foreign policy and talking of war with Russia. On 18 March he sent his resignation letter, which was so abusive that the Kaiser suppressed its publication. In parting he conferred on him the dukedom of Lauenburg and offered him a gift of money. Bismarck answered coldly that he would use the former when travelling incognito and refused the latter, complaining that it was like a tip for the postman at Christmas.

Reaction to the news of Bismarck's departure was generally restrained. Lord Salisbury called it 'an enormous calamity of which the sinister effects will be felt in every part of Europe'. The Empress Frederick told Queen Victoria that she could not approve of the way in which his resignation had come about, calling it 'a dangerous experiment'.[44] Though she could never forget the misery he had caused her and her husband, the Empress admitted magnanimously that he had been ousted for all the wrong reasons, and that despite his advancing years his 'genius and prestige' could still have been useful for Germany and for the cause of peace. Ironically, the Kaiser was writing to his friend Poultney Bigelow at the time and stated that one of the reasons he had asked for his chancellor's resignation was because of the offensive manner in which he spoke of the Empress Frederick and the treatment given to her by 'his official press'.[45] He asked the British ambassador to inform Queen Victoria of the circumstances that had brought about Bismarck's dismissal from office, among them the 'complete subjection' of his ministers who did not dare support their sovereign's measures of social reform, and his treatment of the Kaiser 'like a schoolboy'. The Queen must have been amused to receive her grandson's letter telling her that he and his former chancellor parted tearfully 'after a warm embrace', and that the doctor had assured him that had Bismarck remained in office for a few more weeks, he would have died of apoplexy; 'I resolved to part from him, in order to keep him alive.'[46]

The only major figure who seemed to approve was his fellow monarch and ally in Vienna, Emperor Franz Josef. He remarked that, like the late Count Metternich, Bismarck 'had the misfortune to be unable to find his exit from the stage, and to remain too long'. According to Kaiser Wilhelm, Tsar Alexander III, who had sensed what was coming, told him that Bismarck's 'disobedience to the Emperor brought his fall. In your place I should have done just the same.'[47] In view of Alexander's assessment of his young fellow sovereign, this is open to doubt. Several newspapers printed a summary of the Kaiser's declaration that 'the position of officer of the watch on the ship of state' had fallen to him, and the course remained the same – 'full steam ahead'.[48] The nautical metaphor was taken up in London by Sir John Tenniel of *Punch*, who marked the event with his renowned cartoon, 'Dropping the pilot'.

Bismarck's successor, General Leon von Caprivi, had been told by the Kaiser some weeks previously that he was being considered as the next chancellor. Caprivi's resignation from the Admiralty less than two years earlier had convinced the Kaiser that he was a man of principle. A former state secretary of the imperial navy, now commander of the 10th corps in Hanover, he was aged fifty-nine; he was a model Prussian officer and a non-smoking bachelor who led a Spartan life, with few intimate friends and few enemies. Stubborn, loyal and modest, he accepted the position for the simple reason that his monarch had commanded him. Even his predecessor took the news of his appointment gracefully, telling Caprivi on the day he left the Wilhelmstrasse that 'if anything can lighten for me the oppressiveness of this moment, it is the fact that you are to be my successor'.[49] Waldersee had expected the position to be his, a promotion which the Kaiser's brother Henry had almost taken for granted to the extent that when he heard the announcement he thought a mistake had been made. However, Waldersee was prepared to wait 'until at least one successor to Bismarck' had ruined himself.

Caprivi's promotion meant little change in the ministry. The Kaiser appreciated the importance of continuity, to the extent of asking Count Herbert von Bismarck several times to remain at his post in the foreign ministry. But the Count was too loyal to his father to do so, and followed him into the political wilderness. Father and son devoted much time and effort to spreading rumours throughout the press of their ruler's instability, saying that Chancellor Bismarck had only wanted to stay in office because he knew of the Kaiser's abnormal condition and wanted to save the German nation from catastrophe. Their cause was not helped by the fact that Herbert was becoming a liability, rarely sober in the evening and sinking deeper and deeper into alcoholism.

Not everybody approved of Caprivi's appointment. As he was reputed to be something of a radical, the Junkers regarded him with suspicion, while the Social Democrats looked at him with foreboding. However he made one significant break with his predecessor's ways by giving full information on governmental matters to all the major newspapers irrespective of their political affiliations. It was something of a victory for the people of Germany, though resented by editors and journalists who had preferred the days when they could fill their pockets with Bismarck's handouts.

Honest and straightforward, regarded as an innocent in government circles, Caprivi came to high office with little knowledge of the empire's relations with foreign powers. Bismarck had retained in effect a more or less secret monopoly on knowledge of all relevant information. Though he had written two long memoranda expounding his views on foreign policy in 1888 and passed them to the Kaiser, it never occurred to the latter to let Caprivi see them. The cornerstone of Bismarck's diplomacy had been the isolation of France. To this end, as well as to maintain control on Russian and Austrian expansion in the Balkans, he had signed a defensive alliance with Austria which provided for Germany to come to the dual monarchy's aid in the event of attack from Russia. His Reinsurance Treaty with Russia, due to expire in June 1890, stipulated mutual assistance if Austria-Hungary should attack Russia, or France attack Germany. The Kaiser alleged that he knew nothing of the treaty until the spring of 1890, when he was informed of its existence by Bismarck. Wilhelm's opinion was that the chancellor hoped that the revelation of such complex treaties would ensure his retention in office as nobody else in the empire would be as capable of handling such a foreign policy. On the contrary, some years later the Kaiser declared that it was such chicanery that strengthened his resolve to dismiss Bismarck.

Nikolai Giers, the Russian foreign minister, had seen through the German chancellor's strategy and warned that if Germany did not renew the alliance, the Tsar would have to consider an alliance with the French republic. Caprivi knew nothing of the treaty, or of assurances that the Kaiser had given Count Paul Shuvalov, the Russian ambassador to Germany, that Bismarck's departure from office would mean no changes in German policy and that the Kaiser would personally give his word that the treaty would be renewed. Baron Holstein, who had been offered but refused the post of state secretary in the Foreign Office left vacant by Count Bismarck, recommended letting the treaty lapse on the grounds that it undermined the Austro-German alliance.

Faced with a combination of Holstein and General von Schweinitz, German ambassador to Russia, Caprivi was advised that the Reinsurance

Treaty was incompatible with Germany's obligations to Austria. The Kaiser was convinced, somewhat against his better judgment, to accept their advice. Shuvalov was astonished to be told by Schweinitz that 'the decision had been reversed'. The Kaiser had inadvertently provoked a crisis of judgment, not to say of broken promises. Faced with the alternatives of going back on his word to Shuvalov, and therefore to Tsar Alexander III and Giers, or accepting the resignation of his new chancellor within a week on a matter of a major foreign policy decision, he chose the former.

The Kaiser had previously assured Tsar Alexander III that he intended to renew the alliance. In order to extricate himself the best he could, he instructed Schweinitz to return to St Petersburg and inform the Tsar that, while Germany still valued good relations with Russia, a less complex diplomatic policy was necessary as a result of recent German ministerial changes. The Tsar was contemptuous of such explanations, convinced that with Bismarck's fall he had lost his only trustworthy friend in Germany, and that the Kaiser was 'as good a liar as his manners are bad'. The more problems Germany had, he maintained, 'so much the better for us'.[50]

Although the Kaiser had unwittingly stirred up problems for his empire in the future, another old family problem was about to be resolved. His twenty-four-year-old sister Victoria, who had almost resigned herself to the dreary life of an old maid since the end of the ill-starred Battenberg courtship, had at last found a husband. Admittedly Prince Adolf of Schaumburg-Lippe did not make a great match. An undistinguished soldier, not very clever, a distant relative of the Württemburg royal family, he was unattached, good-hearted enough, and in him at least she saw a chance of some measure of domestic contentment if not happiness. They were betrothed in the summer and married in Berlin on 19 November.

The wedding was marred by an unseemly argument between the Kaiser and Empress and Sophie, Crown Princess of the Hellenes. Sophie had become a mother in July with the birth of her eldest son George, and had decided to enter the Greek Orthodox Church. Wilhelm would not confront his sister himself and decided the task of 'forbidding' Sophie to act in this way should be carried out by his wife. Perhaps he thought Sophie would be more open to her sister-in-law than to him, and perhaps he thought that she would not dare to argue with the heavily pregnant Empress. Summoned to the presence, Sophie was told by Dona that the Kaiser was head of the evangelical church of Prussia and would never agree to his sister changing her religion. If she disobeyed him, she would end up in hell. Infuriated, Sophie told her she could not accept this, and banged the door behind her as she left. The Kaiser informed their mother that if Sophie persisted he would bar her from Germany, and sent

King George of the Hellenes a telegram containing the same threat. During the excitement Dona gave birth prematurely to an undersized, sickly son, later named Joachim. Beside himself with fury, Wilhelm wrote to Queen Victoria that if their baby died 'it is solely Sophie's fault and she has murdered it'.[51]

As Sophie was Crown Princess of the Hellenes she had every right to change her religion, and did so the following spring. Advised by the Empress Frederick to write the Kaiser a conciliatory letter explaining why, he remained obdurate, but had the good grace to lessen her sentence of banishment. She replied to her mother in a telegram sent *en clair*: 'Received answer. Keeps to what he said in Berlin. Fixes it to three years. Mad. Never mind.'[52]

Early in 1891 the Kaiser decided to try and improve Franco-German relations. Having needlessly alienated Russia over the Reinsurance Treaty, he was faced with the likelihood of an alliance between two powerful hostile neighbours. He had never revised his unfavourable opinion of France as a nation, and in 1890 he refused to let his mother and sisters visit Queen Victoria while she was in Aix-les-Bains, on the grounds that he was duty bound to uphold a law passed by his grandfather in 1887 forbidding any prince or princess of the Prussian house to cross the French frontier.[53]

However, Wilhelm's mother had been a regular visitor to Paris, and as a patron of the arts she would be less likely to attract hostility than he would if he set foot there again. He asked her to go and invite French artists in person to participate in an international art conference to be held in Berlin. When it was suggested by her old friend Count Münster, now German ambassador to France, she was so delighted to have a chance to be of use that she did not realize her son was using her to pull German chestnuts out of the fire. The Empress set off with her daughter Margrethe on a semi-official visit. A small but vociferous right-wing nationalist group in Paris, eager to make political capital out of her presence in order to discredit Germany, watched her every move carefully. When she paid discreet visits to Versailles and St Cloud, scenes of happier days in 1855 when she and her parents had visited the Kaiser and Empress, but later of national humiliation and defeat for the French, the press claimed that she had gone out of her way to insult France. The painters who had accepted invitations to exhibit in Berlin were accused of dishonouring their country, and when the German press replied in kind, feeling between both countries rose to such a pitch that the Empress and her daughter were advised to leave France at once. Though Count Münster had discussed the itinerary with her and accompanied her everywhere, he made no effort to defend her, and joined her son in allowing the Empress to take the blame for everything.

Meanwhile, the Kaiser appointed a new chief of the general staff, Count Alfred von Schlieffen. Waldersee was out of favour and had been demoted to a minor local post after criticizing a military exercise prepared by his staff which the Kaiser resented. This was compounded by his behaviour at the Silesia autumn manoeuvres, attended by Emperor Franz Josef, when the Kaiser assumed personal command of an army corps undertaking an exercise which, he had not realized, was the losing side. Schlieffen was the last man likely to criticize his master, and with his appointment and the fall of the ever-resentful Waldersee, who had still had his eye on the highest office, Caprivi was secure at last.

The new chancellor was enjoying a period of relative calm. Initially handicapped by the burden of succeeding the mighty Bismarck and by his ignorance of foreign affairs, Caprivi had successfully presided over modest reforms in taxation, labour relations and local government. In foreign policy he had strengthened the Triple Alliance by seeking trade treaties linking the German economy with those of Italy and Austro-Hungary. Nevertheless, he had no illusions as to the dependence of government policy on his master's caprices. Baron Holstein shared his unease, hoping that the Kaiser would reach maturity before there was 'any serious testing time'. If they did not want a republic, they would have to 'take our princes as Providence sends them'.[54]

Already one major difference was opening up between sovereign and chancellor. The former had already decided on having a large German fleet and took it for granted that Caprivi, a former head of the navy, would agree. To the Kaiser's irritation the chancellor told him that good Anglo-German relations were vital for the peace of Europe and that to build more battleships was no way to preserve harmony.

In June 1891 the Kaiser and Empress went on a state visit to England soon after minor scandal as a result of the Prince of Wales's involvement in a game of baccarat at Tranby Croft, and the Kaiser sent Queen Victoria a high-handed message protesting against the impropriety of anyone holding the honorary rank of a colonel of Prussian hussars becoming implicated in a gambling dispute with men young enough to be his children.[55] Nevertheless, the visit went smoothly and the Kaiser left Dona, their six sons and tutors, governesses and nursemaids to take a seaside holiday at Felixstowe while he departed for a cruise to Norway on board *Hohenzollern*.

The annual cruise, or *Nordlandreise*, with its exclusively male company, allowed him to indulge in practical jokes and boyish tomfoolery, like applying a foot to the backside of elderly aides-de-camp engaged in physical exercises. Its purpose was originally to give him a month-long break from Court life, but in due course his doctor decided it was counter-productive, as he was physically and mentally upset by the long voyage, diet and exhaustion of various kinds, and it did him more harm than good. His entourage soon tired of these cruises, bored if not repelled by the juvenile atmosphere and behaviour of the Kaiser and some of his officers, who loathed every childish prank and moment themselves but were too sycophantic to say so.

A few weeks at sea also gave Wilhelm time to devote to two of his hobbies, art and music. He had inherited the enthusiasm of his mother and maternal grandmother for sketching and painting, his preferred subject matter being seascapes. Examples graced most of the royal homes and palaces in Germany and England at one time. Another was sent as a gift some years later to Hvidøre, the villa in Copenhagen purchased as a bolthole by Queen Alexandra and her sister the Dowager Empress of Russia. On its arrival they looked at it carefully for some moments, then Queen Alexandra remarked, 'I would really like to know what is supposed to be at the top and what at the bottom.'[56]

A private orchestra played almost continuously on the *Hohenzollern*, with a programme personally devised by the Kaiser, usually containing some of his own compositions. One day he began listening carefully to a piece they were performing and shook his head. 'What sort of a dreadful noise is that?' he asked one of his officers, sending him to find out what it was. Barely able to contain his laughter, the officer returned to tell His Majesty that 'the noise' was a piece of music he had composed. He scowled for a moment, then laughed with the rest of them, but it disappeared from the repertoire forthwith.

Even those who knew him best could never tell when he was joking or when to take him seriously. On this cruise he grew a beard, which he shaved off on return. At first he told the assembled company at dinner with a chuckle that it would 'fix the portrait painters', and that people would collect coins showing him without a beard. A day or so later he was sitting at table, his eyes blazing as he brought his right fist crashing down, shouting, 'With a beard like this you could thump on the table so hard that your ministers would fall down with fright and lie flat on their faces!'[57] If it was his idea of a jest, it appeared a deadly earnest one to those assembled there. Alfred von Kiderlen-Wächter of the foreign office, who accompanied him on these cruises for the first few years, was so disturbed by the incident that he wrote to Holstein to warn him of their sovereign's unstable temperament.

These autocratic tendencies surfaced again later that year. In November the Kaiser paid a state visit to Munich where he gave offence when signing the ceremonial golden book of the *Rathaus* by adding the phrase *'Suprema lex, regis voluntas'* (The will of the King is the highest law). All shades of opinion in the Reichstag were affronted. As his mother told Queen Victoria, 'A Czar, an infallible Pope – the Bourbons – and our poor Charles I – might have written such a sentence, but a constitutional Monarch in the 19th century!!!'.[58] He compounded it a few days later when addressing a parade of recruits at Potsdam that, in swearing loyalty to him, 'You have only one enemy and that is my enemy. In the present social confusion it may come about that I order you to shoot down your own relatives, brothers or parents but even then you must follow my orders without a murmur.'[59] Apologists defended him by pointing out that three different versions of this speech existed, and that this one was tampered with by a hostile press as anti-monarchical propaganda,[60] but his spoken words did not differ substantially from this. Condemnation came not just from England and France, where unfavourable comment could be expected, but also from Russia and Berlin. Caprivi faithfully tried to explain his master's words by saying that he was warning young recruits against the menace of civil anarchy, but nobody was convinced.

In February 1892 Caprivi, eager to gain the political support of the Roman Catholic Centre Party, asked Count Zedlitz, minister for ecclesiastical affairs, to introduce a schools bill giving both Lutheran and Catholic churches some control over state education. It was fiercely opposed by liberals and the left in the *Reichstag*, but nobody knew what the Kaiser wanted. He made his annual speech to the provincial assembly at Brandenburg, without letting Caprivi or Zedlitz know in advance the contents of his message. It was a typically bombastic, rambling affair in which he suggested among other things that those among his subjects who liked criticizing his government should emigrate, so that they would be free of 'grumblers we do not need'. One Prussian newspaper pointed out that if 'the grumblers' took their sovereign's advice and emigrated, Germany would become a third-class power in months.

Caprivi had to wait for another three weeks to hear His Majesty's opinion of the bill. In March the Kaiser attended a crown council and spoke against educational reforms which would favour Roman Catholic schools. He and Zedlitz threatened to resign but the Kaiser was mortified, scribbling on his chancellor's request that 'It is not nice to drive the cart into the mud and leave the Kaiser sitting in it.'[61] Caprivi was persuaded to stay and agreed not to press the offending bill.

In April 1892 the Kaiser told the British ambassador at Berlin, Sir Edward Malet, that as an admiral in the Royal Navy he felt obliged to pass intelligence reports he had received on torpedo boat bases, currently under construction by France between Dunkirk and Brest, to the British Admiralty. It was part of a ploy to go to England for a few days 'if Grandmama lets me'. Malet was in a difficult position, as he realized that while the Kaiser adored going back to Osborne, Queen Victoria found his regular visits increasingly wearisome, and his presence thoroughly irritated the Prince of Wales. It seemed to be part of the Kaiser's dual nationality that whenever he felt in the least threatened by pressures or disagreements from his own ministers, or criticism from journalists in Berlin, he appeared to take comfort from and refuge in his dynastic link with Britain. Suddenly he would remember that he was not just an admiral of the fleet like the great Nelson, but an honorary Englishman as well. The Naval Secretary Admiral Hollmann thought that he was attracted to Cowes not by the sailing, so much as by 'unrestrained conversation with distinguished English society in which he finds what he values most and searches for in Germany in vain', and 'unselfish exchange of opinion with independent, strongly formed characters and personalities'.[62] Accordingly, he invited himself to Cowes for regatta week again, though this time he had the grace to stay on his yacht instead of imposing himself and his vast suite on the limited accommodation at Osborne. All Queen Victoria could do was send a cypher telegram to Malet asking him directly to hint more strongly in future that these annual visits were 'not quite desirable'. They would have been even less desirable if she had known that one member of his entourage at Cowes, the painter Karl Salzmann reduced him to helpless mirth by singing him half a dozen times in succession the British national anthem with the words *'God seefe det Queenchen ein'* (God soap the little Queen).[63]

Perhaps the Kaiser badly needed a rest from affairs of state in Germany at the time. Rumours about his mental instability were rife throughout various courts in Europe that spring. The French foreign ministry had received reports from Berlin that he was 'mentally ill' and 'temporarily of unsound mind'. The former judgment was repeated independently in Russia by Grand Duke Serge, now married to the Kaiser's first love Ella.[64] When Queen Victoria was at Hyères on the French Riviera in April and about to go to Darmstadt, Lord Salisbury hoped she would make a point of seeing the Kaiser; 'if he is in this excitable mood he may be dangerous', and a few hours' conversation with the Queen might 'appease him'. However, she was tired of her grandson, and retorted that she 'really cannot go about keeping everybody in order.'[65]

Fortuitously the Kaiser became calmer and that summer behaved more amiably than usual at Cowes. A general election in Britain that July resulted in defeat for Salisbury and brought a Liberal government under Gladstone to power at Westminster. Salisbury had worked conscientiously despite provocation from Berlin to preserve good relations with Germany and her allies, Austria-Hungary and Italy, while stopping short of outright alliance. On their past records, Gladstone and his Foreign Secretary Lord

Rosebery were more favourably inclined towards Russia and France, who had recently concluded an alliance. The Kaiser looked askance at a change of allegiance by his grandmother's ministers, though he was soon assured by Salisbury that Rosebery did not intend to make any sharp break with continuity in foreign policy.

In September 1892 Dona presented the Kaiser with the last of their seven children, a daughter whom they named Victoria Louise. The first six had been sons: Wilhelm, now Crown Prince, had been followed by Eitel Friedrich in 1883, Adalbert in 1884, August Wilhelm in 1887, Oskar in 1888, and Joachim in 1890. Now the succession was safe, the proud father was more pleased to have a girl than he cared to admit. He spoilt her, and she could often get her own way with him where her brothers failed; the eldest of them later recalled that she was the only one 'who succeeded in her childhood in winning a warm corner in his heart'. One of her favourite tricks was making noises with her mouth and cheek imitating the pop of a champagne cork and the subsequent gurgle of flowing wine. Reproved by her governess for such 'unladylike accomplishments', she answered gleefully that Papa taught her – 'he can do it splendidly'.[66]

'Papa' treated his sons like small recruits to be barked at and strictly disciplined. Erring on the side of generosity, Crown Prince Wilhelm recalled that he was 'always very friendly and, in his way, loving towards us; but, by the nature of things, he had none too much time to devote to us. As a consequence, in reviewing our early childhood, I can discover scarcely a scene in which he joins in our childish games with unconstrained mirth or happy abandon. If I try now to explain it to myself, it seems to me as though he was unable so to divest himself of the dignity and superiority of the mature adult man as to enable him to be properly young with us little fellows.'[67] When they walked into his study – which was infrequently, as he made it plain that they were not welcome – they had to hold their hands behind their backs so they would not knock anything off the tables. When they were old enough he insisted that they accompany him on early morning rides on horseback, galloping excursions which required considerable skill in handling the animals. As Hinzpeter had helped him conquer his fear of riding, so Wilhelm was determined that his sons should never admit to any weakness in that area either. The Empress feared that such demands put too much of a strain on them, particularly on the delicate Joachim. She begged her husband to let her accompany him instead, and though she was always exhausted by the time they arrived back, she took their sons out for a less strenuous ride afterwards, so he could not complain that they were poor horsemen from lack of practice.[68]

The Empress, everyone who knew them agreed, 'bored and agitated' her husband. She doted on him with cloying admiration, imbued him with her naïve optimism which made her the despair of his officials, and the more she tried to calm him, the more she contributed to his nervous and restless character. As she knew her husband disliked plump women, she subjected herself to various medicines and strict dieting in order to retain her figure. In addition to seven pregnancies she had at least two miscarriages, which she tried to keep secret from him. Her own health suffered as a result and General Adolf von Deines, who was in charge of their sons' education, lamented having 'to deal with a nervously ill woman and an unreasonably anxious mother, who, despite many excellent qualities, hurts at least as much as she helps – strictly from anxiety'.[69] Sometimes she tried the Kaiser's patience so much that he wanted to send her away, persuading her that it would be for the good of her own health, but she always resisted. In 1894 she cajoled her way into accompanying him on his *Nordlandreise*, with the result that the atmosphere was strained and subdued throughout, and those around them found the situation even more unbearable than the customary cavalcade of childish pranks. In order to compensate for her shortcomings in taste and dress, he sometimes chose – and occasionally attempted to design – her hats, clothes and jewellery, another of his fleeting enthusiasms that soon waned, especially as the results were not particularly successful.

Their sons grew up with an exaggerated sense of their own importance and talents. August Wilhelm was inordinately proud of his artistic skills, and as a boy delighted in making 'crude and feeble sketches', which he presented to any lady or gentleman at Court whom he wished to show kindness. As Fraülein Clare von Gersdorff, one of the Empress's ladies-in-waiting, remarked sadly after becoming the less than gratified recipient of one, it was a pity 'that our young Princes think so much of everything they do. They never seem to compare it with what others do, but believe it to be admirable simply because they did it.'[70]

Another common fault of the youngsters was impatience. Miss Topham often helped Victoria Louise with taking photographs, and assisted her in developing and printing them at the end of the day. She agreed to demonstrate the process to Joachim, but in his desire to hurry everything he upset a large paraffin lamp. Though she managed to catch it as it fell and avoid serious damage, she sustained a painful burn and blistering on her wrist. Fortunately, Joachim decided not to pursue the art of photography after that.

In 1893 the last of the Kaiser's sisters was married. Margrethe, aged twenty, had briefly been considered as a suitable wife for her cousin the late Albert Victor, Duke of Clarence, and then for the Tsarevich. Neither were sufficiently enraptured with her, ostensibly as she was said to be 'not regularly pretty', but perhaps as neither really wanted 'Wilhelm the Sudden' as a brother-in-law. At length she was betrothed to Friedrich Karl, son of the Landgrave of Hesse. His family was not wealthy, and since the Austro-Prussian War had owned no land, only a few castles. Nevertheless, as the youngest of the family she was of no dynastic importance, and after huffing and puffing about a 'poor match', mainly to irritate his harassed mother, the Kaiser gave his consent. The couple were married in Berlin on 25 January 1893, the thirty-fifth wedding anniversary of the bride's parents.

This time the ceremony was not spoilt by any family arguments, only by the behaviour of Duke Ernst Gunther of Holstein, the black sheep of the Empress's family. If his sister was insufferably pious, he was an unashamed rake who set out to prove himself a more entertaining host to the Tsarevich than the Kaiser could ever be. He treated the future Tsar to a bachelor entertainment of Roman punch and dancing girls, thus missing a dinner laid on partly for him at the Russian embassy by the ambassador, Count Shuvalov, on 27 January, the Kaiser's birthday. The latter was furious, and though Shuvalov and the Empress Frederick begged him not to take it to heart, he despatched a priggish letter to the Tsar complaining of his son's 'proclivities for vice' and his 'disregard for the decencies of life'.[71]

Such censorious remarks might have been justified if the Kaiser's own tastes in entertainment had been more dignified. Only a few months earlier Georg von Hülsen-Haseler, a military attaché at Munich, had devised a party piece for his and the Kaiser's friend Count Emil von Görtz. The portly count, he said, should be paraded by him as a circus poodle. 'Just think: behind *shaved* (tights), *in front* long bangs out of black or white wool, at the back under a genuine poodle tail a marked rectal opening and, when you 'beg', in front a fig-leaf. Just think how wonderful when you bark, howl to music, shoot off a pistol or do other tricks. . . . In my mind's eye I can already see H.M. laughing with us.'[72]

In June 1893 the Kaiser was back at Cowes, looking forward to competing in the Queen's Cup competition in his cutter *Meteor* against the Prince of Wales' new yacht *Britannia*. It had been a difficult summer for him, particularly as there had been heated debates in the *Reichstag* over a proposal to increase the size of the army by 18 per cent, as a compromise, cutting the length of conscripted service from three years to two. However, there was a brief but alarming interlude in which the Kaiser feared that war might break out. French warships were provoking the English by blockading Bangkok, and when two British gunboats were warned to keep the French under surveillance the French admiral immediately asked British vessels to withdraw. Rosebery sent an ultimatum to Paris on 30 July, the day after the Kaiser's arrival at Cowes. Just before midnight Sir Henry Ponsonby arrived at Osborne with a telegram from Rosebery which suggested the French were threatening war after the incident off Bangkok. Rosebery sought an urgent meeting with the German ambassador to see how much Britain could rely on German support or collaboration.

The Kaiser had been his usual bombastic self on board *Britannia* at dinner, constantly referring to the growing strength of Germany. However, once back on board *Hohenzollern* his true reaction became evident. Desperately worried, he confided to Eulenburg how France and Russia had the initiative, and how neither his army nor the British fleet were ready for war. If Germany could not demonstrate her strength as a decisive world power, the reputation he had worked so hard to build up since his accession would be shattered. Two German diplomats were called by Eulenburg to help him convince the Kaiser that he need not worry, but it was evident that their master's nerve had temporarily gone. Whether it was a complete 'nervous collapse' is debatable, but his aggressive euphoria of only a few hours earlier had given way with startling suddenness to the opposite.

The situation was retrieved when the French foreign office rescinded the order given by the French admiral to the English gunboats off Bangkok. Once he had recovered his composure the Kaiser was furious, believing that either Rosebery had overreacted or the Prince of Wales and Ponsonby between them had made excessive drama out of the incident in order to test his reaction. Rosebery sent an explanation via the German ambassador to say that he had only thought it fair to keep the Kaiser informed of the situation while he was in England, to which the Kaiser's response was that there were other ways of doing this than through a private secretary at midnight. The rest of the visit was not a success, with the Kaiser making up for his panic by a further display of aggressive banter. As he left England after Cowes week he was angry to find that Caprivi welcomed the war scare as a possible catalyst for expanding the Triple into a Quadruple Alliance. A reprimand from the Kaiser had Caprivi ready to threaten resignation, until Eulenburg intervened again, pointing out that if he forced Caprivi from office while returning home from a pleasure trip, his people would criticize him for having spent a week sailing at a time of political crisis.

During his four and a half years as chancellor, Caprivi offered or threatened to resign ten times. By the end of 1893, Kaiser and chancellor knew that they could not work together much longer. The former said openly that he would soon be choosing a successor, a younger man who would not have enough past experience to oppose him. Caprivi admitted that his relations with the sovereign had become intolerable, and nobody could imagine 'how relieved I will feel out of here'.[73] The catalyst was a disagreement between the chancellor and Count Botho von Eulenburg, minister-president of Prussia, over renewing anti-socialist laws about to go before the *Reichstag*. An escalation of anarchist violence throughout part of Europe in the summer of 1894 had convinced some ministers that repressive measures were required. The Kaiser supported Eulenburg, somewhat hesitantly, while Caprivi felt that such measures would never get through the *Reichstag*. The Kaiser snubbed him publicly and privately, and refused another letter of resignation in October until Eulenburg wrote his, saying he could not work with Caprivi any more. Tired and weary of the conflict, the Kaiser was persuaded to let them both go.

## CHAPTER FOUR

# 'A Great Ruler and a Sensible Man?'

Despite the Kaiser's intention to appoint someone younger as his chancellor and minister-president, he chose a man of seventy-five, some months older than Bismarck had been at his resignation. Prince Chlodwig zu Hohenlohe-Schillingsfürst, governor of Alsace-Lorraine, a distant kinsman of the houses of Coburg and Schleswig-Holstein, was jocularly called 'Uncle Clovis' by the Kaiser. As his predecessor had done, he accepted the post largely as he felt it would be disloyal to refuse. Self-deprecatingly he claimed he was too old, too ill and had too poor a memory; he was a poor public speaker with no knowledge of Prussian laws and politics; and as he had been in public life for thirty years he did not want to begin something that he knew would prove to be too much for him.[1] Major-General Swaine, now serving out the last two years of his appointment as military attaché in Berlin, regretted the actions of the ruler in whom he had tried hard to see the best. The Kaiser, he wrote to Sir Henry Ponsonby (3 November), had dispensed with two chancellors and replaced the second with a man whose age would limit the period of his usefulness, purely in order to 'pull the strings without opposition and in order that the new man should carry out the same identical policy of the last. Is this the action of a great ruler and a sensible man?'[2]

Two days after the appointment was announced, Tsar Alexander III of Russia, in the Kaiser's words, 'the barbarian', died of Bright's disease at the premature age of forty-nine. The accession of his diffident, unprepared son as Tsar Nicholas II gave Kaiser Wilhelm a golden opportunity, or so he believed. In April both had been guests at the wedding of his cousins Princess Victoria Melita of Coburg and Ernest, Grand Duke of Hesse, the only surviving brother of his old flame Ella. While they were there, the Kaiser had added his efforts to those of several other guests to persuade the Grand Duke's youngest surviving sister Alix to accept the hand of 'Nicky', then Tsarevich, in marriage. By so doing he hoped to win and retain the young Tsar's confidence, weaning him away from Russia's alliance with republican France. 'The blood of their

Majesties is still on that country,' Wilhelm wrote. 'Look at it, has it since then ever been happy or quiet again? Has it not staggered from bloodshed to bloodshed? Nicky, take my word for it, the curse of God has stricken that people for ever.'[3]

The Kaiser had another curse with which to deal. Since the autumn of 1892 Berlin society had been troubled by an epidemic of anonymous letters sent to prominent people at Court, from the Kaiser and Empress downwards. All in the same handwriting, they told of intrigues, cabals and accused the recipients or their families of fraud, calumny and illicit love affairs. The in-depth knowledge of personalities they revealed made it evident that the person or persons responsible were either courtiers, or members of the imperial family. Some letters contained montages based on pornographic photographs from Paris with the heads obscured by cut-out portraits of well-known courtiers and members of the royal family. The Kaiser called in a private investigator and then the Berlin police, but the culprit or culprits still eluded detection. Judging by the volume of scurrilous communications, it appeared that at least two pairs of hands were involved – between three and four hundred letters were sent in less than two years.

When the imperial master of ceremony, Baron von Schrader, received one of these collages, he decided it must be the work of his main enemy at Court, Count Leberecht von Kotze, a close friend of the Kaiser. He asked the investigators to search Kotze's possessions thoroughly, and they found a piece of blotting paper on his desk with handwriting very similar to that of the letters. The Kaiser ordered Kotze's arrest, but while he was in custody awaiting trial the missives continued to be sent. To make amends the Kaiser presented Kotze with an Easter egg made of decorated flowers, some bottles of wine and his uniform and old position back. Embittered by his wrongful imprisonment, Kotze demanded a military trial to establish his innocence and then began a series of duels with those who had accused him of being responsible. From these he emerged maimed but unbowed, and in a duel early in 1896 he killed Schrader. At about this time the letters stopped, and the police apprehended the culprits – the Empress's reprobate brother Duke Ernst Gunther and his French mistress. He was informed that in future his time at Court would be restricted to no more than a week at a time, and he would not be permitted to open any establishment of his own at Berlin or Potsdam. His mistress was escorted to the German–French border by a police guard, and she was banished from Germany for life.

The Kaiser's brother-in-law was not the only difficult member of the family. One of the first suspects had been his sharp-tongued, tittle-tattle-loving sister Charlotte. She and her husband Bernhard had been close friends of Baron and Baroness Kotze, and the couples had made a joint expedition to Greece and Palestine in 1892, just before the letters started. While abroad the couples had quarrelled and fallen out, and Charlotte lost her diary, full of poisonous gossip. Somehow, perhaps through the Baron and Baroness, it came into the possession of Duke Ernst's mistress, and then into the hands of the police. When they showed the Kaiser his sister's diary, he was enraged by her betrayal. Since his marriage, relations between them had cooled. While his anger against her fell short of outright banishment, it was made clear to her and her husband that they would not be welcome at Court, and the Kaiser never forgave her. Soon afterwards Bernhard was transferred to a regiment at distant Breslau, a subtle sentence of banishment which removed them as far as reasonably possible from the bright society life on which Charlotte thrived.

Another sensation at Court, albeit more short-lived, occurred at Easter 1894 with the publication of a pamphlet *Caligula, A Study in Roman Megalomania*. Written by Professor Ludwig Quidde, a member of the *Reichstag*, it compared Kaiser Wilhelm with the mad Emperor of Rome, and sold very well. Everyone expected that Quidde would be sued for libel, until a comic journal produced its idea of the likely dialogue in court between defendant and prosecution:

Q: Whom had you in mind in writing this book, Professor?
A: Caligula, of course! Whom have you in mind, Mr Prosecutor?[4]

To his credit, the Kaiser read the pamphlet and took it with good humour. When his English landowning friend the Earl of Lonsdale came to stay at the palace, he was presented with a bust of his host on leaving. No plinth was available and a courtier removed one from a piece in the corridor. Presenting it to the Earl, the Kaiser chuckled as he said that the plinth had surely come from a bust of Caligula.

Meanwhile, there was a new cause to kindle national and patriotic sentiment in Germany. In January 1895 the Kaiser told members of the *Reichstag* that a substantial increase in the fleet was the empire's prime focus as a great power. His *eminence grise* was the new navy secretary Captain Alfred von Tirpitz, a specialist in torpedoes whom he had first met on exercises in the Baltic Sea. Like his master, Tirpitz was familiar with England, and his wife and daughter had been educated at Cheltenham Ladies' College. One recent historian has suggested that at the height of his power, after Bismarck, Tirpitz was the ablest, most durable, most influential and most effective minister in imperial Germany.[5] Resentful of what he saw as England's patronizing attitude towards the German navy, he resolved to build the latter into a formidable fighting force, more than a match for British seapower. For Tirpitz Britain was the German empire's most dangerous enemy, and the most effective way to challenge her was to concentrate on building battleships instead of cruisers. His enthusiasm was bolstered when the Kaiser read *The Influence of Sea Power upon History*, an account by the American naval captain Alfred Mahan of the struggle for maritime supremacy in the seventeenth and eighteenth centuries, which suggested that the growth and prosperity of nations depended ultimately on command of the seas. Adding weight to this argument was Japan's recent victorious war against China over the future of Korea, and French military operations on the island of Madagascar in the Indian Ocean. At the same time German traders in Mozambique and the Transvaal reported President Kruger's plans to complete a railway that would free the economy of the Transvaal. If Germany had naval bases in the China seas and southern Africa, the Kaiser believed, he could conduct a world policy commensurate with his empire's prestige and economic strength. A coaling station in Mozambique would be necessary to protect German interests in southern Africa, and a solid base in China. Hohenlohe and Marschall, the foreign secretary, were left to discover how to acquire the outposts of empire necessary for such a world policy.

Germany's future, the Kaiser had proclaimed in a widely reported speech at Stettin in 1891, was 'on the water'. However, few Germans, apart from Tirpitz, agreed with him. Prussia had long believed that defence funds should be spent on the army, while the *Reichstag*, suspicious of anything that might encroach on its already limited constitutional prerogatives, was reluctant to do too much to enhance its sovereign's delusions of grandeur and gratify his more ambitious designs. While most of the deputies resented British naval superiority to some degree, they were not prepared to risk coming to blows with England merely to gratify the whims of the Kaiser. Even fewer were prepared to take him seriously when he spoke of a dream he had in which German warships combined with the British Royal Navy to destroy the French and Russian fleets, and celebrated their joint victory with a ceremony in London at which Queen Victoria would greet him in Trafalgar Square at the foot of Nelson's column.[6]

The Kaiser's persistent intervention in German foreign policy exasperated his ministers, who were frustrated at feeling that they never enjoyed his confidence. In December 1894 Eulenberg wrote to Holstein of his conviction that 'the Guiding Hand of Providence lies behind this elemental and natural drive of the Kaiser's to direct the affairs of the kingdom in person. Whether it will ruin us or save us I cannot say'.[7] Two months later Eulenburg was begging the Kaiser to show support for Hohenlohe and Marschall if he did not want to plunge Germany into a severe constitutional crisis. The Kaiser was already intervening in domestic and foreign affairs to an extent unknown during the time of Caprivi. It was clear that he had chosen Hohenlohe largely because he was too old and lacking in energy to defend his rights as chancellor against the sovereign who had boasted at the beginning of his reign that he meant to be his own Bismarck. Privately, the Kaiser felt he had no reason to keep his ministers informed of his personal dealings with the other sovereigns of Europe. He believed that he understood the British better than anybody else in Berlin. The Liberal government, in which Gladstone had just been succeeded as prime minister by Rosebery, was divided between imperialists and radical isolationists, and he felt it would be most sensible to wait for the return of a Conservative administration led by Lord Salisbury, to whom he ascribed undue influence over the London press.

In June 1895 a general election in England produced this result. The Kaiser sent Salisbury a telegram of congratulation direct from Potsdam, and came to the Cowes regatta again in August for what proved to be a troublesome few days for everyone involved. The Prince of Wales was irked at his nephew using the occasion to celebrate the silver jubilee of victories in the Franco-Prussian War aboard his warships, and the Germans complained that the Prince was snubbing their sovereign in public. Both men were losing patience with each other, and in their anger were starting to complain about the other to their entourages, though as everyone was aware of the tension between them, it was no more than confirmation of what they had long known. But of the two the Kaiser was less circumspect, and English and Germans alike were shocked when he openly referred to his uncle as 'the old peacock' at a dinner on board *Hohenzollern*. The Grand Duke of Mecklenburg was horrified by his sovereign's behaviour at Cowes, of which this episode was but one example. When Queen Victoria's son-in-law Henry of Battenberg asked why the German princes put up with so much from a man who was only *primus inter pares*, the Grand Duke shrugged and said that it was 'no use one kicking by himself; they must all do it together, and to line them up and loose them off together against the Kaiser seems to me an impossibility'.[8]

To add to their woes there was a misunderstanding over a meeting with Salisbury, who received an invitation to call on the Kaiser at a time when he already had an appointment with Queen Victoria at Osborne. He was detained there by a heavy storm until early evening, and then had to cross to Portsmouth because of various commitments in London. The

Kaiser hoped to secure himself an invitation to Hatfield, where he could have private talks with the prime minister. Instead he went back to Germany in high dudgeon.

That winter two episodes involving the Kaiser kept gossips well supplied with ammunition. The first had no repercussions beyond Berlin and Potsdam, apart from reminding everyone of his petty sense of family tyranny. On 28 December 1895 his sister-in-law, Princess Friedrich Leopold, went skating on the lake near Schloss Glienecke, her home at Potsdam. The ice gave way, and had she not been rescued promptly she would have risked death from hypothermia in the freezing water. Yet she feared death less than the reaction at Court, for her sister, the Empress, was coming to visit her later that day. In an attempt to cover up her folly she asked her ladies to tell Her Majesty that she was indisposed with a severe cold. That would have been the end of the matter, had an enterprising reporter not ensured that news of her rescue would make the afternoon papers.

The panic-stricken Princess wrote to her sister to apologize, but to no avail. Next morning her husband was summoned to appear before the Kaiser. After an angry meeting he was escorted home by the Kaiser's aide-de-camp and the commanding officer of the Potsdam garrison, who took his sword away and put an armed guard around the castle. The Prince and Princess were under house arrest for a fortnight, forbidden to communicate by any means with anyone, or to receive visitors. Military guards were stationed in their home, an officer shadowed the Prince in his garden, and another visited every evening to check he had not absconded. In an unduly high-handed letter the Kaiser informed his brother-in-law that 'in spite of frequent admonitions you have not been lucky enough to guide and keep your wife in the conception of life proper to a Prussian Princess, which she has the high honour to be', and he had 'the power to insist on the observance of the laws of tradition, decency and custom'.[9] An old family feud had been rekindled, for Prince Friedrich Leopold was the son of Wilhelm's late uncle Friedrich Karl, who had loudly derided the inadvisability of letting a one-armed prince become their sovereign. Nevertheless, the Kaiser's reaction seemed out of all proportion to such a trifling misdemeanour. Even the Empress Frederick, who knew the unpleasant side of her son too well, was aghast at such high-handed action, but after the events which followed her husband's death, 'I can believe *anything* and *everything* of him.'[10]

This trivial episode was soon eclipsed by events in Africa. On new year's eve news reached Berlin of Dr Storr Jameson's raid into the Transvaal prior to an anti-Boer rising in Johannesburg. German capital accounted for one-fifth of foreign investment in the Boer republic and German-born settlers held high positions in the administration of President Kruger. Convinced that it held what *The Times* called 'a moral protectorate' in the Transvaal, the German government was indignant and the Kaiser reacted angrily. 'I hope that all will come right,' he wrote to the Tsar (2 January), 'but come what may, I shall never allow the British to stamp out the Transvaal.'[11] He was convinced that Jameson had been encouraged by the British government, particularly the colonial secretary Joseph Chamberlain. Jameson and his force were captured by the Boers within four days, but the Kaiser made matters worse by sending a telegram to President Kruger congratulating him on 'restoring tranquillity against the armed bands which have broken into your country as disturbers of the peace and in protecting your country's independence against attacks from without'.[12] The English press carried the message word for word, and within hours there were anti-German demonstrations throughout London; seamen were attacked in the docklands, and windows of German-owned shops were smashed. While Salisbury and Chamberlain maintained that there had merely been misunderstandings, the furious Prince of Wales demanded that Queen Victoria should make the nation's feelings known for her grandson. She wrote him a conciliatory letter, pointing out that while Dr Jameson's action had been wrong, the telegram was considered very unfriendly towards England, which she felt sure was not his intention. 'Our great wish has always been to keep on the best of terms with Germany, trying to act together, but I fear your Agents in the Colonies do the very reverse.'[13] In his defence he replied that he did not rejoice at the discomfiture of English officers and gentlemen, but at the defeat of rebels against Her Majesty.

All the same, the Kaiser was so alarmed at English press attacks on Germany and the resulting Anglophobia in Berlin that he felt he should exploit the mood by gaining approval in the Reichstag for naval expansion. He told Hohenlohe that the only way to impress foreign seafaring powers was to build a large navy. When Hollmann warned him that the deputies would not be convinced merely because of criticism in the British press, Wilhelm threatened angrily to wait until he could find ministers and a *Reichstag* who would share his patriotic spirit.

By now 'Uncle Clovis' was no longer the passive, compliant soul he had seemed at the time of his appointment. When Bismarck, now a widower of eighty-one in poor health but still strong enough to alarm his sovereign, revealed to the press the previous existence of the Reinsurance Treaty with Russia and criticized the Kaiser for not renewing it in 1890, the Kaiser angrily threatened to have him imprisoned for treason. Hohenlohe told him the minimum sentence for such a crime was two years' hard labour. If Bismarck was jailed and died in custody, would it be 'worthy' of His Majesty to have the funeral cortège of imperial Germany's first great chancellor coming from a second-rate fortress like Spandau? And would it not invite ridicule to bring such a charge against such an esteemed servant of the house of Hohenzollern?

Having made him see sense on the matter, Hohenlohe had a second bone of contention when the Kaiser announced he would set up a committee at the highest level of government. To do so, Hohenlohe warned, would 'diminish' the constitutional office of the chancellor. Wilhelm retorted that he knew no constitution: 'I only know what I will.' Making no apology for expressing his views frankly, Hohenlohe insisted that he was not the author of the constitution, but he was bound by it. Astonished by such defiance, the Kaiser talked excitedly of a *coup d'état* against the *Reichstag*, and warned Waldersee to be ready to take over the chancellorship if necessary, telling him that he would 'do the job well if shooting becomes necessary'.[14] While alarmed at his sovereign's autocratic manner, Hohenlohe stood firm. If the Kaiser intended to be his own chancellor, he said, 'he will have to appoint a straw doll. I have no desire to be one.'[15] At length the Kaiser realized that he had overreacted, and Hohenlohe remained in office for another three years, albeit virtually powerless. He was asked to place his signature on state documents while the Kaiser supervised the preparation of new legislation, often drafting bills himself. Holstein was so appalled by the constant atmosphere of intrigue, tension and uncertainty which threatened to paralyze the government that he consulted Eulenburg. Holstein proposed adopting a policy of allowing the Kaiser to follow his own inclinations, no matter how wild or unworkable, and then confronting him with the mass resignations of his ministers, as the resulting débâcle would be the only way to save the monarchy. Even the Kaiser's loyal friend Eulenburg informed Count Bernhard von Bülow, secretary of state for foreign affairs, that all the foreign office believed their sovereign was mad, that they had joined the Bismarcks in spreading rumours to this effect, and that there was a movement afoot within the family – probably involving the Empress Frederick and her other son Henry – to have him 'put into care'.[16]

The Kaiser also wrote his brother Henry's speeches, or so he led the Court to believe. As most of the sovereign's speeches were ghost-written to some extent, it strains credibility to believe that the officially sanctioned addresses with which he provided his brother, whom he often dismissed as a 'political child', were really his own work. A less combative character, the easygoing Prince was careful to avoid friction with his brother. Keen to flatter him and avoid charges of having said the wrong thing, he asked the Kaiser to perform this fraternal task which Wilhelm discharged good-humouredly, telling his sycophants cheerfully that 'to be the intellectual giant of one's family has its drawbacks'.[17] Brotherly relations were amicable enough on the surface, though the more discerning thought them 'never hearty and frequently strained'. Their wives disliked each other; the Empress took exception to the good-natured Irene's devotion to Queen Victoria and her English relatives; and the Kaiser resented Prince and Princess Henry's ready welcome at Windsor and Osborne, as well as his brother's popularity in the navy.

In April 1897 Prince Henry read to the officers of his flagship a telegram from his brother in which members of the *Reichstag* were referred to as 'rascals' and 'scoundrels who knew no Fatherland'. It was widely reported and criticized in the press, and a few weeks later a prominent radical Liberal, Eugen Richter, led an attack in the *Reichstag* on irresponsibility in the highest places. Nobody rose to speak in the sovereign's defence. Holstein gloomily warned Count Paul von Hatzfeldt, German ambassador in London, that feeling in the country was turning more and more against the Kaiser as a result of the telegram, and he had undermined the prestige of the throne: 'I regret this whole unnecessary complication so very much because I am firmly convinced that it will finally end with a powerful landslide to the Left, into democracy.'[18]

The Kaiser wanted to attend Queen Victoria's diamond jubilee celebrations in June 1897 in London, not as a reigning sovereign but as the eldest grandson. He was advised gently but firmly that no invitation would be forthcoming. In siding with Turkey in her quarrel with Greece over the possession of Crete, he had gone against family loyalties by snubbing King George of the Hellenes and the King's daughter-in-law, his sister Sophie, and had outraged feeling in Britain, which was solidly pro-Greek. The Queen could not help comparing his behaviour with that of Tsar Nicholas II, the 'dear young Emperor' in St Petersburg, whom she found so much more sensible as well as more eager to promote good relations with Britain. Kaiser Wilhelm resented his exclusion bitterly, writing to his grandmother (10 June) that he felt 'like a charger chained in the stables who hears the bugle sounding, stomps and chomps his bit, because he cannot follow his regiment'.[19] Instead his mother, his brother and three of his sisters took part in the festivities. It was fortunate for Wilhelm that he did not go, as the crowds groaned audibly when a German general rode by in the procession to St Paul's Cathedral. As Prince Henry passed, a cockney voice informed him loudly that if he wanted to send a telegram to Kruger, he would find a post office round the corner. Had the Kaiser been there, the Londoners' displeasure would have been considerably less restrained.

Despite this gesture Henry was more popular in England than his elder brother. The days when he had taken the path of least resistance and joined Wilhelm and Charlotte in provoking their parents were long past. His marriage to the level-headed Irene had been partly responsible for the change in him, but a certain resemblance in character to his late father became increasingly obvious with maturity. Straightforward, modest, devoted to his wife and children, he was sometimes compared unfairly with Wilhelm, largely as his critics failed to see that with his trusting nature he was no master of political intrigue. As Bülow readily pointed out, 'his simple decency and modesty failed to reckon with the evil always in mankind'. Hinzpeter once remarked to Bülow, with perhaps more praise than he intended, that 'you can see in Prince Henry what the Kaiser would have become if I had not taken him in hand'. The future chancellor was not the only person to wonder if 'the German Empire might not have been better served with Prince Henry as Kaiser, than with his much more gifted but also much more difficult, capricious and unreliable elder brother'.[20] Henry and Irene had set up their first home at the Schloss at Kiel, and the Empress Frederick often stayed with them; she found them good company, 'so happy and their home so peaceful and harmonious because they are away from Berlin, and mischief-making'.[21] In 1896 Henry bought the estate of Hemmelmark near Kiel, which remained their home for life.

With Anglo-German relations becoming ever more chilly, the Kaiser felt that the time had come to make overtures to the Tsar. In August 1897 the Kaiser and Empress went on a cruise on board *Hohenzollern* to St Petersburg. He wanted to sound out the Tsar's reaction if German warships were to anchor off the northern Chinese port of Kiaochow. The Tsar agreed that he would not make any objection to a German presence at the port, as long as his naval authorities in the Pacific were advised in advance.

During the previous year the Kaiser had become convinced that Germany needed a colony and port which would free the navy from dependence on the Hong Kong dockyards and act as a terminus for railways to Peking and northern China. The foreign ministry disliked the idea of encroaching on an area where there was already Russo-Japanese competition, but the Kaiser was not to be dissuaded. His visit to the Tsar assured him, he believed, that he could 'count on Nicky', and he thought that German – and his own – prestige would benefit from a spectacular success in foreign policy. The catalyst was the attack and murder of two German missionaries by Chinese brigands in southern Shantung. When the news reached Berlin, the Kaiser telegraphed to the Tsar that he was sending a German squadron to Kiaochow, 'the only port available to operate from as base against marauders'. The Tsar replied evasively that he could neither approve nor disapprove of such an action.

In December an expedition sailed under the command of Prince Henry, who delivered a stirring speech to his men and their sovereign, declaring that he was not motivated by the desire for fame or laurels, only 'to proclaim, to preach the gospel of your Majesty's sacred person to all who will hear it, and also to those who do not want to hear it'.[22] This oration was received coldly by the more liberal German press and by papers abroad. Worse still from Henry's point of view was the reaction of his English in-laws, his grandmother, the Prince of Wales and his sisters. After an icy reception when he touched at Portsmouth on his journey to the Far East, he was readily forgiven. Everybody knew who was responsible for the speech. A few days later German marines landed in Kiaochow Bay to seize control of the town and harbour. Five months later the whole district was formally transferred from China to Germany on a lease of ninety-nine years, and subsequently declared a colonial protectorate within the German empire.

Among the Kaiser's ministers, approval was by no means unanimous. Some at the foreign office feared that he had destroyed the fragile Russo-German peace, while others dreaded a war with China. However, the Kaiser was sure that he had almost single-handedly scored the foreign policy triumph that he had sought.

Germany now had a footing in Asia and the Kaiser, encouraged by Tirpitz, was still obsessed with the benefits of naval expansion. Tirpitz proposed to submit a parliamentary bill, the Navy Law, to determine and secure revenue for warship construction until the year 1905, by which time Germany would have a fleet comprising nineteen battleships and twenty-four cruisers. At the opening of the *Reichstag* session on 30 November 1897 the development of Germany's battle fleet was a prominent theme of the speech from the throne. Tirpitz went about the business of propaganda with thoroughness in order to win the support of a sceptical public for the rightness of their mission with a special news section in Berlin to answer hostile criticism in the national and local press. A German colonial society was formed to organize lectures on the need for a navy, distribute pamphlets, sponsor talks and meetings addressed by university professors. With public opinion solidly behind the mission, the Navy Law was passed by the *Reichstag* by a comfortable margin in March 1898, and the Kaiser was delighted with Tirpitz's work. In April a group of businessmen, industrialists and aristocrats founded the navy league to help support national consciousness throughout Germany, and it was with wholehearted confidence that Wilhelm could deliver a speech in September declaring that their future lay 'on the water'. As yet reaction from England was restrained. Most of the press thought that Germany was doing no more than taking reasonable defence precautions in the light of hostility from France and Russia. Only one journal, the *Saturday Review*, saw the Navy Law, like the Kruger telegram and the seizure of Kiaochow, as evidence of German ambitions to rival if not overtake British pre-eminence as a world power. Queen Victoria similarly understood and distrusted her grandson. In October 1898 she found it necessary to warn Lord Salisbury that Lord Charles Beresford, the commander of one of her battleships, should be watched with care and not shown anything, 'as I know it for a fact (the Duke of York told me) that he writes every week to the German Emperor who is better informed about our navy than I am'.[23]

By this time Bismarck was dead. The Kaiser had visited him for the last time in December 1897 and found him in a wheelchair, but still as mentally alert as ever, keen to engage his sovereign in serious conversation, much to the latter's discomfort. In the new year he sank into a slow decline and passed away on 30 July 1898. The Kaiser was informed while cruising in the North Sea and hurried back for the funeral, held privately at the old man's estate of Friedrichsruh as he had refused a state ceremony. As he was buried the Kaiser and his suite stood on one side of the grave, his son Herbert and the rest of the family on the other, unforgiving to the last.

Throughout much of the year the Kaiser renewed his efforts to bring about an Anglo-German *rapprochement*. In this he had the eager participation of Baron Eckardstein, an official at the German embassy in London. Salisbury welcomed the move, and during the summer the Empress Frederick encouraged the British government to this end, hoping on behalf of her son that England could meet him halfway. Yet none of his senior ministers shared his enthusiasm, seeing no German advantage in such an alliance, and apprehensive lest any general agreement with Britain might make it appear to Russia that Berlin was taking sides against St Petersburg.

In October 1898 the Kaiser and Empress undertook a journey to Constantinople, Jerusalem and Damascus. Their acceptance of hospitality from Sultan Abdul Hamid was criticized by those who noted his failure to protect adequately the Armenian Christians in his empire. The French press was particularly scornful, as was the Dowager Empress of Russia, writing acidly to her son the Tsar of the German Emperor's vanity and desire to be talked about: 'That pose of Ober-pastor, preaching peace on earth in a thunderous voice as though he were commanding troops, and she wearing the Grand Cross in Jerusalem, all this is perfectly ridiculous and has no trace of religious feeling – disgusting!'[24]

Germany's new interest in the Middle East was inspired by a desire for economic penetration. A German company had begun building railways in Asia Minor a few years previously, but Britain did not see it as a threat. The French press was angry, but Anglo-French relations were bad at the time and conservative newspapers in London treated the Kaiser indulgently. The colonial confrontation at Fashoda, once again, made the English government more than ready to come to an agreement with Germany.

In January 1899 the Kaiser informed Sir Frank Lascelles, the British ambassador in Berlin, that France and Russia had invited Germany to join them in a coalition against Britain but he had no intention of doing so. It was to be a difficult year for family relations. In February the Kaiser's young cousin Alfred, heir to the duchy of Saxe-Coburg Gotha, died from self-inflicted shotgun wounds. He left no brothers or children, the Prince of Wales had long since renounced the Coburg succession for himself and his issue, and Arthur, Duke of Connaught, was therefore now heir. The reigning Duke, the Prince of Wales's and Duke of Connaught's brother Alfred ('Affie'), was frequently unwell and believed to be drinking himself slowly to death, and it was evident that the next Duke would succeed him before long. Without consulting the Kaiser, Queen Victoria gave her immediate blessing to Arthur taking up his position as heir presumptive.

Angry at not being asked for his permission, the Kaiser insisted that the Duke of Connaught and his eldest son would have to live in Germany and enter the German army, or else the *Reichstag* might declare foreign princes ineligible to succeed to German thrones. Now in his late forties, the Duke made no secret of resenting the idea of having to uproot himself and his family. At a meeting with the Dukes of Connaught and Saxe-Coburg in April, the Kaiser strongly denied threatening to introduce any bill preventing the succession of foreign princes to German thrones, but said that national sentiment required the heir to the duchy to serve in the German army and have his principal residence in the empire. Queen Victoria was angry with the Kaiser, who had 'been tiresome and has interfered', and deprecated his 'threats' to Lord Salisbury.[25] The issue was settled some weeks later when the Duke of Connaught renounced the succession for himself and his son in favour of his fifteen-year-old nephew Charles of Albany. Charles succeeded sooner than anticipated, for Duke Alfred succumbed to throat cancer in July 1900.

Becoming Duke of Coburg did not prevent Charles from becoming the butt of the Kaiser's bullying sense of humour. The controller of the Kaiser's household, Count Robert Zedlitz-Trutschler, recorded an unpleasant scene in March 1905 when the Kaiser playfully set about pinching and smacking his cousin 'so hard that it is hardly an exaggeration to say that the little Duke gets a good beating'.[26]

A further cause of misunderstanding was the situation in Samoa, where disorders had reached a situation involving intervention by the three protecting powers, Britain, Germany and the United States of America. Convinced that Germany was being snubbed, the Kaiser wrote Queen Victoria a long, anguished tirade (27 May), accusing Salisbury's government of 'high-handed treatment', and giving the impression that the prime minister despised Germany. Public feeling in Germany against Britain 'has been very much agitated and stirred to its depths', and all 'on account of a stupid island which is a hairpin to England compared to the thousands of square miles she is annexing right and left unopposed every year'.[27] The Queen immediately put him in his place, replying to him (12 June) that 'I doubt if any Sovereign ever wrote in such terms to another Sovereign, and that Sovereign his own Grandmother, about their Prime Minister.'[28]

The dispute continued throughout the summer, and by mid-September Count Hatzfeldt feared that if relations between both countries deteriorated any further he might be recalled from his post. At length, under persuasion from Cabinet colleagues, Salisbury conceded and an agreement enabled Germany to acquire the island of Upolu, where the Kaiser wanted to set up a coaling station. Delighted with this latest acquisition, another 'success for world policy', he agreed to visit Windsor in November.

Accompanied by the Empress and a large suite, he arrived on 20 November 1899. It was not a propitious time, for five weeks earlier war had broken out in South Africa between the British and the Boers, and public opinion throughout Europe, especially in Germany, was overwhelmingly pro-Boer. In Berlin the Kaiser took advantage of the patriotic mood to announce a second navy law, to come before the *Reichstag* early in the new year, saying that he was as yet in no position to go beyond neutrality. When he had his fleet, he would be able to talk differently. But Windsor transformed him instantly into the respectful grandson of Queen Victoria, even more English than the English. Each morning he pointed to the tower, telling his resentful military entourage that 'from this tower the world is ruled'.[29] Lady Salisbury died at Hatfield at the start of the visit and the Kaiser did not see her widower, in mourning, but he had talks with Balfour and Chamberlain. Queen Victoria was relieved to find that her grandson and Bülow both deplored 'shameful attacks' on England in the German press. With Chamberlain he was more circumspect, dismissing the colonial secretary's favourite project of an Anglo-German-American alliance as contrary to the traditions of all three nations, and also as it might threaten conflict with

Russia. However, he was sympathetic to suggestions of limited Anglo-German co-operation in areas such as Morocco and Asia Minor where there was a potential conflict of interests. If there could be no alliance, as he suggested, they could at least come to 'an understanding'.

Two days after he left England, the Kaiser and his ministers were irritated by a speech by Chamberlain proposing an alliance between Britain, America and Germany. The German press suggested that a secret bargain had been struck at Windsor. Matters were exacerbated in January 1900 when it was learnt in Berlin that British warships had intercepted three German vessels suspected of carrying supplies for the Boers. The navy league exploited this in its demands for more battleships, and the Navy Law was carried in June by a comfortable majority. The law stated a rate of expansion that would produce a fleet of thirty-eight modern battleships and three cruisers by 1916, and a new battleship launched at an average rate of every four months over the next five years. Throughout this time the Kaiser seemed keen to maintain good relations with Queen Victoria and the Prince of Wales, even to the extent of sending detailed notes on the military conduct of the Boer War to the latter, and making lighthearted sporting metaphors. The Prince declined to see his nephew's parallels between 'our conflict with the Boers' and the Lord's Test match of the previous summer, in which Australia beat England by ten wickets. The Kaiser congratulated Queen Victoria on the relief of Kimberley, as if to make amends for his telegram to Kruger, and sent the Prince of Wales details of attempts by the Russians to form a continental league aiming to 'enforce peace' in South Africa. While the Queen and Prince of Wales thanked him, more out of good manners and family feeling than from a genuine belief that he was providing an instant solution to the world's major problems, the prime minister remained suspicious that he was over-dramatizing a conventional diplomatic initiative.

The Kaiser had made some rather odd comments to others, including a remark to Lascelles about Russia, adding that the British government 'would be a set of unmitigated noodles if they cared a farthing' for anything the Russians might do.[30] Later he discussed the matter again with Lascelles, saying that Tsar Nicholas II was as weak as King Louis XVI, and only told him because he was the grandson of Queen Victoria, 'for whom I have always retained the deepest affection'. As Salisbury suspected, the Russians had no intention of bringing pressure to bear, their role being limited to suggestions of joint amicable pressure rather than any coercive measures. All the same, the Kaiser's claim that he was England's greatest ally on the continent during the Boer War was not as empty as it may have sounded. While sympathies in Berlin were overwhelmingly pro-Boer, the Kaiser's insistence on strict neutrality in Germany effectively prevented intervention by any effective alliance of European powers. It was one of the few occasions on which he genuinely assisted British foreign policy. The unduly flattering remarks of one of his most fervent English admirers did a certain amount to reinforce this impression. While in Berlin in June, the composer Sir Arthur Sullivan told him he hoped he would visit England, as 'you would receive a grander reception than ever Your Majesty has had before'. His Majesty and Lord Roberts, he went on, were the two most popular men in England.[31] These remarks were ill-received at home, especially by the Prince of Wales, but the ailing Sullivan did not live long to ponder his indiscretions; within five months he was dead.

In the summer of 1900 the Kaiser made what Bülow considered in retrospect was perhaps the most harmful speech of his reign. Resentment in China against foreign domination had exploded in the Boxer rising; Europeans were besieged for three months in the diplomatic quarter of Peking, and on 20 June Baron Clemens von Ketteler, the German minister, was murdered while attempting to negotiate with Chinese officials. A European military expedition was quickly raised to rescue the international community in Peking. To the Kaiser, this murder was as great a blot on German honour and as much an insult as General Gordon's murder at Khartoum in 1885 had been to the British. He brought back Waldersee, who had spent the last few years out of favour if not exactly in disgrace, promoted him from general to field-marshal, and appointed him overall commander of the relief force.

Had the Kaiser stopped there all would have been well, but he could not resist taking matters further. As the troops were about to sail from Bremerhaven the Kaiser inspected them, climbed on to a wooden dais on the quayside, and delivered a stirring oration with phrases which were destined to return to haunt him in years to come. 'There will be no quarter, no prisoners will be taken!' he proclaimed in ringing tones. 'As, a thousand years ago, the Huns, under King Attila, gained for themselves a name which still stands for a terror in tradition and story, so may the name of German be impressed by you for a thousand years on China, so thoroughly that never again shall a Chinese dare so much as to look askance at a German.'

Even his ministers knew, once the speech was finished, that he had rarely made himself look so foolish. Ashen-faced, Hohenlohe turned to Bülow, saying he could not possibly answer for such a speech in the *Reichstag*. As a damage limitation exercise, Bülow released a discreetly edited version to the press. When the Kaiser saw the papers that evening he was disappointed to find only an expurgated report, telling his minister, 'You have struck out the best parts of it.' Another paper produced the full, more inflammatory speech, which had been taken down by a reporter in shorthand at the time. The Kaiser was pleased until Bülow told him after dinner that such outbursts would 'produce sorrow and mortification among good Christians'. To this Wilhelm countered that Moses, Joshua and other Biblical heroes had used even harsher language in addressing their hosts of fighting men, only to be told that the speech would still have political repercussions guaranteed to produce dismay among their friends and be used against them by their enemies. Chastened, the Kaiser admitted he would count on Bülow's friendship and 'famous eloquence' to resolve the problems his speech would create in the *Reichstag*.[32]

The speech coincided with further fears that the Kaiser was losing his reason. Eulenberg, on board *Hohenzollern* during the cruise of July 1900, reported with alarm that His Majesty had such a violent attack of rage that he himself was quite frightened, fearing the Kaiser was 'no longer in control of himself', while his doctor feared a weakening of the nervous system. In September bad temper gave way to paranoia, and he complained about a 'suffocating web of senseless court ceremonial'. Boredom with a routine of monotonous regularity could be excused, but less easy for those close to him to accept was his feeling, so he told Eulenburg, that he was 'constantly surrounded by a network of spying lackeys of the Empress'.[33]

For once Wilhelm seemed to find his wife even more trying than usual. For a few years she had been suffering from a nervous condition. Her hair suddenly turned white, and her face looked blotched, puffy and aged. She flew into rages over trivial matters, complained bitterly that he preferred the company of Eulenburg to hers, and made terrible scenes because he refused to take her on his frequent trips around Germany. They often argued about the upbringing of their sons, who were always closer to her than to him. In 1896 he had decided to send the two eldest, the Crown Prince and Eitel Friedrich, to a cadet academy at Plön, in Schleswig-Holstein, partly to provide her with some respite. Though she begged him not to, he remained obdurate, but she insisted on visiting them regularly at Plön. Now, four years later, he decided that Princes August Wilhelm and Oskar, now thirteen and twelve, should go there too. She had hysterics, demanded that they should stay in Berlin with her, wept through the night, and accused her husband of not loving her. Again he told her that his word was law, and the boys went to Plön. The Empress's mother had had similar mental problems, and he was alarmed that his wife might be suffering from a hereditary disorder which would make it necessary for her to be confined in a sanatorium, a development that would render the dynasty less an object of sympathy than one of enduring shame. When he confided his woes to Eulenburg, he advised him to sleep in a separate bedroom and lock the door.[34] Fortunately the Empress's behaviour soon returned to normal.

By October 1900 Hohenlohe had resigned the chancellorship. Aged eighty and suffering increasingly from heart trouble, he had long since been regarded as no more than a rubber-stamp for the Kaiser's decisions. He complained that he had personally been told nothing about Waldersee's expedition to China, and that foreign affairs were settled by His Majesty and Bülow. The latter, formerly state secretary for foreign affairs, was appointed as his successor. Unlike his three predecessors, he was adept at managing people and established a good relationship with the Kaiser by praising him to his face for his foresight, strength and wisdom, and for possessing the rare gift of always saying the right thing. The Kaiser was naïve enough to accept this flattery at face value. Little did he know that his new chancellor would soon be complaining to others behind his back of the Kaiser's boundless vanity and immaturity, or that he had no illusions about the need to keep his sovereign in his place. Bülow told Count Szögyényi-Marich in 1903 that he could contradict the Kaiser when they were alone as long as he formulated his responses carefully. Shortly before his death, Prince Bismarck had again revealed his anxiety about His Majesty's 'abnormal mental condition', fearing that he was 'hereditarily burdened' on his descent from the English and Russian sides.[35] While it would be more difficult to remove Kaiser Wilhelm from the middle of all his generals than it had been to secure the abdication of the hapless King Ludwig II of Bavaria in 1886, the precedent was borne very much in mind. In November, a few weeks after taking up office, Bülow told Eulenburg it would only take 'one false move' by the Kaiser for the formation of a coalition of the German princes (led, probably, by his Uncle Friedrich, Grand Duke of Baden) and the *Reichstag* against him to have him declared unfit to rule.[36]

Despite the fighting talk, the Far East emergency was over long before Waldersee and his relief expedition reached China. Had they covered themselves with glory, the effect of the Bremerhaven speech might have been justified in some small way. As it was, the Kaiser had confirmed his reputation as the *enfant terrible* of European sovereigns and, not for the last time, made himself look either menacing or foolish throughout Europe.

However, the speech proved no obstacle to talk of an Anglo-German alliance, which had been steadily gathering pace. After Salisbury's government won an election in October 1900 he retained the premiership but resigned as foreign secretary on health grounds; Lord Lansdowne was appointed to the post instead. Joseph Chamberlain, the new colonial secretary, was sympathetic to Germany, and early in 1901 Chamberlain and the Duke of Devonshire discussed the matter. The days of Britain's 'splendid isolation' were over, and England had to look for allies elsewhere – either Russia or France or the Triple Alliance – and Chamberlain preferred the latter, news that Berlin received with guarded welcome.

Suddenly negotiations were interrupted by grave news from Osborne House. For several weeks Queen Victoria's health had given cause for concern. In the third week of January her younger surviving son Arthur, Duke of Connaught, was in Berlin with the Kaiser, attending bicentenary celebrations for the kingdom of Prussia, when he was summoned by telegram to Osborne where she was not expected to last for more than a few days. The Kaiser, who had always maintained close contact with the Queen's personal physician, Sir James Reid, on the subject of his grandmother's personal health, also received a wire informing him that 'Disquieting symptoms have developed which cause considerable anxiety.'[37] He cancelled his engagements at once, and on 19 January sent an uncoded telegram to the Prince of Wales confirming that he would reach London the following evening. The Duke was on better terms with his nephew than the rest of the family, and he tactfully suggested to Bülow that the Kaiser ought to consider carefully whether it was in his best interests to go. While it 'might be an expression of his kindness of heart', he felt unsure as to how the family would receive such a visit. Though public opinion in England would surely appreciate the gesture, in Germany it would probably turn opinion against England even more. Nonetheless, Wilhelm insisted that his proper place at such a time was by his grandmother's side. Throughout the journey he masked his concern beneath a display of high spirits and banter, explaining to his suite that 'Uncle Arthur is so downhearted we must cheer him up.'[38]

They took their place at the hushed vigil at Osborne with the Queen's children, all except the Empress Frederick, who was suffering from cancer and too ill to travel from Germany. By the time the Kaiser arrived, his grandmother's mind was wandering and she mistook him for his father. As her remaining strength ebbed away he helped to support her with his right arm, and she died on the evening of 22 January. When his uncle, now King Edward VII, left for the traditional accession council in London, it was the Kaiser who remained behind at Osborne in charge of the arrangements. At his suggestion a Union Jack was draped on the walls of the room where his grandmother's coffin lay in state. Though he would have celebrated his forty-second birthday on 27 January, he requested that no special notice should be taken of it, as mourning for 'his unparalleled grandmama' must come first.

The Empress had strongly disapproved of her husband's visit to England. Reluctant to acknowledge the deep emotional bond between him and his grandmother, she asked Bülow to try and dissuade the Kaiser from staying in England for the funeral, insisting that he could quite easily allow the Crown Prince or Prince Henry to attend instead. Her main reason, she said, was that the Empress Frederick was particularly anxious to see him again, but to no avail. He telegraphed back that his aunts were 'quite alone and I must help them with many things, I must give them my advice, whenever advice is necessary. They are so kind to me, they treat me like a brother and a friend instead of like a nephew. . . . It has been a terribly difficult and exciting time.' When she heard three days later that King Edward had made her husband an English field-marshal, she immediately saw it as evidence of English scheming: 'If this is not an irony in present circumstances, I do not know what is. It is supposed to be a gracious act, but I consider it tactless.'[39]

The Empress was not the only one alarmed by her husband's excessive fraternization with his family on the other side of the North Sea. In the light of Chamberlain's recent overtures regarding an Anglo-German alliance, Bülow and Holstein looked askance at their sovereign's presence in England at a time when he was bound to be emotionally vulnerable and thus more Anglophile in his mood. As a precaution they had instructed Baron Hermann von Eckardstein at the German embassy to meet him on his arrival and try to restrain him from discussing an alliance or any other political matters with ministers in Britain while on what was technically a family visit. Accordingly, Eckardstein gave the Kaiser a full report of conversations with Chamberlain and the Duke of Devonshire in which he had been involved; at the same time he advised him not to discuss the alliance, and even to act as if he had no knowledge of these conversations. To this the Kaiser agreed, and promised that he would only 'discuss Anglo-German relations generally'.[40]

Yet the Kaiser's ministers had been right to express anxiety. Within a couple of days he was telegraphing to Bülow that he intended to accept the hand of friendship, even alliance, as proposed by Chamberlain. Eckardstein, he said, had told him confidentially that it was 'all over' with Britain's 'splendid isolation', and her choice lay between the Triple Alliance and that of France and Russia. Chamberlain himself favoured the former. It was the answer that Germany had been waiting for, but Bülow and Holstein advised their sovereign to be patient. With unreliable if not downright hostile powers on all sides, not to mention the possibility of defeat in South Africa, England would soon need every friend in

Europe she could find, and consequently the price Germany could demand for an alliance would rise.

When Lord Lansdowne called on the Kaiser at Osborne to discuss foreign affairs, nothing was said about an Anglo-German alliance. Instead the Kaiser held forth on the fickleness of Russians and the personal inadequacy of the Tsar, who was 'only fit to live in a country house and grow turnips'.[41] Russia, he declared, was 'really Asiatic', while Britain, being European, should join in a general concert of Germany and France. When Lansdowne said the old doctrine of the balance of power between European states was still in the hands of England, the Kaiser retorted that the balance now rested with the twenty-two German army corps instead: 'England was no longer in a position to keep apart from the rest of Europe, but must combine with the Continent.'[42]

The Kaiser stayed in England for the Queen's funeral at Windsor on 2 February and interment in the mausoleum two days later. King Edward was touched by his nephew's uncharacteristically subdued behaviour, and wrote (7 February) to the Empress Frederick that his 'touching and simple demeanour, up to the last, will never be forgotten by me or anyone'.[43] For his sister's peace of mind he did not dwell on one of the Kaiser's motives for prolonging his time in England. According to the French ambassador, Paul Cambon, at one stage during the Empress Frederick's three troubled months as consort of a reigning Kaiser, she and the Jewish financier Baron Hirsch had advanced the Prince of Wales a loan of between 15 and 25 million French francs. Deeply in debt at the time, Cambon reported to his government that the Prince was afraid to ask Queen Victoria to come to his financial rescue yet again. Now that the spendthrift heir was King and therefore presumably well provided for, the Kaiser wanted to use what might be the only chance to settle his mother's claims in the intervals between attending the funeral rites of his grandmother.[44]

Having accomplished both missions – attendance at the funeral and, presumably, reimbursement of the loan – the Kaiser was ready to accept the hand of British friendship. Acceptance by his grandmother's family, and the obvious warmth of crowds in London wherever he went, had convinced Wilhelm that he was genuinely beloved in Britain. Anxious messages of restraint from the Berlin foreign office in the Wilhelmstrasse dismayed him and he conveyed his frustration to Count Paul von Metternich, German ambassador in London, saying he could not 'wobble forever between England and Russia'. As instructed by his superiors in Berlin, Metternich repeated their words; an alliance between England and Germany would come, but it was politic to wait until Germany could extract a higher price for the privilege. Anxious to show the Kaiser how England's prestige was sinking, he drew his attention to the military ranks they had seen at the funeral, a muster of 'pitiable human beings', evidence that the English had reached the end of their military capacity. What he omitted to add, and what the Kaiser had presumably forgotten, was that at the time there were still over quarter of a million British troops on active service in South Africa.

On the Kaiser's last day in England, at luncheon at Marlborough House, the King proposed his nephew's health. The latter answered in ringing terms of 'the two Teutonic nations' which would stand together to help in keeping peace throughout the world: 'We ought to form an Anglo-German alliance, you to keep the seas while we would be responsible for the land; with such an alliance, not a mouse would stir in Europe without our permission, and the nations would, in time, come to see the necessity of reducing their armaments.'[45]

As he left for his homeward journey, the Kaiser was cheered enthusiastically throughout London, with several buildings displaying the German flag beside the Union Jack. On saying farewell at Charing Cross station, he gripped the King's hand emotionally. His passion for everything English survived his return to Berlin. For the next few days Wilhelm continued to wear civilian clothes, including a red enamel tie pin with a monogram VRI set in diamonds. His table talk was full of references to Osborne and Windsor, and how well everything was done in England, much to the irritation of his entourage. Knowing that the Kaiser was bound to maintain pressure for an Anglo-German alliance, Bülow was not alone in sharing his belief that Germany was England's only natural ally in Europe, and thought that the likelihood of Britain being drawn into the Franco-Russian camp was remote.

The two wisest and best sovereigns who had ever lived, the Kaiser told his officers, were Queen Victoria and Kaiser Wilhelm I. With two such grandparents, he said with a laugh, 'I should not be a bad ruler.' As a sovereign, Wilhelm said openly, he took both as his exemplars, and whenever he was in a difficult position he asked himself how they would have acted under similar circumstances.

Uncle and nephew met again two weeks later. The Kaiser had returned from his grandmother's funeral to visit his mother, whom he had not seen for three months. Her condition had worsened; her left arm was completely paralysed, her feet were very swollen, and she could hardly digest food properly. 'Poor mother is simply in a horrible state of suffering & discomfort,' he wrote (9 February) to King Edward VII, 'so that one really sometimes is at a loss as to think whether she could not be spared the worst.'[46] The King was determined to see her for what he rightly feared would be the last time. As he was still in mourning, there was no question of a state visit to Berlin – or indeed any foreign capital – for several months. His expedition to Friedrichshof was to be a purely private affair. It irked him when the Kaiser, who had decided that to wear civilian clothes any longer would tax his entourage's patience too much, was waiting for him at Frankfurt station attired in the uniform of a Prussian general. Having arrived to the sound of a 'hymn', which turned out to be the Boer national anthem, King Edward was not in the best of tempers.

The visit was fraught with tension throughout. Dinner every evening was subdued, with the Kaiser making a forced effort to maintain the small-talk. His two youngest sisters were there, and Sir Frederick Ponsonby, the King's private secretary, observed that they would cut in tactfully 'if the conversation seemed to get into dangerous channels, and one always felt there was electricity in the air when the Emperor and King Edward talked'.[47] Another member of the King's suite was his physician-in-ordinary, Sir Francis Laking. His presence was regarded with hostility by the German Court, as they rightly suspected the King's motive. He hoped that Laking might be able to persuade the German doctors to give the Empress Frederick larger doses of morphia than they had done so far in order to mitigate her sufferings, and for which she sometimes begged in her agony. Queen Victoria had repeatedly offered, even begged, her grandson to receive Laking the previous autumn, but he had sharply refused; 'I won't have a repetition of the confounded Mackenzie business, as public feeling would be seriously affected here.'[48] It was noticed that Wilhelm showed his dying mother less solicitude than he had demonstrated towards his grandmother during her last days.

One evening Ponsonby was asked to see the Empress in her sitting room. In great pain, mentally she was as alert as ever, plying him with questions about England and the war in South Africa. Then she asked him to take charge of her letters and bring them back to England with him. She would send them to his room at 1 o'clock that night. It was important that nobody else, least of all her eldest son, should know. Before the Empress could explain further the nurse interrupted them and, seeing how tired her patient looked, asked him to go. Confidently expecting a small packet or parcel of letters to slip into his luggage, Ponsonby was aghast when there was a knock on his door at the appointed hour and four men arrived carrying two enormous trunks. Suspecting the castle was full of secret police, he feared he might be unable to carry out his sacred trust. Hoping for the best, he marked them 'China with care' and 'Books with care' respectively, and had them placed in the passage with his luggage later that morning. As he was a member of the King's suite, he trusted that nobody would try and search his belongings without a major incident arising, and they went safely with him to England a few days later. His godmother's dying wish was granted.

Ironically, a month later uncle and nephew were to close ranks against another member of the family who dared to publish a book treading on sacred family ground. The culprit was Lord Lorne, the estranged husband of King Edward's sister Louise, whose acceptance of a commission by the publisher Spottiswoode to write a biography of Queen Victoria was viewed with dismay. The Kaiser said that any such book should be only for the family itself; 'on *no account can a real "life"* of Grandmama be published before the *next 20 years* are over'.[49] Agreeing wholeheartedly, the King told Louise to ask Lorne to restrain himself in future. As the eccentric Lorne was very much a law unto himself and had inherited large estates from his family, which entailed a severe drain on his finances, it was doubtful whether he paid his wife's request any heed.

Meanwhile, the momentum for an Anglo-German alliance gradually weakened. Discouraged by delaying signals from Berlin, Chamberlain reaffirmed his view to Eckardstein in March that he thought such an agreement would be valuable, but in view of the tortuous pace of events he had 'no desire to burn his fingers again'. Bülow proposed an Anglo-German defensive alliance to last initially for five years, the terms of which stated that each power would remain benevolently neutral if the other was attacked by one other European country; only if it was attacked by two states would the ally intervene. Eckardstein was optimistic, but in his letters he made his enthusiasm too evident. Convinced that he had gone native with a vengeance, Bülow decided he would send a more senior diplomat from Berlin, who could be trusted to defend German conditions more vigorously, to England to conduct negotiations. Eckardstein resigned in disgust, and although Holstein declined to accept his resignation, in England he was no longer regarded as an influential figure. As if to make amends to his chancellor and foreign office for his unbounded Anglophilia earlier in the year, the Kaiser impetuously referred to British ministers as 'unmitigated noodles' in a conversation with Sir Frank Lascelles and, having become rather proud of the phrase, repeated it in a letter to King Edward. The King showed the letter to Eckardstein, who advised him to treat it as a joke and he agreed, adding ruefully that 'unluckily I have already had to put up with many of these jokes of the Kaiser's'.[50] Hatzfeldt was entrusted with the alliance negotiations, but his suggestion that Britain should join the Triple Alliance of Germany, Austria and Italy as a junior partner, subordinate to Germany, and guarantee the interests and frontiers of each other member against threats from Russia and France seemed untenable to Lord Salisbury. His dismissal of the scheme effectively put an end to any serious efforts by either side to secure an agreement.

The Kaiser was at Kiel week in July when he wrote to the King about his mother's state of health. When he had seen her the previous week he found her still in great pain, but taking an interest in everything that was going on in the world. The doctors said that there was 'nothing to inspire any momentary anxiety; if things go on like this at present the doctors think that it may go on for months, even into the winter possibly'.[51]

Fortunately for the Empress Frederick, her agonies were not prolonged. On 4 August a bulletin announced that her strength was 'fading fast' and her children were summoned to her bedside. The Kaiser had been cruising in the North Sea when a telegram called him back. Dona met him at Kiel, and he scolded her in front of his entourage for not remaining at his mother's bedside, though the patient had asked her not to stay. At Friedrichshof he joined the vigil by his mother's bedside. Late the following afternoon his sisters Sophie and Margrethe, who had been in attendance almost constantly for the last few weeks, went out to the garden for fresh air, and when they returned she was gone. It was their eldest brother who was still at her side when she breathed her last.

The death of the Empress was followed by similar events to those that occurred immediately after that of her husband. Cavalry was posted around Friedrichshof, while special police patrolled the interior of the castle, and every room was searched. She had been wise to entrust her letters to Ponsonby. Some writers suggested that the only troops to arrive were twelve NCOs from her own regiment, the royal Prussian fusiliers, who were to act as bearers at her funeral. If this was the case, and if they had not come to prevent the removal of private papers, that they should have been guarding her home before she was dead on the pretext of coming for her funeral indicates remarkable punctuality.

The next morning, according to Bülow, the Kaiser walked with him in the gardens at Friedrichshof. Wilhelm told him that his mother had left instructions for her body to be wrapped unclothed in the Union Jack, and her coffin to be sent to England as she wanted to be buried there.[52] In fact she had left precise instructions during the summer with her sister Helena, stating that her body was to be covered by the Prussian royal standard, and she was to be interred in the mausoleum at Potsdam beside her husband and two youngest sons. Never a personal enemy of the Empress, Bülow readily concurred with British opinion that her fate was a tragic one. He therefore had no motive for blackening her name. If he was telling the truth, it is a tale from which her eldest son emerges with no credit whatsoever. Either he was trying to undermine his mother's last shred of credibility with his subjects in case the letters should ever come to light,[53] or else Bülow (writing more than twenty years later, by which time he had little reason to speak well of his master) was embroidering fact with scurrilous fiction.

King Edward was also on board his yacht, preparing for Cowes week, when he learned that his sister's condition had worsened. He and Queen Alexandra prepared to leave at once, and were about to depart when a telegram announced the news of her death; they reached Germany four days later. Whatever grief the Kaiser felt at his mother's death, he could not stop himself from reproaching his uncle for lack of feeling as he had taken so long to arrive. It was an undeserved rebuke as, apart from her daughters, King Edward had been closer to the much-misunderstood woman than anybody else since her husband's death. He felt the Kaiser was trying to take him to task over the behaviour of his ministers and lack of progress on an Anglo-German alliance. The tension between uncle and nephew on this occasion was in stark contrast to the feeling that had been evident at Queen Victoria's funeral.

On his journey to Germany the King took a memorandum containing confidential notes on Anglo-German relations from Lord Lansdowne. When he met the Kaiser at Homburg on 11 August he was still overwrought at his sister's death and so anxious to avoid any controversial talk that he handed Wilhelm his minister's 'confidential' notes. Maybe he was acting on impulse; perhaps it was done in a genuine moment of absent-mindedness. Though no harm was done, Lansdowne was horrified.

The Empress's funeral took place on 13 August at Potsdam, and her son could not resist another chance to create a military display out of the occasion. The streets were lined with German troops, while both monarchs wore the blue uniform of the Prussian dragoon guards, marching at the head of the procession to the Friedenskirche. Having treated his mother so callously, perhaps the Kaiser was making amends by giving her the sort of burial that would have been accorded to a reigning Empress. It was an almost unrecognizable Kaiser Wilhelm, pale and trembling, who arranged the wreath on his mother's coffin at the altar, fell to his knees and placed his face in the folds of the pall as he silently broke down.

'What awful times of suffering and agonies my poor dear mother went through in the last two years no human being can conceive', he wrote to Princess Daisy of Pless four days later. 'It leaves a blank in our home, for she was the spiritual centre for all of us, in her activity and liveliness, in the interest she took in everything. Poor dear mama! Thank God the last days she was without pain and went to sleep quite quietly and peacefully.'[54]

All the same, King Edward found the constant jingle of Prussian spurs at such a poignant time distasteful. It was not over, for after a few peaceful days at Homburg uncle and nephew met again the following week at Wilhelmshöhe for what were intended to be serious political talks. The proceedings began badly when the King uncomfortably squeezed into his Prussian colonel-in-chief uniform. As the Court was still in mourning he had expected no pomp or ceremony, yet he was still greeted by a parade of 15,000 German troops. The talks achieved nothing, and the King was perturbed to find his nephew better informed on certain foreign policy matters than he was. A rumour that the British government was considering granting Malta independence without reference to him made the King angry; but he was uninterested in affairs in the Middle and Far East, and prepared to leave such matters to his ministers and civil servants. For Edward, the meeting ended not a moment too soon.

While an Anglo-German alliance remained doubtful, the Kaiser was determined to maintain good relations with Tsar Nicholas II. Perhaps he thought that the Tsar and his ministers might be able to influence their ally France, thus reducing the risk of war at a time when British pre-eminence was being challenged by Germany. Later in August the Kaiser joined the Tsar at Reval for Russian warship manoeuvres. He introduced the Tsar to Bülow as 'the Admiral of the Pacific', a pun on Nicholas's patronage of international disarmament, which he did not find amusing. The Kaiser was so pleased with his wit that as the *Hohenzollern* sailed away he signalled to the Russian imperial yacht, 'The Admiral of the Atlantic bids farewell to the Admiral of the Pacific'. To British journalists, this could only mean some kind of secret agreement by both emperors to divide the oceans of the world between them.

In Britain the Admiralty knew that Germany's newest battleships were short-range vessels designed for action in the North Sea and not on distant oceans. Anglo-German relations had not improved with a forthright speech by Chamberlain in October 1901 defending the British army's tactics in South Africa and condemning the hypocrisy of other European nations that had accused Britain of barbarous behaviour. If the British had acted forcefully against the enemy, he pointed out, there were many precedents from continental powers, notably the behaviour of the German army during the Franco-Prussian War. The Kaiser angrily told Colonel Wallscourt Waters, the British military attaché in Berlin, that the colonial secretary should be taken to South Africa, marched across the continent and then shot. Chamberlain's 'foolish oratory' had made relations between their countries worse than ever, the Kaiser declared, for while he was still full of goodwill towards England, Germany had a right to continue its policy of *Weltpolitik* (world politics), but it ought to be carried out with England's cooperation.[55] Count Metternich was officially informed by Lansdowne in December 1901 of the British

*1. Prince and Princess Friedrich Wilhelm at Windsor, 29 January 1858. The Royal Archives © Her Majesty The Queen*

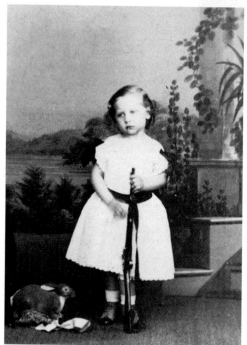

*2. Prince Wilhelm, February 1862. The Royal Archives © Her Majesty The Queen*

*3. Kaiser Wilhelm I.*

*4. Queen Victoria (left) and Queen (later Empress) Augusta, 1867.*

*5. Prince Otto von Bismarck.*

*6. Crown Prince Friedrich Wilhelm,
1883.*

7. *Kaiser Wilhelm II during the early years of his reign.*

*8. Empress Augusta Victoria ('Dona').*

9. Charlotte ('Charly'), Hereditary Princess of Saxe-Meiningen, the Kaiser's eldest sister.

10. King Edward VII.

11. *Count Philipp von Eulenburg.*

12. *Prince Bernhard von Bülow. Mary Evans Picture Library*

*13. The children of Kaiser Wilhelm II. Left to right: Oskar, Eitel Friedrich, Victoria, seated on knee of Crown Prince Wilhelm, Adalbert, Joachim (in front), August Wilhelm.*

*14. The Empress Frederick, 1900.*

15. *Crown Prince Wilhelm.*

16. *Crown Princess Wilhelm, the former*
*Princess Cecilie of Mecklenburg-Schwerin.*

17. Empress Augusta Victoria.

18. Kaiser Wilhelm II in naval uniform.

19. *Princess Victoria Louise.*

20. *Prince Henry, the Kaiser's only surviving brother, and his wife, formerly Princess Irene of Hesse and the Rhine.*

21. *Kaiser Wilhelm II. Theo Aronson Collection*

22. *Admiral Alfred von Tirpitz. Mary Evans Picture Library*

23. *Kaiser Wilhelm II and his cousin,*
*King George V, 1913.*

Look at William! There he stands,
With the blood upon his hands.
His moustaches daunt the sky,
Pointing to his great Ally.
What of Heaven William thinks
Is no riddle of the Sphinx,
But a matter much more dim
Is what Heaven thinks of him.

24. *'Swollen-headed William', a satirical*
*adaptation from 1914 by E.V. Lucas (verse)*
*and George Morrow (drawing) of 'Shock-*
*headed Peter', from* Struwwelpeter, *by*
*Heinrich Hoffmann, 1903.*

25. *General Paul von Hindenburg.*
*Walter Petersen/Mary Evans Picture*
*Library*

26. *General Erich von Ludendorff.*
*Mary Evans Picture Library*

*27./28. Kaiser Wilhelm II with an aide-de-camp, Doorn, 1922. These photographs were taken without Wilhelm's approval or knowledge by a photographer with a zoom lens under the direction of Count de Radowitz. Dale Headington, Regal Reader*

29. *Kaiser Wilhelm II in old age.*

30. *Empress Hermine. 'Empress' was a purely honorary title, always used at her request and that of her second husband.*

government's decision to suspend Anglo-German alliance negotiations on the grounds that 'the temper of the two countries was not in a particularly favourable state'.[56] Public opinion in both countries did not favour such a policy; the British government had no wish to alienate France or Russia by involvement with the Triple Alliance, and it was necessary to avoid irritating the United States, displeased by recent anti-American statements from Germany.

Though disappointed, the Kaiser did not give up hope and wrote to King Edward (30 December) at the end of the year that it had 'been one of care & deep sorrow to us all'. With admiration and envy he commented on the 'magnificent realm' Queen Victoria had left him, and the mutual relations between their countries that belonged to

the great Teutonic race, which Heaven has entrusted with the culture of the world; for apart from the Eastern races, there is no other race left for God to work His will in and upon the world except ours; that is I think grounds enough to keep Peace and to foster *mutual* recognition and *reciprocity* in all that draws us together, and to banish everything which could part us. The Press is awful on both sides, but here it has nothing to say for I am the sole arbiter and master of German Foreign Policy and the Government and Country *must* follow me even if I have to 'face the music'. May your Government never forget this, and never place me in the jeopardy to have to choose a course which would be a misfortune to both them and us.[57]

## CHAPTER FIVE

# The Quill and the Sword

Kaiser Wilhelm II had rightly seen in Joseph Chamberlain the British government's main proponent of an Anglo-German alliance. While Chamberlain's speech of December 1901 hardly made him a 'dangerous and implacable foe' of Germany, it was evident that his sympathies no longer lay with Berlin. Bülow saw an opportunity for strengthening his popularity among the Anglophobes in Berlin, and demanded an apology for the speech, but despite requests from Metternich none was forthcoming on the grounds that no insult had been intended. King Edward had proposed to send his son and heir George, Duke of York, to Berlin for the Kaiser's birthday, but he was so incensed by constant personal attacks on himself in Germany and violent anti-British speeches in the *Reichstag* that he threatened to cancel the visit. The Kaiser ignored his letter and the King's ministers persuaded him not to imperil relations between both countries; the Duke accordingly went to Germany, and on his departure the Kaiser telegraphed to the King that they were 'very sorry to have to part so soon from a merry and genial guest'.[1]

This was more than could be said for the Kaiser's eldest son and heir. Crown Prince Wilhelm, now aged nineteen, paid a private visit to England soon afterwards. From an early age he had shown signs of becoming a compulsive womanizer, and while staying at Blenheim Palace he had an affair with an eighteen-year-old American, Gladys Deacon. It did not escape the notice of the European press, and one paper said he had given her a valuable ring, his confirmation present from Queen Victoria. Furious with his son, the Kaiser thundered that the example of his decadent 'uncle Bertie' was solely responsible for his transgression. He refused to let the Crown Prince represent him at the King's coronation in June, and sent his brother and sister-in-law Henry and Irene instead. As they were more popular with their English relations than the touchy Kaiser and Anglophobic Empress it was a wise choice, though soon after they arrived they were involved in a petty argument over precedence in a carriage ride for a reception at Buckingham Palace. Waldersee, representing the German army, had been allocated a coach behind the Prince and Princess, but flatly refused to go last. The situation was only retrieved when the easy-going Prince Henry declared that it did not matter to him who went first.

The coronation was postponed from June to August after the King was suddenly taken ill with appendicitis. At once family considerations rose to the fore; genuinely concerned, the Kaiser asked the embassy in Berlin to keep him informed as to his uncle's condition. His relief at hearing of the successful operation was heartfelt. Even so, during the King's convalescence prior to the postponed ceremony taking place, the Kaiser's careless talk almost caused a diplomatic incident. In July an American-owned yacht cruising off Norway put in at a harbour where the *Hohenzollern* was moored, with the Kaiser on board. He visited the Americans on board their yacht, and wasted no time in launching a political tirade against England. Lord Salisbury, who had recently resigned the premiership because of ill-health, was denounced as not a man, 'just a protoplasm', and his uncle's permissive lifestyle was a scandal. If he, the Kaiser, behaved himself like King Edward, the German people would soon get rid of him. One of the yachtsmen, a former attaché in the British diplomatic service, immediately reported everything to the foreign office in London. It was a salutary reminder to officials in London of the German Kaiser's fickleness and instability.

Later in August three Boer generals came to London seeking more favourable terms in the peace settlement signed at Pretoria in May. Having failed, they decided to try and capitalize on Boer sympathies in the rest of Europe. Oblivious to his advisers' warnings that to do so would jeopardize any chance of improved relations with Britain, the Kaiser announced he would receive them in Berlin. King Edward wrote to Sir Frank Lascelles warning that for the Kaiser to do so just before another visit to England would be inadvisable. The Kaiser cancelled the audience, but when pro-Boer feeling in Berlin made him hesitate he decided to receive them after all. Further objections from a united front of his ministers and officials in London persuaded him to change his mind again, and the generals returned to South Africa empty-handed.

Plans therefore went ahead for the Kaiser's visit to England in November 1902, to coincide with King Edward VII's sixty-first birthday. The Empress did not accompany her husband; on the contrary, she complained bitterly when he went. 'My mother is always in a fever if I or my father go to England', the Crown Prince scoffed; while Daisy, Princess of Pless, remarked gleefully that the Empress 'must have an extra supply of breath to enable her to gasp at her fantastic notions of all the horrible temptations that her husband and son have to resist in the dangerous little island: poor dear, she looks more like the Emperor's mother than his wife'.[2]

As Anglo-German alliance discussions were in abeyance, the King intended to keep the visit as informal as possible, with a few days' shooting at Sandringham, where the King always celebrated his birthday, and no appearances at Windsor or London. As the Kaiser particularly wanted to meet some of the ministers, Arthur Balfour, the new prime minister, and cabinet members were invited at various times. All were instructed to keep politics at arm's length and be non-committal to the Kaiser, even when the latter made tentative efforts to convince Balfour of Germany's need for a large fleet.

Having failed to achieve any diplomatic feats, the Kaiser resorted to trying to blind his host with science. When King Edward proudly showed off his new motor car, the Kaiser asked whether it ran on petrol or any other fuel, and proceeded to lecture him on the merits of potato spirit and the internal combustion engine. A few days later he presented the inwardly fuming King with a collection of glass bottles and chemical samples sent from Germany post-haste to prove his point. By the time he left for Germany on 20 November the King had had enough, muttering 'Thank God he's gone!' at the entourage sailing across the North Sea.

Nevertheless, the customary courtesies continued by letter. The King sent his nephew good wishes for his birthday in January 1903, and the latter replied (2 February) with thanks, though he could not resist a few mildly chauvinistic barbs:

I fully reciprocate what you say about the Peace of the World, & I fervently hope & pray that the sword may never be recurred to! With regard to the pen – which is certainly more desirable – in settling international difficulties, I am under the impression that in some cases it is in the act of doing a great deal of mischief. Because there are sundry persons – master in the art of using the pen – who make a sport of it to use it for the purpose of inflaming the hatred of one country against the other, & thereby play with a danger they do not perhaps wish to bring about, but where they decidedly try to loosen the sword by means of the quill – I hope & trust that the British Press & the Reviews will soon come to their senses & stop the inane ravings with which they are trying to poison Public opinion & to undo the work of King & Ministers. The Quill & Sword must both be kept under restriction!'[3]

Though the Kaiser claimed that he never read newspapers, he kept a careful eye on them, especially British publications, and deeply resented any criticism of Germany or himself. Such attacks, he believed, hampered if not destroyed his personal efforts at Anglo-German diplomacy. The hostile British press, he was convinced, was mainly under Jewish control, and part of an international conspiracy that involved the British, French, Russia, Belgian and American press; he resented the inability of successive prime ministers in Britain to prevent attacks on Germany, and in his more paranoid moments believed that the British government was bribing journalists abroad to join them.

In May 1903 King Edward's state visit to Paris, and a reciprocal one by President Loubet two months later, helped to soften Anglo-French hostility, and the Entente Cordiale was signed in April 1904, much to the Kaiser's alarm. The year 1903 had not been good for the Kaiser; during the summer floods in Silesia claimed several lives, and Eulenburg was distressed to hear his friend complain heartlessly that 'a few old women have drowned because they were left in their rooms for that express purpose – and now people are making all this fuss!'.[4] His temper had not improved by the time of his *Nordlandreise* in August, when he outlined his plans to quell the coming revolution. It would be revenge for 1848, he proclaimed; he would mow down the Social Democrats, 'but only after they had first plundered the Jews and the rich'.[5]

In February 1904 war broke out between Russia and Japan, with Britain sympathetic to the Japanese while Germany stood by Russia, and concluded a valuable trade agreement with her in July 1904. Germany pondered the likely impact of these events on the rest of Europe; as France was an ally of Russia and England of Japan, the Kaiser had hoped that this might prevent the Entente from being concluded. If war broke out between Germany and France, Bülow asked the general staff, did Russia have the military strength to intervene effectively against Germany along the Polish Frontier? Schlieffen, chief of the general staff, was convinced that if hostilities did break out in the continent, Germany would gain rapid victory in the West, and many staff officers supported him in what seemed to be a call for a march on Paris. When the Kaiser opened a new bridge across the Rhine at Mainz in May 1904 he seemed to share their view, speaking belligerently of Germany's past triumphs and her present strength in the field. While it pleased high-ranking officers in the German army who had complained about their sovereign's vacillations in world policy, other countries criticized it as a gesture of defiance against the Entente Cordiale.

However, he was still obsessed with the navy above all else, and determined to impress the British with his growing fleet. In June 1904 he invited King Edward VII to the Kiel regatta, where every available warship was moored as though for a major naval review. At the state banquet the Kaiser expressed his delight that his uncle should have been greeted by the thunder of the guns of the German fleet, while the King refrained from rising to the bait, commenting wryly that he looked forward to sailing at Kiel. Tirpitz viewed the Kaiser's boasting with some alarm, thinking it unwise to make so much of the fleet's fighting strength and dreading the prospect of a 'Copenhagen', particularly after the success of a Japanese attack on the Russian fleet at Port Arthur. All the same, British officers were suspicious of the efficiency of the German warships. In July a British war plan for destroyer operations was drawn up by Prince Louis of Battenberg, a brother-in-law of Prince Henry of Prussia and of Tsar Nicholas II, who had accompanied the King to Kiel. Some British officers were less alarmed. Rear-Admiral Montagu, a friend of the Kaiser since his first visits to Cowes who corresponded regularly with him until the beginning of 1914, noticed with pride that improved cutters and gigs which he had introduced himself into the Royal Navy were being modified for service on German warships. He might have reacted differently had he known that his letters were carefully annotated by the Kaiser, circulated among members of his naval staff and sometimes forwarded to the chancellor. Yet he was aware of the growing danger, asking him only half in jest (17 October 1904) not to 'build any more fleets, Sir, or some day Germany will want to fight us'.[6]

A chilling reminder of the fragility of peace, the 'Dogger Bank incident' occurred on 21 October 1904. *En route* for the Far East during the Russo-Japanese War, the Russian Baltic fleet opened fire on a group of English fishing smacks in the North Sea, mistaking them for Japanese torpedo boats, and killed seven fishermen. When British warships trailed the Russians down the Channel and towards the Bay of Biscay the Russian government, fearful of another ignominious naval defeat, agreed to submit the incident to international arbitration. The Kaiser tried to make capital out of the tension by urging Tsar Nicholas to take the initiative in forming an alliance of the three major continental powers – Germany, Russia and France – as a counter-balance to the Anglo-Japanese partnership. The Tsar initially showed interest, but to the Kaiser's disgust did not pursue the matter, perhaps after being persuaded by his ministers to think better of it. Just how inconsistent the Kaiser's views were towards other powers became evident with his attitude to the revolt in Russia in 1905, the year which began with 'Bloody Sunday' and the assassination of Grand Duke Serge and ended with the Tsar's reluctant assent to the creation of a *Duma*. The leaders of the revolt, Kaiser Wilhelm told the Tsar, were Jews who worked with their kinsmen in France who had the press under their influence.

In 1905 the Kaiser was persuaded by Bülow and Holstein to pay a courtesy visit to Morocco. Germany, the chancellor and his advisers maintained, needed to provide France and Britain with a stern reminder that they could not act unilaterally in European matters where German interests were involved. On 31 March he spent four hours in Tangier, and in a speech he proclaimed to a handful of German officials and merchants that the Sultan was lord of a free and independent country and that Germany would support his efforts to keep Morocco open for peaceful competition in trade among all nations. His own presence there was a pledge of Germany's 'great and growing interests'. The Kaiser had underestimated how sensitive the British were to anything that could be regarded as intriguing by Germany for a naval station so close to such vital trade routes, and his cool reception at Gibraltar angered him. While there he met Prince Louis of Battenberg and stated that he was determined to prevent France from swallowing Morocco as she had done with Tunisia. Throughout most of Europe it was accepted that Morocco was about to become a French protectorate, and the pact on North Africa featured prominently in the Anglo-French alliance. King Edward saw the Kaiser's conduct as a 'gratuitous insult' to Britain and France.

The Germans wanted an international conference on the future of Morocco and refused to negotiate with France alone. In June Prince Radolin, German ambassador to Paris, declared that as long as Delcassé, the French foreign minister, remained in office there was no chance of an improvement in Franco-German relations, and unless France accepted a Moroccan conference she risked attack. To the Kaiser's delight Delcassé resigned on 6 June, and Bülow was raised to the dignity of prince. At the same time the Kaiser refused a courteous invitation from Loubet to visit France, and while his reply was polite enough, he expressed his true feelings in a speech at Cassel exhorting his audience to 'keep your powder dry – keep your sword sharp – and keep your fist on the hilt!'.[7]

For the moment the Kaiser had triumphed, but at no little cost to his reputation. He had created a climate of uncertainty in which the threat of European war was not far away, and justified any concerns that King Edward (if not privately other European sovereigns as well) had regarding his nephew's emotional stability and the consequences for Europe in the future. To Marquis Luis de Soveral, Portuguese ambassador in London, the King remarked that Kaiser Wilhelm was vain, cowardly and he would tremble before his circle of sycophants when they called upon him to draw the sword in earnest; 'He won't have the courage to talk some sense into them, but will obey them cravenly instead. It is not by his will that he will unleash a war, but by his weakness.'[8]

The crisis coincided with another occasion in Germany which should have been a cause for family and national happiness, but did not turn out that way – the wedding of Crown Prince Wilhelm. In September 1904 he had become betrothed to Princess Cecilie of Mecklenburg-Schwerin, younger sister of Alexandrine, wife of Prince Christian of Denmark, later King Christian X. During their engagement the Princess had shown jealousy of her future husband's regimental friends, a bone of contention which augured ill for their marriage. For the Crown Prince the wedding, on 6 June 1905 (coincidentally the date of Delcassé's resignation in France), was overshadowed by the unhappy state of Anglo-German relations. As a fervent Anglophile he was disappointed that King Edward VII, his godfather, neither attended the ceremony nor sent the Prince of Wales. The only representative from England was Prince Arthur of Connaught. On the honeymoon the Crown Prince longed for his bachelor company, and rather tactlessly told his wife that she was not to interfere with his friends.[9]

Russia's internal, financial and military desperation, the Kaiser believed, would make her receptive to Berlin's plans to replace Paris as her main ally. The result would be to isolate France and Britain, and produce a strong Russo-German bloc in Europe powerful enough to meet the challenge of the Anglo-Japanese alliance. In July 1905, a month after his son's wedding, Wilhelm put to sea aboard *Hohenzollern*, to meet Tsar Nicholas II on board his yacht *Polar Star* at Björkö on the Finnish coast. Wilhelm telegraphed to Bülow for a copy of his draft treaty prepared the previous November, copied it in his own hand just before arriving at Björkö on 23 July and had it in his pocket when he walked on to the Tsar's yacht. It made provisions for each country to help the other if attacked by a third power, and was to come into effect as soon as peace was signed between Russia and Japan. In order to limit German obligations, the Kaiser inserted on the original draft a clause confining the treaty to Europe. The Tsar read it three times and signed, the Kaiser adding his name underneath. Two naval aides, one representing each sovereign, countersigned. The Kaiser thought he had achieved a major triumph, declaring emotionally that the treaty was 'a turning-point in the history of Europe, and a great relief for my beloved Fatherland, which will at last be emancipated from the Gallic-Russo strangle-grip'.[10] When the Tsar asked how Franco-Russian relations would be affected, the Kaiser explained that, with Moroccan difficulties out of the way, the Germans and French could be friends.

In Berlin and St Petersburg, ministers were aghast. After her defeat by Japan, Russia saw the treaty as an ill-thought-out initiative incompatible with the Franco-Russian alliance. Bülow believed that for the Kaiser to commit his empire to major agreements in foreign policy without consultation would leave the ministers as little more than clerks. The treaty was seriously flawed as the addition of the words 'in Europe' would make it impossible for them to threaten British garrisons in India, to which the Kaiser replied that the threat to British India was a total illusion. Nevertheless, Bülow was so angry that he threatened to resign. The Kaiser begged him to remain in office, and the chancellor later claimed in his memoirs that he was deeply moved by the Kaiser's appeal. A more likely explanation was that, after hearing such a pathetic outburst from his master, he now had high hopes of ruling supreme over Germany's affairs.[11]

The meeting at Björkö was one of Kaiser Wilhelm's most ambitious efforts at personal diplomacy. Had it succeeded, his personal power and prestige would have been considerably enhanced. Instead it was a disastrous failure. He tried to rival King Edward VII as the supreme diplomat-sovereign of the time, but when faced with a ministerial showdown he gave way like the weakest of constitutional monarchs. For a sovereign who considered himself an autocrat, he had supremely little backbone. This defeat – which it was in effect – was not lost on the other crowned heads of Europe, least of all his uncle in Britain.

It was a subdued Kaiser who wrote to his chancellor on new year's eve 1905. He seemed to dread the possibility of war, which he was anxious to avoid at least until Germany had concluded a formal alliance with Turkey; they could not unleash a conflict against France and England single-handed. The year 1906 would be particularly unfavourable for war, partly as the army had embarked on a major programme of renewing artillery, to take at least a year; partly as he was obsessed with the 'socialist menace at home', and thought they could not take a single man out of the country. To do so would jeopardize the property and lives of their citizens. 'Shoot down the Socialists first, behead them, put them out of action, if necessary, massacre the lot – and then war abroad! But not before, and not *a tempo!*' The letter closed with a demand for the chancellor to direct his foreign policy in a manner which would avoid any warlike decision, 'for the time being at any rate and as far as you consider this possible. But don't back out as the French did over Fashoda!'[12] In his memoirs Bülow used this letter as evidence of the Kaiser's fear of war and 'aversion to serious conflict' and to refute 'the lie' that he deliberately brought about conflict in 1914. At this stage Wilhelm was still equivocal. Whether he actively canvassed war in Europe or merely regarded it as inevitable is open to argument.

A conference convened at Algeciras, Spain, in January 1906, was a diplomatic defeat, if not disaster, for Germany. Her delegates, supported only by Austria, had hoped to drive Britain and France apart, but they only succeeded in isolating Germany. On its conclusion in April the conference authorized France and Spain to police Morocco for the Sultan under a Swiss inspector general; and Germany could take some pleasure in seeing a principle established that the country was under international, not French, control. But the Entente Cordiale had been strengthened, not weakened, thanks to the Kaiser's folly; and Russia, her prestige at a low point after the war with Japan, could now see the advantage of an understanding, if not an alliance, with Britain. While Italy had been bound to Germany in the Triple Alliance since 1882, King Victor Emmanuel III and his government, repelled by Kaiser Wilhelm's high-handed attitude and his ministers' efforts to drive a wedge between them and France, had done nothing to support Berlin. That Italy was at heart on the Anglo-French side was not lost on the Kaiser. Most important of all, it marked the first time for thirty-five years that major powers in Europe had seriously contemplated war. The complacency of the late nineteenth century was eroded by the beginning of a crisis of confidence in Kaiser Wilhelm's leadership of Germany, a sense of growing fatalism and worst of all a resigned belief in the inevitability of conflict that would culminate in the events of 1914.

On 4 July 1906 the Kaiser became a grandfather for the first time with the birth of a son to Crown Prince Wilhelm, also named Wilhelm. *The Times* wrote of 'family ties which unite the Royal Houses of Prussia and Great Britain', adding rather over-generously where the father was concerned that the Crown Princess had 'added her own popularity to that which the Crown Prince himself has always enjoyed'.[13]

Nonetheless, relations between both countries were still strained. The Kaiser had actively supported the claims of one of his own sons as King of Norway, following the country's declaration of independence from the crown of Sweden, only to be forestalled by the Norwegians' preference for Prince Charles of Denmark, a grandson of King Christian IX and son-in-law of King Edward VII, who was elected and took the name of King Haakon VII. Britain regarded Germany's new navy law with suspicion, as it would supply the German fleet with six new battle-cruisers. In turn Germany looked askance at the vogue for futurist fiction in England. Erskine Childers' *The Riddle of the Sands*, a spy story about a German invasion of England published in 1903, was to some a sensational novel unlikely to improve Anglo-German relations. Yet it was mild in comparison with William Le Queux's melodramatic *The Invasion of 1910* three years later. This was the brainchild of Lord Northcliffe, publisher of the *Daily Mail*, and Lord Roberts, who persistently warned that a weak complacent England was vulnerable to German invasion. Le Queux was commissioned to write a story in which the German army battled through major cities and towns in England, aided and abetted by German spies who had settled there and found ready civilian employment, with imaginary proclamations issued at Potsdam, signed 'Wilhelm'. Roberts used the book to advance his belief in conscription and a larger army, views he shared with the author. To Northcliffe it was primarily a circulation-booster when serialized in his paper prior to publication in book form and advertised by sandwich men in spiked helmets and Prussian military uniforms parading along Oxford Street. Both book and newspaper enjoyed healthy sales, while the public became alarmed at the apparent presence of enemy agents and German plots throughout England. The Liberal government was irritated by what it saw as Lord Roberts' mischief-making, while King Edward resented these provocative attempts to portray Germany as 'the enemy'. Much to the author's disgust, in a German edition the story ended with a triumphant German army marching on the shattered remains of a smoking London. The Kaiser read English and German editions, passing copies to his general staff and the German Admiralty to analyse for useful information.

After these ruptures in Anglo-German relations, it was deemed necessary to re-establish personal contact between both sovereigns. Friendly letters between King and Kaiser continued apace, but a meeting was still important. King Edward VII was going to Marienbad for 'the cure' that summer, and he could hardly refuse a meeting with the Kaiser, especially as ambassadors and ministers in both countries were pressing him to do so, as were Wilhelm's Anglophile brother and sister-in-law, Henry and Irene. The King accordingly came to Friedrichshof, and in their conversation they kept clear of contentious matters. As the Kaiser was disappointed that no member of the British government had yet visited Germany, the King promised to make good this omission. At the end of August Richard Haldane, secretary of state for war, came to Berlin. His command of German was excellent and he was a great admirer of German literature. In September Winston Churchill, colonial under-secretary of state, was the Kaiser's guest at the autumn manoeuvres at Breslau. Both men got on very well, and Churchill was impressed by all he saw but when he returned home he told a relative he was 'very thankful that there is a sea between that army and England'.[14]

That autumn the Kaiser was due to spend a few days hunting at Liebenberg with Eulenburg, as he did every year. At first he cancelled his visit as he had a cold, a decision which had unexpected repercussions. In April he had accepted Baron Holstein's resignation from the foreign ministry. Holstein and Eulenburg had quarrelled four years earlier, and the former blamed his downfall on the latter, especially as perhaps by coincidence Eulenburg had lunched with the Kaiser on the same day that he co-signed Holstein's resignation. Holstein tried to provoke a duel with Eulenburg and began a whispering campaign to discredit him and their Liebenberg circle. When the Kaiser suddenly cancelled his visit there were fears that he was not genuinely ill, but had been listening to Holstein's allies. Later the Kaiser had decided that his cold was better, and he would accept the hospitality after all. But Eulenburg's other guests were beginning to disperse, and he had to find new companions to invite. Unwisely he chose a friend of some twenty years' standing, Raymond Lecomte, first secretary at the French embassy. A foreign diplomat had never been invited to one of these gatherings before; it was thought to be error of judgment to invite a Frenchman so soon after Algeciras; and, worst of all, in the words of Bülow, he 'had the reputation of indulging in unnatural vice and had been under police surveillance on that account'.[15]

As Bülow feared, Lecomte's presence led to rumours, and the implication that Eulenburg was wielding undue power behind the throne. Having retired as ambassador at Vienna in 1902 ostensibly due to ill-health, but in fact after a threat to expose his private life, Eulenburg had remained a close confidante of the Kaiser. His sharp tongue spared almost nobody, from the military to the business community and the Jews; and he had made numerous enemies. Bülow had owed his advancement partly to Eulenburg, but by now he feared that the Kaiser might be planning to replace him with his old friend, or another candidate from the Liebenberg circle, 'the inner circle of the Emperor's Round Table' on whose sinister pacifist influence Germany's conciliatory attitude towards France at Algeciras and subsequent defeat was blamed.

In the *Reichstag* Bülow referred to a camarilla behind the throne and subtle hints about the dangers of personal rule, to which the Kaiser reacted indignantly. Anxious to defend his position from those whom he feared were plotting his downfall, the chancellor encouraged a campaign against them by feeding information and gossip about their dangerous political influence and homosexual activities to the press. These were received eagerly by Maximilian Harden, editor of the influential weekly *Die Zukunft*. As a Jew he had a vested interest in discrediting Eulenburg with his pacifist and anti-Semitic views. They were assisted by the vengeful Holstein, with his own scores to settle, not to mention his desire to humiliate France and destroy the Anglo-French Entente. Others were also sympathetic to Harden's campaign, among them Prince Max von Fürstenberg, General Dietrich von Hülsen-Häseler, chief of the Kaiser's military secretariat, and perhaps the Kaiser's sister and brother-in-law, Prince and Princess Bernhard of Saxe-Meiningen, whose names were a byword for malicious gossip and mischief at Court.

The last thing Bülow wanted was for any scandal to be attached to the Kaiser's name. By accusing the sovereign's closest friends of 'unnatural vices', he knew, Harden was striking at the heart of the German monarchy and imperilling its good name if not its existence. Homosexuality was a criminal offence in the German empire, punishable by imprisonment. Few cases rarely led to such a penalty, as evidence of what was in legal terms a 'victimless' act (taking place in private without witnesses), was almost impossible to establish, yet they still provoked moral outrage and social ruin. Even the highest in the land were not immune from its consequences. Eulenburg's only brother Friedrich, a cavalry officer, had been convicted of a homosexual offence in 1898, and asked to resign from the army. Philipp was ordered by the Kaiser never to see or speak to his brother again, a sentence which greatly upset him. Four years later another of the Kaiser's friends, Fritz Krupp, head of the family armaments firm, had been accused of paedophile activities on the Isle of Capri. His convenient sudden death soon afterwards was probably suicide, and the Kaiser, sure he had been hounded to his grave, made an impassioned speech at his funeral. In Vienna Emperor Franz Josef's brother, Archduke Ludwig Victor, was exiled after being convicted of gross indecency with a boy in a public bath.

When the attacks in *Die Zukunft* persisted, a worried Eulenburg asked Bülow to see if anything could be done to silence Harden. The chancellor advised him to go abroad until the scandal died down. In December 1906 he went to Switzerland, and the press campaign promptly ceased. As yet the Kaiser was blithely unaware of these events. Carefully shielded by his personal staff and ministers from disquieting articles in the press, Wilhelm was only shown the more anodyne ones, and nobody had yet dared to inform him of the bitter personal campaign being waged against one of his oldest friends.

Once Eulenburg was out of the country, Bülow was convinced that he could no longer intrigue for a change of chancellor, and asked the Kaiser to dissolve the *Reichstag*, with elections to be held six weeks later, on 25 January 1907. They resulted in a victory for the chancellor and his conservative allies, with the strength of the Social Democrats almost halved. The Kaiser saw this as a vote of confidence in his plans for naval expansion and world policy, and the reputation of Bülow, rather dented in the eyes of his sovereign since the Moroccan crisis and its aftermath, was restored. However, Eulenburg returned to Germany on the eve of the election, and the Kaiser summoned him to Berlin where he invested him with the Order of the Black Eagle. Three months later *Die Zukunft* renewed its attacks on him, hinting first that his friendship with Lecomte made him a security risk, and later that three imperial aides-de-camp were homosexuals. All three belonged to the Liebenberg 'Round Table', and were close friends of the commandant of the Berlin garrison, Count Kuno von Moltke, and of Eulenburg. Two of the Kaiser's aides persuaded Crown Prince Wilhelm that 'as future bearer of the throne and as the first subject of His Majesty'[16] it was his duty to bring these articles to his father's attention.

The Kaiser reacted with horror. His son wrote loyally if unconvincingly in his memoirs that his father's 'moral purity' was such that he could 'hardly imagine the possibility of such abnormalities'.[17] But Kaiser Wilhelm was no paragon of virtue, and the real cause of his distress was shock at the exposure of his friend, who had in late-twentieth-century jargon been 'outed', and that his own tendencies might inevitably be made public knowledge. Only twenty years later, when the climate of moral opinion had barely altered, his biographer Emil Ludwig could write in thinly veiled terms that His Imperial Majesty 'was not ignorant of any phase in the interrelated phases of perverted practices and unnatural tendencies'. It strained credibility, he went on, 'that he could not account for the difference between Eulenburg's languishing grace and Kiderlen's angular sturdiness, between the elegance of Kuno Moltke and the virility of Tirpitz, or that he should not have perceived that between a crudely perverted Colonel and a subtly abnormal artist there runs a devious path whereon no woman sets her foot'.[18] The Kaiser's unfortunate association with such men was as yet only known to well-informed gossips in Germany, none of whom could state facts openly without incurring major libel actions. But two decades later, there was no reason for biographers to conceal such controversial material about a former sovereign.

While the Kaiser may not have been 'addicted to such a filthy vice',[19] in the words of his uncle Bertie, he was well aware of it. His fruitful marriage and extra-marital affairs before ascending the throne made it unlikely that he was homosexual. Eulenburg was also a husband, the father of eight children and had had occasional adulterous affairs with other women. Nevertheless, the researches of Professor Röhl concluded that 'dear Phili' was not homosexual in the narrower sense of the term, but homoerotically inclined and certainly bisexual.[20] The Kaiser's intense feelings for Eulenburg had long been an open secret. Only three months after Wilhelm's accession, Herbert Bismarck was told by a Court official that His Imperial Majesty loved Philipp Eulenburg 'more than any other living being'. Disturbed by the relationship, Chancellor Bismarck wrote to his son discreetly that he did 'not wish to commit to paper' his thoughts on the subject, and wished to speak to him on the matter, but would not write down 'very much that I want to talk to you about'.[21] The Kaiser's fondness for the appearance of good-looking young men in uniform had been evident to a select few since his fascination with young Russian recruits on his St Petersburg visit in 1884. Some years later Brooke Heckstall-Smith was struck by his attention to Royal Navy officers; his admiration of them and their appearance 'amounted to worship. I have often known his eyes [to] follow one of our young naval men who was, of course, quite unaware that he was the object of any special attention. He once told me: "I like to look at your naval officers."'[22]

The Kaiser demanded the immediate resignation of Moltke and his aides, on the grounds that if they were innocent they would have already sued Harden for libel. Eulenburg was asked why he had not taken similar action. Already ill with a heart condition, he said that he hesitated to as he feared the political consequences of a possible trial, and he wished to protect the throne. Enraged by this ambiguous and evasive message, the Kaiser told Bülow that he insisted Eulenburg should ask to be retired at once. 'If this accusation against him of unnatural vice be unfounded, let him give me a plain declaration to that effect and take immediate steps against Harden. If not, I expect him to return the Order of the Black Eagle, and avoid a scandal by forthwith leaving the country and going to reside abroad.'[23] Eulenburg resigned, sent back the insignia of his Order, and in obedience to the Kaiser's command he and Moltke, in their capacity as former government officials, applied to the Prussian crown prosecutor to begin legal proceedings against Harden. The prosecutor refused on the grounds that it was a personal matter and that public interest was not affected by the allegations.

By now Bülow and most other figures in public life, even those who personally disliked Eulenburg, wanted to let the matter rest. German society was becoming a laughing-stock throughout the rest of Europe, particularly in France, where Lecomte had been recalled and the Parisian press was speculating on the behaviour of prominent personalities in Berlin and Potsdam. Convinced that he had embarked on a great moral crusade against corruption close to the throne, and adamant that he possessed material which would seriously compromise the monarchy, Harden was not anxious to desist.* He claimed to have similar evidence of homosexuality against other royal figures, among them the Kaiser's cousins Charles, Duke of Coburg, Ernest, Grand Duke of Hesse, and Prince Aribert of Anhalt, who had been married to and divorced from Princess Marie Louise of Schleswig-Holstein, another cousin.

---

*Most of the Eulenburg–Moltke correspondence was destroyed in 1907 when the scandal broke, and material collected by the prosecution was destroyed in 1932.[24]

Eulenburg retired from the fray but Moltke brought a libel action against Harden, which came to court in October 1907. The defendant's case was helped by Moltke's and Eulenburg's prompt compliance with the Kaiser's demand that they both resign, as well as the declaration of Moltke's divorced wife that Eulenburg had gone down on his knees begging her to give up her husband. Much to the Kaiser's fury Harden was acquitted and the Liebenberg 'Round Table' further discredited in the process.

After so many years of mutual suspicion, the Kaiser was disturbed by signs of reconciliation between Russia and Great Britain. Tirpitz wanted to avoid Anglo-German tension while a supplementary naval law was under discussion, especially as he suspected the British First Sea Lord, Admiral Sir John Fisher, of planning a surprise attack on the German fleet. When King Edward VII visited his nephew at Wilhelmshöhe in August, he said he would be glad to receive him on a state visit to Windsor later that year.

The visit, arranged for November, was almost cancelled. On 31 October the King received a telegram from the Kaiser saying that he was feeling tired and weak after 'bronchitis and acute cough effect of a virulent attack of influenza'. As he was unable to meet the strain of the programme so kindly prepared for him, would it be in order for him to send the Empress and Crown Prince instead, or should they postpone everything until next spring or summer? King Edward saw through the ruse, telling his private secretary Lord Knollys that after recent scandals at home his nephew 'dare not "face the music" and has practically been told he will get a bad reception in England'.[25] Later that day the Kaiser informed Bülow that during the afternoon he had been resting on a sofa, fallen in a fainting fit and caught his head a stunning blow on the floor. Dona later admitted to the chancellor that her husband had done no such thing. On his way to discuss the cancellation of the visit with the chancellor, Sir Frank Lascelles was startled to notice the Kaiser, hale and hearty, riding at a gallop in the Tiergarten. At the theatre that evening, Wilhelm told Bülow that the afternoon's ride had cured him completely and he felt fit enough to go to Windsor after all.

On 11 November the Kaiser and Empress arrived at Portsmouth on board *Hohenzollern*. At a lavish banquet at Windsor the King made a gently teasing reference to his guest's wish to postpone the visit; 'recently we had feared that, owing to indisposition, it would not take place; but, fortunately, their Majesties are now looking in such good health that I can only hope their stay in England, however short, will much benefit them'.[26] In reply to an address of welcome at a luncheon hosted by the lord mayor at the Guildhall on 13 November, the Kaiser said, 'The main prop and base for the peace of the world is the maintenance of good relations between our two countries, and I shall further strengthen them as far as lies in my power. Blood is thicker than water. The German nation's wishes coincide with mine.'[27]

Throughout the visit the King avoided political discussions, and entertained his nephew on a round of shooting parties and gala theatre performances. Yet the Kaiser could not refrain from attempting diplomatic initiatives. One matter on his mind was that of a railway from Berlin to Baghdad. Germany had obtained a concession from the Sultan of Turkey to build the Turkish section of the new line, but it was delayed by British fears that the railway would open a potentially hostile approach to India through the Persian Gulf. To Haldane, the Kaiser expressed regret at friction between their countries on the matter, and wanted to know exactly what England required. Haldane replied that they wanted a 'gate', or control of the section of the railway near the Persian Gulf, to protect India. 'I will give you the gate,' the Kaiser promised. Early next morning Haldane was woken by a knock on his door from a helmeted guardsman with a message from the Kaiser, confirming his message of the night before. Haldane immediately got up and left for London to discuss it with Lord Grey, the foreign secretary, who advised him to tell the Kaiser that, while they were pleased to discuss the suggestion, it was necessary to involve France and Russia in talks as their interests were also involved. Meanwhile, the Kaiser had been shooting with the King, and raised the matter with him. Privately irritated by his nephew's incessant obsessions, the King tactfully advised him to continue the conversation with Haldane. On seeing the Kaiser again Haldane found him enthusiastic about the possibility of an agreement, until told that it was imperative for the discussion to be continued *à quatre* instead of *à deux*. At this the Kaiser demurred, saying that public opinion in Germany would object to the inclusion of France and Russia. After consulting the ministers in his suite that evening he withdrew his objections, and agreed to make a formal proposal to Grey for British co-operation in the matter. All parties assumed there would be no difficulty, until Bülow firmly vetoed a four-power conference in Berlin some weeks later. It was striking proof of the Kaiser's inability to let well alone, to say nothing of his endless potential for half-baked personal initiatives creating one problem after another for his hosts and ministers in Britain and Germany.

On another issue entirely Lord Esher was disturbed by what he saw of the German monarch. 'Our King makes a better show than William', he noted. 'He has more graciousness and dignity. William is ungrateful, nervous and plain.' In addition his anti-Semitism shocked Grey. There were far too many Jews in his country, the Kaiser insisted. 'They want stamping out. If I did not restrain my people, there would be a Jew-baiting.'[28] Harden had evidently touched a raw nerve.

The state visit ended on 18 November. Dona and her ladies returned to Germany, but the Kaiser stayed in England for three more weeks. Before leaving Berlin he had asked if there was a suitable residence in southern England where he could enjoy 'a short convalescence'. The King had visited Highcliffe Castle, the home of Colonel Edward Stuart-Wortley near Bournemouth. The colonel had never met the Kaiser, though some years previously he had entertained Prince Henry briefly at Malta, and he was related by marriage to the diplomat Sir James Rennell Rodd, who had served in Berlin. His family was very sympathetic to Germany, distressed by the prevailing anti-German tone of the press, and welcomed any chance to try and improve relations between both countries. He was happy to lend Highcliffe to the Kaiser and his party, on condition that he could remain on the estate and act as host.

The Kaiser relished this interlude as an English country gentleman, and stayed for three weeks instead of the fortnight originally planned. He sat at Highcliffe with his hands in his pockets, he told Mrs Patsy Cornwallis-West, mother of Daisy Princess of Pless, and never opened a newspaper. 'When I said I would not be a King for all the world,' she wrote to her daughter, 'he replied: "Ah yes you're right; if I could have chosen my life I would have been a country gentleman and quite content with a home like this."'[29] Dressed in English clothing, including a checked suit and boater, it was said by one amused observer that he looked 'even more of an incongruous cad than most Bank Holiday trippers to Margate'.[30] To Houston Chamberlain, he wrote in an unusually relaxed frame of mind that he was sampling all the delights and comforts of English home and country life, as he had long wanted to do, and enjoying conversation with gentlemen 'on an equal footing without all the ceremonial of royalty. . . . The way these British refrained from discussing our affairs made me ashamed. *Such a matter in our Parliament would be an utter impossibility.*'[31]

During the third week the colonel received a letter from an old friend asking if he could arrange for the Kaiser to give an interview to the journalist W.T. Stead. The Kaiser initially declined; Stead had already asked him for one in Berlin, but on his chancellor's advice he had made it a rule never to give interviews.

Having said as much the Kaiser proceeded to do the next best thing – which in this case turned out to be one of the worst mistakes he ever made. He talked freely with Colonel Stuart-Wortley about his previous efforts to improve relations with Britain. Queen Victoria, the Kaiser said, had appealed directly to him during the Boer War; he had spoken with his general staff, and then recommended a certain line of military action for which she was deeply grateful. He spoke of Bismarck's resignation, and about the possibility of war between the United States and Japan. Twenty years previously he had foreseen 'the danger of the Yellow Peril', and had built his fleet to be ready to lend a helping hand. Apart from Admiral Fisher, 'a most dangerous and overrated man',[32] he refrained from censuring any individuals in particular.

After the mounting tension of those troublesome months at Berlin, the Kaiser felt thoroughly at ease at Highcliffe, and talked even more than usual. Returning to Berlin for Christmas, he sent the colonel a postcard from Potsdam in English, saying he was 'quite in love with your lovely place' and would 'only be too glad to come again'.[33] He was convinced that he had single-handedly improved Anglo-German relations. It had escaped his notice that while he was in England the naval race had accelerated, with Tirpitz's proposals for shortening the effective life of German battleships laid before the *Reichstag*, speeding up modernization of the fleet by 25 per cent each year. Confidential reports from the British naval attaché in Berlin confirmed the worst fears of the press to the extent of suggesting that by 1911 the German fleet would have two Dreadnoughts more than the British.

Just before Christmas the Kaiser wrote to Houston Chamberlain summarising 'a very difficult year' which had caused him a great deal of acute worry. 'A trusted group of friends was suddenly broken up through Jewish insolence, slander and lying. To have to see the names of one's friends dragged through all the gutters of Europe without being able or entitled to help is terrible. It upset me so much that I had to have a holiday and rest. The first after nineteen years of hard uphill work.'[34]

That same month, December 1907, the German government overturned the verdict in the Harden-Moltke case and ordered a second trial. Eulenburg was summoned as a witness, denied under oath that he had ever 'practised any abominations' and the testimony of witnesses at the first trial, particularly that of Moltke's former wife, was discredited. In January 1908 Harden was found guilty and sentenced to four months in prison. Legally vindicated but now a social outcast, Moltke retired to his country estate.

Three months later Harden, freed on appeal, promised evidence of Eulenburg's homosexual behaviour. Eulenburg was arrested in May and taken into custody at Berlin to await trial on a charge of perjury. Although his enemies accused him of malingering, his health was obviously deteriorating; he suffered from heart trouble and rheumatoid arthritis, and after his doctors pleaded for him not to be imprisoned, he was admitted to Berlin Charity Hospital. When the trial began at the end of June he was carried into court every day on a stretcher. Harden and

Max Bernstein, crown prosecutor of Bavaria, had assembled 145 witnesses to testify against Eulenburg, but during the first week of proceedings all but two were discredited and dismissed. Of these, one was disqualified after it was learned that he had attempted to blackmail Eulenburg. That left only Jacob Ernst, who had accompanied Eulenburg as a boatman and personal servant as a boy of seventeen nearly thirty years earlier. Despite his denial at an earlier trial that he was innocent of homosexual practices, Ernst, now a partly deaf alcoholic, agreed to give evidence as to his master's suspicious behaviour twenty-five years previously. After three weeks of legal proceedings Eulenburg collapsed in court and the case was adjourned again. It was suspected that Bülow still feared that Eulenburg was a rival for the chancellorship should he himself fall out of favour, and it was only through his persistence that legal proceedings had not been dropped altogether the previous year. Certainly Eulenburg's disgrace came at a convenient time for the chancellor.

The year 1908 had opened with a crisis, just before the *Reichstag* met to approve Tirpitz's new naval estimates. On 6 February *The Times* in London published a letter by Lord Esher that attacked the Imperial Maritime League for criticizing Admiral Fisher and his insistence on building Dreadnought-class ships; it also said that if forced into resigning his office it would be very good news for Germany. Eight days later, without his chancellor's knowledge, the Kaiser wrote to Lord Tweedmouth, First Lord of the Admiralty. His letter, signed 'Wilhelm, I.R., Admiral of the Fleet', was an attempt to calm fears in Britain regarding the threat from Germany, which he asserted was 'built against nobody at all', but solely for Germany's needs in relation to her rapidly growing trade. It was never intended to be a threat against Britain, whose navy he estimated to be about five times as large; but he defended the right of any nation to build as many warships as she felt she needed. The letter was treated confidentially by the British government, not shown to Fisher or any of the sea lords. Tweedmouth discussed the matter with Grey, and the letter was shown to King Edward VII. The Kaiser had sent a courteous note to the King informing him that he had written, as an admiral in the British fleet, to the first sea lord. Angry that a foreign sovereign should write directly to a senior member of his government (though he himself had sent personal messages directly to foreign statesmen, such as Delcassé in France), the King made his objections clear to the Kaiser. Bülow was likewise exasperated by his sovereign's action. A polite, evasive reply, drafted and re-drafted several times in association with Grey and the foreign office, was sent personally by Tweedmouth. While he regretted the tone of the press, as a gesture of goodwill he enclosed a copy of the statement including naval estimates for the forthcoming year, due to be presented to Parliament shortly. A copy of the letter came into unauthorized hands while Tweedmouth was at a country weekend in Hertfordshire, and *The Times* was indignant at the thought of a British cabinet minister sending such sensitive communications to the German Kaiser before the House of Commons was informed. A few weeks later the ailing Tweedmouth resigned and was succeeded as First Lord of the Admiralty by Reginald McKenna.

The Kaiser refused to accept that either he or any of the German ministers were to blame. He told Bülow that the British had to 'accustom themselves' to the existence of the German fleet, 'and from time to time we should assure them the fleet is not built against them'.[35] From London Count Metternich reported to the Kaiser: 'No one will ever persuade the English that a German fleet of thirty-eight battleships, twenty armoured cruisers, and thirty-eight small armoured cruisers, with corresponding torpedo and submarine craft – the total of our units in commission for 1920, if the Navy Law is carried out – is a matter of indifference to England. All the technical arguments we adduce to justify this rate of construction only make the English more mistrustful.'[36] Outraged, the Kaiser declared that he had never heard such insolent talk before, and he did not want 'a good understanding with England' at the expense of an extension to the German fleet. The German navy law was being carried out to the very last letter; 'whether the British like it or not does not worry us. If they want a war, *they* may *start* it, we are not afraid of it!'[37]

In August 1908 the Kaiser met Sir Charles Hardinge, the foreign office permanent under-secretary accompanying King Edward VII when he broke his journey to Marienbad at Friedrichshof in August. When their conversation turned to naval limitation, Hardinge stressed that while the British government was still friendly, the pace at which German naval construction was being pursued was causing concern in London. Lulled into a sense of false security by the Kaiser's amiability, he spoke of 'grave apprehensions' in England. Afterwards, according to the Kaiser, he assured Hardinge that he himself, as an admiral of the British fleet, knew far better than him, 'since you are only a civilian'. When Hardinge asked bluntly, 'Can't you stop building. Or build less ships?', the Kaiser retorted that they would fight, 'for it is a question of national honour and dignity'.[38]

While Germany hardly hoped for more than outwardly friendly relations with Britain, at least she could rely on her old ally Austria – or so she thought. Kaiser Wilhelm had taken care to cultivate good relations with Emperor Francis Joseph and his heir, his nephew Archduke Francis Ferdinand. The latter had incurred his uncle's displeasure by falling in love with Countess Sophie Chotek, a lady-in-waiting at Court, and insisting that he would marry no other. A morganatic marriage took place in 1900 and the heir's wife was created Princess von Hohenberg, but still treated by Court officials as if she were of lower rank. On his subsequent visits to Vienna Kaiser Wilhelm went out of his way to treat the Princess with respect, a gesture which flattered her and her husband after all the petty humiliations of Court protocol constantly inflicted on them. His commendable refusal to regard her as beneath his dignity was in stark contrast to his earlier attitude towards the late Alexander von Battenberg, though he could evidently accept morganatic marriages as long as they did not involve Hohenzollern flesh and blood.

Another Habsburg connection had been sealed in 1907 when the Kaiser purchased the Achilleion, a Gothic folly of a marble palace built on the island of Corfu for the late Empress Elizabeth, from her daughter Archduchess Gisela. He, his family and suite visited Corfu every April until the war, 'my favourite way of leading the simple life', as he described it, although the Greek royal family considered that his vast retinue hardly gave the impression of simplicity. King George of the Hellenes thoroughly disliked the Kaiser; like his elder sister, Queen Alexandra of England, he had never forgiven Prussia for wresting the duchies of Schleswig and Holstein from their father's Danish kingdom in 1864. Even so, he always arranged to be there at the same time, or arrive a day or two early. When Queen Olga asked her husband why he made such an effort for a man he could not stand, the King replied that if he did not Wilhelm would think he was the King of Greece.[39] Nobody else enjoyed these sojourns. The Kaiser was bored with his wife's presence and, his officers considered, treated her even worse than usual. Admiral Müller gloomily told Tirpitz that the Kaiser would 'concentrate his life on the excavation of the miserable temple ruins and demand that his entourage do the same. No one does this from inward motivation, and only a few adhere to the outward appearance of doing so.'[40] Every time Wilhelm and his suite left Corfu, the excavation sites would be closed and then restocked with fragments collected elsewhere, so that he would be able to make further 'discoveries' on his next visit.[41]

Relations between the German and Austrian Emperors were always formal and restrained. They were too dissimilar in personality, and Franz Josef resented Wilhelm's patronizing, almost discourteous manner towards him on his over-frequent visits to Vienna. There was more than a touch of poetic justice in the events of September 1908, when Kaiser Wilhelm's confidence in the elderly Emperor was shaken after the latter wrote letters to all his fellow monarchs informing them of the annexation of Bosnia and Herzegovina, two states nominally part of the Turkish empire though occupied and administered by Austria since the congress of Berlin in 1878. Throughout Europe monarchs were dismayed and angered. King Edward, unaware that Kaiser Wilhelm had not been informed of the annexation either, suspected Germany had encouraged Austria to make these acquisitions, in order to strengthen the Austro-German grip on the Balkans and humiliate Russia. Wilhelm told Bülow that he was deeply offended at not being taken into the Austrian Emperor's confidence, called the action of Baron Aehrenthal, the Austro-Hungarian foreign minister, 'a piece of brigandage' which made it impossible for them to protect their allies the Turks, and thought King Edward was secretly pleased at destroying their Turkish policy. Yet Germany had no choice but to support Austria-Hungary, her one real ally. The Kaiser had unbounded, not to say misplaced, confidence in Field-Marshal Count Franz Conrad von Hötzendorf, Emperor Franz Josef's chief of staff, praising him as 'a wonderful character', and calling a pact between Germany and Austria-Hungary the best military combination in the world, 'a granite-like foundation'.

Meanwhile, repercussions from the events of the previous autumn were beginning to haunt the Kaiser. In September Colonel Stuart-Wortley was invited to imperial manoeuvres at Metz and held further conversations with his host. On returning to England he contacted the staff of the *Daily Telegraph*, at that time the only major British newspaper sympathetic to Germany, with a proposal that he should 'write up' the Kaiser's remarks at Highcliffe and Metz as 'a supposed communiqué' to give His Imperial Majesty a fair hearing in the press. He sent the article to the Kaiser with an appeal from Lord Burnham, owner of the *Daily Telegraph*, saying that its publication would surely reduce friction between both countries. The Kaiser showed everything to Tirpitz, who strongly counselled against publication as it might create an unfortunate reaction in England. Reluctant to abandon the idea, Wilhelm decided to consult Bülow, who was on holiday. The article was read first by Martin Rücker-Jenisch, Prussian minister to Hamburg and a foreign office adviser to the sovereign, who forwarded it to the chancellor with a request to study it closely and correct any factual errors, adding his own recommendation that the article would be better left unpublished. Though reluctant to become involved as he felt ministers were responsible for concentrating 'on great matters' and should leave such business to their subordinates, Bülow read through it and returned it to Jenisch, suggesting that certain passages seemed 'undesirable'. The article and a revised, supposedly more tactful draft both passed through the hands of several ministers, secretaries and other functionaries, but the original document was returned to the Kaiser with the non-committal advice that there were no grounds for preventing publication. He made a few minor corrections and returned it to Colonel Stuart-Wortley with a letter stating that the article correctly embodied all the principal items of their conversation and authorizing him 'to make a discreet use of the article' in whatever manner he thought best.[42]

Based on Stuart-Wortley's notes made from the Highcliffe conversations, with some asides from the Kaiser made at Metz, the 'interview' was published in the *Daily Telegraph* on 28 October 1908. It castigated the English as 'mad as March hares' in their suspicion of German intentions; one day, when faced by the menace of Japan, England would be glad of the German fleet, and would appreciate his 'repeated offers of friendship'. His Imperial Majesty, it went on, had refused to join Russia and France in a continental league during the Boer War, and the plan of campaign he had sent to Windsor resembled a strategy later followed by Lord Roberts. He strove unceasingly to improve relations, and the British retorted that he was their arch-enemy. Why did they make it so hard for him?

The remarks caused a sensation throughout Europe. British reaction was mild, seeing the interview as confirmation that Kaiser Wilhelm was his own best Court jester, and the government in London refrained from making any official comment. But King Edward VII was furious, telling Hardinge that 'of all the political gaffes which H.I.M. has made, this is the greatest'.[43] *The Times* asked why a great naval force was concentrated in the Baltic and the North Sea if it was intended for use in the Pacific. Puzzled by references to 'a continental league', Tsar Nicholas II summoned the British ambassador to Peterhof and explained that Russia had only wanted peaceful mediation in 1900, while the Japanese wanted to know how they were threatening Germany and Britain.

In Germany there was outrage at their monarch's frank admission that he was more sympathetic to the British than most of his subjects, and that he had employed his general staff to draft a war plan for the British at a time when most of them supported the Boers in South Africa. Radicals in the *Reichstag* who wanted the sovereign to be made more accountable to the deputies found themselves in broad agreement with their right-wing opposites who criticized him for his excessive Anglophilia. His sister Charlotte, with whom he had long ceased to be on amicable terms, remarked that the only salvation for Germany and Europe was the institution of a collective regency of all the German princes to curb such initiatives in future.

Colonel Stuart-Wortley wrote to the Kaiser of his sadness at 'the fuss made by the villainous press' in both countries, but he was sure the tone of the newspapers would improve. He was wrong. Bülow offered his resignation for having failed to check it more fully, pleading pressure of other business. His critics, and perhaps Wilhelm himself, thought he had read and approved it in the belief that publication would deal such a crushing blow to his sovereign's power that he himself would find his own power more firmly entrenched than ever. Though he had been partly responsible for the débâcle, the Kaiser begged him to stay; he could say what he liked, but 'get us out of this'.

Bülow accordingly advised the Kaiser to proceed as if nothing had happened. After a few days' shooting with Franz Ferdinand in Austria, and a visit to airship trials with Count Zeppelin, he went to stay at Prince Fürstenberg's estate at Donaueschingen. After Eulenburg's disgrace, Fürstenberg became the Kaiser's closest friend. He never forgot the safe haven that the Prince and his family gave him during this, the unhappiest period of his reign, and after the visit thanked him for giving him 'the courage and energy to believe in myself'.[44] While one of the imperial entourage was critical of 'this boisterous and not always tasteful Austrian', it was generally acknowledged that with his optimistic personality and calm nerves, he could handle the Kaiser better than anybody else. Unlike Eulenburg, he got on well with the Empress (and, remarkably, had also been respected by the Empress Frederick), feeling sorry for her as he could see that she was treated unfairly by her husband, and was one of the few people who had the tact to smooth over unpleasant situations between husband and wife. While at Donaueschingen a full report of the debate in the *Reichstag* reached the Kaiser, and he was disappointed with Bülow's lukewarm defence of him, regarding his comments that the Kaiser would later maintain more reserve in his private conversation as akin to treachery.

Fürstenberg was so moved by his guest's downcast spirits that he decided to stage some entertainment to cheer him up, but his well-meaning efforts culminated in grim farce. An orchestra was engaged to play in the hall of the castle while General Dietrich von Hülsen-Haseler, head of the military cabinet, appeared in one of Princess Fürstenberg's ball gowns, complete with feathered hat and fan. He executed a graceful dance to the music, described by those who had seen it on previous occasions as a beautiful performance if rather too dainty for a man in his position. The General acknowledged the applause gratefully, blew kisses to his audience, exited to a passage off the improvised stage, and then a loud crash was heard. Two doctors were hastily summoned, but in vain. The fifty-six-year-old general had died of heart failure, rigor mortis was setting in and it took a great deal of effort by several onlookers to dress him in normal attire. At this particular time, the last thing His Majesty wanted was for his subjects to know that one of his most loyal associates had expired in his company in drag.

When Bülow came to see the Kaiser at Potsdam on 17 November, the Empress warned him to be gentle with her husband who was 'quite broken up'.[45] Dejected and pale, the Kaiser looked as if he was expecting a severe lecture from his chancellor. After a long and calm discussion about affairs of the last few years, in which Bülow did not shrink from advising His Majesty 'to be more discreet and cautious in future', he took a prepared statement from his pocket. It was a report he planned to make to the *Reichstag* announcing that as the result of an audience he had had with His Majesty, 'uninfluenced by the exaggerations of public criticism, which seem to him unjustified, His Majesty the Emperor regards it as his chief Imperial task to assure the continuity of Imperial policy, while, at the same time, maintaining his constitutional responsibilities'.[46] The Kaiser gave his immediate consent, and the chancellor added a final clause affirming that the Kaiser had approved all declarations by him, 'at the same time assuring Prince von Bülow of the continuance of his confidence'. The Kaiser signed it, and grasped Bülow's hand convulsively, crying, 'Help me! Save me!' Returning home, the chancellor told his wife that once more he had managed 'to get the Crown and the Emperor out of a scrape'.[47]

When Bülow had gone the Kaiser suffered a nervous collapse. On 21 November he was sufficiently recovered to attend a function in Berlin and read a speech Bülow had written for him. However, the following day, breaking down in tears, racked by spells of giddiness, shivering and facial neuralgia, he took to his bed and Bülow received a phone call telling him the Kaiser intended to abdicate. The Crown Prince assured the chancellor that he was ready to succeed his father if it was for the essential good of the empire. Realizing that he owed it to the German people to save them from such a catastrophe – for the Crown Prince possessed his father's faults but in even greater measure – Bülow hurried to Potsdam. The Empress met him, her eyes red with tears as she asked him, distraught, 'Must the Emperor abdicate?' He attempted to calm her, assuring her that thanks to his speech in the *Reichstag*, the storm had begun to abate; he left without seeing the Kaiser. To the Crown Prince his father 'seemed aged by years; he had lost hope and felt himself to be deserted by everybody'.[48]

At twenty-six, Crown Prince Wilhelm was a major in the army. He had recently been appointed to train in the ministry of the interior, the finance ministry, the naval office and the ministry of agriculture. One of his tutors found him 'very liberal, by no means an adherent of the theory of the divine right of kings' and 'a charming and sincere young man' but like his father at the same age, 'he could not be brought to real work'.[49] Despite his shortcomings he was allowed to deputize for his father for a few weeks while the latter withdrew to the privacy of the Neue Palais.

Though rarely far from tears herself, the Empress mothered the Kaiser, staying with him for hours at a time, helping to mend his frayed nerves and restore something of his self-confidence. She sent for their younger sons in turn, hoping their presence might cheer him. Though they behaved with circumspection, he seemed to find no pleasure in their company. He acted as if he was in deepest mourning, speaking but seldom and then in an undertone, as if somebody he had loved was dead, attending meals 'in a kind of stony stupor, eating and drinking at meals in a vacant way'.[50] Nobody around him dared to speak above a whisper for fear of disturbing the hush. Wilhelm had gradually come to depend on his wife more as one of the few people close to him who could be trusted, whereas in the early years of their marriage he had treated her as little more than a child. With this crisis, the worst he had yet faced, the transformation became complete. If he was never quite the same again, at least her calming influence ensured his partial recovery and prevented him from sliding into complete dejection. The spectres of the Kaiser's great-great-grandfather King George III of England, his great-uncle King Frederick Wilhelm IV and his third cousin Charlotte, former Empress of Mexico, were not far from her mind – or from those of others. Lord Esher noted in his diary (21 November) that he was sure 'the taint of George III is in his blood'.[51]

On 22 November an 'interview' with the Kaiser was published in the *New York World*. Based on conversations he had had that summer on his Scandinavian cruise with the reporter William Bayard Hale (whom the Kaiser had mistakenly supposed was a clergyman, not a journalist), it contained much of a similar nature to the *Daily Telegraph* article. Most of its criticisms were reserved for King Edward VII who, the Kaiser said, was corrupt, his Court was rotten, his country was heading for disaster, Anglo-German war was inevitable, and the sooner the better. London would be humbled, it stated, as its allies, France and Russia, were militarily worthless, and from any such war Germany and the United States would emerge as the world's leading powers. The German foreign office denounced it as 'baseless invention', and the German ambassador in Washington was asked to try and secure its suppression, but he was too late. However, Bülow managed to obtain an official apology from the paper in which it averred that it could find 'no convincing basis for its published synopsis of the Hale interview with His Majesty' and accepted that 'the alleged interview ascribed to the Emperor stupidly absurd words which he cannot have uttered'.[52]

At a meeting between the Kaiser and his chancellor a few days later, Bülow extracted a pledge from him that never again would he grant anyone an interview for publication without first submitting the full text to his ministers. Much as he privately questioned such restraint, the tarnished autocrat had no choice but to agree. As the chancellor knew, the Kaiser dared not risk his resignation.* But by the beginning of 1909 Wilhelm had come to the painful conclusion that Bülow was no longer the trusted friend he had believed. As yet he hesitated to precipitate yet another crisis by dismissing him too soon. For all his faults, he had a majority in the *Reichstag*, and with his grasp of international affairs he was the only man who could be trusted to weather the storm engendered by Austria's annexation of Bosnia and Herzegovina in October 1908. Moreover, the Empress had begged him to stay in office, and she made it plain that he had her full confidence.

By Christmas the Kaiser's spirits had recovered, and with it his bitterness against those whom he believed to be his enemies. On new year's eve he wrote to Archduke Franz Ferdinand that the British were conducting a 'premeditated campaign' against Germany and Austria, with the aim of causing 'a great continental war of all against all so that they may then fish in troubled waters and weaken everyone else'.[53]

---

*In 1912 an anonymous article, 'The Kaiser as he is', written 'by someone who knows the Emperor very closely', was published in *The Strand Magazine*. A German translation appeared later that year in *Zürcher Wochen-Cronic* (The Zurich Weekly Chronicle) to coincide with a visit by Wilhelm to Switzerland. The article was prefaced by a statement that His Imperial Majesty had approved the article, and that it was the first time he had given a British magazine permission to publish such a feature.

# CHAPTER SIX

# *The Approaching Storm*

By the beginning of 1909 there was a formidable war party in Berlin. Schlieffen's successor as chief of the general staff, Helmuth von Moltke, nephew of the strategist of 1866 and 1870, was authorized by Kaiser Wilhelm to exchange letters with Count Hötzendorf, chief of the Austro-Hungarian general staff, so that the armies of both empires could co-operate in case of war breaking out in Europe. Moltke assured Hötzendorf in January 1909 that as soon as Russia mobilized, Germany would follow suit. General von Lynker, new chief of the Kaiser's military secretariat, chosen presumably more for his strategic prowess than any ballet skills (Hülsen-Haseler had been his predecessor), also believed that an Austro-German campaign would soon triumph over any force sent into the field by Russia and France. He and Moltke thought Germany had a favourable opportunity for war that would not recur for a long time, and they were irritated by the Kaiser's intention to hold back. Had Wilhelm not been plunged into such nervous prostration by the events of 1908, and had the navy been a little stronger, they might not have found it so difficult to persuade him.

It was against this background that the long-delayed state visit to Berlin of King Edward VII and Queen Alexandra eventually took place in February 1909. In personal and diplomatic terms it was little short of a disaster. The visit began inauspiciously with the Kaiser, Empress, chancellor and others waiting on the railway platform to meet them, their ceremony having been meticulously rehearsed beforehand with the welcoming party drawn up exactly where the King's carriage was to stop. However, the King had decided to alight from the Queen's carriage with her and their imperial majesties, in their full regalia, had to move with undignified haste more than a hundred yards down the platform. During the state drive through the icy streets of Berlin, the coach in which the Empress and the Queen were travelling suddenly stopped and the horses refused to move any further. Both ladies had to transfer to another coach to complete their journey. Meanwhile, King and Kaiser shivered in the bitter wind as they waited apprehensively in the palace courtyard, fearing an assassination attempt. When the rest of the procession arrived the Kaiser was furious, feeling he had been made to look ridiculous in front of the English.

The bronchial King looked tired and bored throughout his stay in Berlin. It was rumoured that the Kaiser had kept him waiting in the courtyard on the first day in the hope that pneumonia would carry him off, an unfair jibe as he had taken special efforts to ensure that rooms for the King and Queen were as comfortable and tastefully decorated as possible. After a luncheon at the British embassy the King was sitting in his tight-fitting Prussian uniform on a sofa talking to friends, puffing on a cigar, when he collapsed in a choking fit. For a few minutes the other horrified guests feared the worst. As Daisy, Princess of Pless, put it rather tactlessly, he looked as if he was dying; 'Oh! Why not in his own country?' Fortunately he recovered once Queen Alexandra had loosened his collar, and that evening he attended a ballet at the opera house, *Sardanapalus*, devised by the Kaiser, in which stage effects culminated in an astonishingly lifelike furnace effect, complete with leaping flames and rolling billows of smoke. Exhausted by the day's events he had nodded off, only to wake up and demand angrily what had happened to the firemen. It took all the Empress' powers of tactful persuasion to reassure him that they were in no danger.

Before he had left for Germany King Edward was advised that any attempt at political talks would be 'highly inappropriate'. Nevertheless, he saw fit to raise the highly explosive issue of Germany's shipbuilding programme with his nephew at the end of his stay, either on the drive to the railway station or even on the platform itself. The only account of their conversation was left by the Kaiser himself, who noted that it was a polite exchange in which they agreed that relations between their countries 'would henceforth move into safer and calmer channels of mutual trust' and the King accepted his nephew's argument that Germany had no aggressive intentions towards any other power, certainly not England. The latter had a navy 'according to its interests and to be able to safeguard them and its shores', and Germany was merely doing likewise.[1]

The English visit left a sour taste. When one of Queen Alexandra's ladies-in-waiting openly expressed astonishment that the palace had bathrooms, dressing tables, soap and towels, having been told in London that such facilities were non-existent in Berlin, the Kaiser was angry. Another member of the entourage was surprised to see handsome hotels and large stores on the streets of Berlin. 'The worthy British', the Kaiser wrote (12 February) in exasperation to Archduke Franz Ferdinand, 'seem to have got the impression that they were going to the Eskimos in the farthest backwoods!'[2]

By now Bülow's chancellorship was drawing to a close. While the Kaiser had refrained from dismissing him after the crisis of 1908, he was only waiting for the right moment. He had told confidantes that he no longer trusted his chancellor, and that their 'reconciliation' was 'a comedy'. By spring 1909 naval expenditure had created an economic crisis in

Germany and in deference to conservative strength in the *Reichstag*, 400 million marks, or some 80 per cent of the new revenues, were to be raised from sales tariffs, hitting the lower and middle classes hardest. Concessions had to be made to the liberals, and Bülow proposed that 1 million marks, 20 per cent of the required sum, should be raised from property owners by an inheritance tax. The right- wing deputies opposed death duties, which had never yet been levied in Germany. With reluctance the Kaiser supported his chancellor, making it clear that if he failed to deliver the vote, he must resign. On 24 June the measure was defeated by eight votes and five days later he travelled to Kiel to lay down his seals of office at a meeting on board the *Hohenzollern*.

Ever a partisan of Bülow, the Empress tried to persuade her husband to retain him in office but Wilhelm was adamant. Instead, he appointed Theobald von Bethmann-Hollweg, who had been responsible for internal affairs for the last four years. Both men quickly developed respect for each other, though the chancellor complained to others about the Kaiser's threats to send his adjutants into the *Reichstag* 'if I am not tough enough', or ally himself with the other German princes in order to chastise the *Reichstag* if not eventually abolish it – words the new chancellor was wise enough not to take seriously. The Kaiser dined regularly with him, full of praise for his wife, 'the very model of a genuine German wife', though he misconstrued the chancellor's tough personality, saying later that he 'eventually developed an increasingly strong inclination towards domination; in discussions this tended to make him obstinate and caused him to lay down the law as dogmatically as a school teacher to those who differed from him'.[3]

Politically the new chancellor seemed to represent a kind of reforming, moderate conservatism. His plans included universal suffrage for elections of the Prussian *Landtag*, which had been based on a complicated three-tier voting system largely unchanged since 1849; detaching Britain from her French and Russian sympathies by offering naval concessions in return for a political treaty to end the naval rivalry and secure a pact of neutrality with the British government; and seeking to reform and modernize the German constitution.

Meanwhile, the curtain was about to fall on the Eulenburg saga. The previous trial had been adjourned indefinitely, and in July 1909 he was judged fit to return to court. Proceedings only lasted for a few hours before he collapsed again and the trial was adjourned once more. From time to time over the next few years court-appointed doctors were sent to check on his medical condition, but they always returned with the same verdict: he was not fit to stand trial. Eulenburg lived for another twelve years on his estates, ostracized by society and his health broken.

Never again did he see or correspond with the sovereign whose throne his friendship had inadvertently threatened.

For all his faults, Eulenburg had been a loyal supporter of the Kaiser. Now he and his rival Bülow had left the stage, the Kaiser turned increasingly to his wife for companionship and advice. Though she still alternately bored and irritated him, the Empress had gradually matured from the 'poor, insignificant, foolish little princess' of Queen Victoria's judgment to a shoulder to lean on in times of crisis. It was ironic that Wilhelm had married a woman who, he thought at the time, 'knew her place' and would not attempt to express strong views or exert a fraction of the influence on her husband that her two predecessors had over the previous German Kaisers. Nevertheless, it was regrettable that the third Empress was a prejudiced, xenophobic woman with none of the liberalism or broad outlook of the first two.

More importantly, the crises of the last year had seriously undermined German confidence in the Kaiser, as well as his own belief in himself. With Eulenburg gone, there was one less voice of pacifist restraint against the sabre-rattling influence of the military chiefs, who were tightening their grip on the sovereign and his ministers. It was a turning point in the weakening and ultimate destruction of the German monarchy as well as the collapse of the old order throughout Europe. At one stage during the libel trials Harden had claimed that he possessed evidence which, if laid before the Kaiser, would result in his abdication. The latter felt less secure at his capital, and was always glad to escape to other parts of his empire. He wrote to Lady Mary Montagu (1 May 1910) of his joy at leaving for Bad Homburg 'after a heavy three months at Berlin, full of tedious Court and Society obligations!'. Berlin Court life was 'a Society that burns to be invited on every possible occasion, and laughs at you behind your back!'.[4]

While Bethmann-Hollweg set great store by an Anglo-German understanding, with the Kaiser's approval, Admiral Tirpitz was less amenable. He was asked to submit proposals as a basis for naval discussions, but he had other ideas. He knew that the fleet could not yet hope to emerge victorious from war, and for the next four or five years Germany's outlook was uncertain. It was prudent to avoid total estrangement from the British during this period. Tirpitz was prepared to put forward proposals to limit naval armaments, secretly hoping they would not be accepted. This policy was favoured by German steel barons and shipbuilders, who were growing fat on the proceeds of naval rivalry. The admiral felt there was nothing to be lost from discussions with the British as long as nothing was finally settled. With the retirement of Sir John Fisher as first sea lord in January 1910 the prospect of a naval preventive war looked even less likely.

Yet the Kaiser's obsession with 'his navy' had not abated. Miss Topham, the Kaiser's daughter's governess, was invited to see part of the fleet anchored at Kiel, and when asked by a young naval lieutenant for her opinion of the warships which met her gaze, she agreed diplomatically that they were very fine, 'nearly as fine as ours at home'. When he became angry with her, she pointed out that they burnt Welsh coal as the best German coal was inferior. On her return to the Neue Palais she told Princess Victoria Louise that she had seen the German fleet at Kiel. The Princess told her scathingly that she had only seen a tiny part of it and Germany would soon have a much bigger fleet than England. This conversation got back to the Kaiser, who likewise asked his daughter's governess what she had thought of the ships. She told him that she had admired them, and with a forced laugh continued that the British would have to keep on building with no reduction in the navy estimate. Defensively he retorted that it was nonsense to talk as if the German navy was remotely near that of Britain in size, and he could not understand why England was so concerned about Germany's shipbuilding programme. 'Here you are building Dreadnoughts by the dozen, and if we build one or two there is a tremendous outcry in the press.' She admitted that perhaps the British should 'keep quiet and say nothing, but keep on building, too', though it was an expensive business. His Majesty, she was sure, thought it 'petty-minded to be trammelled by financial considerations' and that it was the job of others to find the money.[5]

Miss Topham's employment as governess ended in October 1909 with Victoria Louise's confirmation. Four days later the Kaiser made his daughter the colonel of the death's head hussars, a position previously held by the Empress Frederick. When she appeared for the first time in her uniform, he proudly declared that she would ride at the head of the first regiment that invaded England.[6]

On 6 May 1910 King Edward VII died. On his last visit to Paris weeks earlier, he despondently told his friend the Comtesse de Greffuhle that he had not long to live, 'and then my nephew [Emperor William] will make war'.[7] His nephew had similar views on what he saw as his uncle's bellicosity, as a passage in his memoirs would later recall: 'The death of the "encircler," Edward VII – of whom it was once said, in a report of the Belgian Embassy at Berlin, that "the peace of Europe was never in such danger as when the King of England concerned himself with its maintenance" – called me to London.'[8] Nonetheless, he was shocked by the sudden news; even in England, the first bulletin warning that His Majesty was 'indisposed' had only been issued twenty-four hours before his death. When told that his uncle was gone, the Kaiser put his head on his arm and wept silently for a few moments, before pulling himself together and announcing gruffly that he would leave for England at once. Though he was but one of nine crowned heads at the funeral at Windsor on 20 May, the courtier Lord Esher felt that 'of all the royal visitors the only mourner was this extraordinary Kaiser'.[9]

With King George V and Queen Mary now on the British throne there was none of the tension that had existed between the late King and the virulently anti-Prussian Queen Alexandra. King George did not share his father's enthusiasm for France or for foreign travel, and had none of his mother's bitter hatred for Wilhelm, seeing in his appointment of the less abrasive Bethmann-Hollweg a chancellor who could help to repair some of the damage done to Anglo-German relations by his shifty predecessor. He suggested to Wilhelm that he might like to return to London in the spring of 1911 for the unveiling of the memorial to their grandmother in front of Buckingham Palace, an invitation that was accepted with delight. On the surface there seemed to be a genuine new spirit of friendship between Germany and Britain. The Kaiser believed that his own personal successes in London outraged the 'anti-British mentality' encouraged by some of his ministers, notably Baron Holstein, who had died in 1909. If anybody needed proof of his love for England, he declared, one need look no further than the annual invitations he sent to British army leaders to attend German military manoeuvres and to join him at his table for dinner afterwards. As far as he was concerned, Britain could colonize the world with his blessing, as long as German traders were permitted to go about their business in their own ports, and the German navy could be maintained without interference.

However, Bethmann-Hollweg needed to check a swing to parties of the left in the *Reichstag* and thought that some major achievement in German diplomacy would be the answer. With little experience of foreign affairs, he recommended the appointment of Alfred von Kiderlen-Wächter as state secretary for foreign affairs. The Kaiser did so reluctantly, warning his chancellor that he was 'putting a louse in the pelt'. Earlier in the reign, Kiderlen-Wächter had accompanied his master on board the *Hohenzollern* cruises as foreign ministry representative for some years. Soon wearying of the Kaiser's false heartiness and schoolboy intrigue, his rudeness to the Prince of Wales and his boorish behaviour at Cowes, he wrote privately of his feelings to state secretary Baron Adolf Marschall von Bieberstein. The letters fell into the hands of Bülow and eventually the Kaiser, who banished him from the yacht and in 1898 had him transferred to the embassy at Bucharest for ten years in what was nearly the end of his career.

Convinced he could achieve a victory for foreign policy before the next elections in January 1912, Kiderlen-Wächter had set his sights on Morocco. In the spring of 1911 ministers in Paris complained that the Sultan could no longer maintain law and order in the interior of Morocco and sent an expeditionary force to assist him. Kiderlen-Wächter argued that as France was about to set up a Moroccan protectorate in contravention of the Algeciras agreement, Germany was entitled to compensation. If the French were going to establish themselves in the town of Fez to protect their nationals in Morocco, Germany should follow suit with warships stationed peacefully in harbour, awaiting a French offer of compensation. As the ports were some distance from the Mediterranean, Kiderlen-Wächter imagined the British would not object. The Kaiser agreed reluctantly to the plan, anxious about the British reaction, especially as he was going to London for the unveiling of the Queen Victoria memorial.

Wilhelm and Dona spent three days in London in May, cheered in the streets and applauded by a standing audience at the theatre, and he was pleasantly surprised to find such a friendly atmosphere at Buckingham Palace. As it was strictly a family visit, he had no discussions with ministers. But just before leaving England, he raised the question of Morocco with King George V. It was a hurried exchange, and when the Kaiser was back in Berlin he assured his chancellor that King George would 'never wage a war for the sake of Morocco', though his government might seek compensation elsewhere in Africa if the French strengthened their position there. England would be afraid to go to war with Germany for fear of losing Egypt, India and Ireland; 'she would not dare to risk the loss of her colonies overseas'.[10] All the same, on the Kaiser's last visit to London, he was sure that England, her people, monarch and government were more well disposed towards Germany. His sister Charlotte was in an equally Anglophile mood as she attended the coronation of King George V in June and spent several weeks in the country, writing enthusiastically that 'there is no place in the world like England, & if possible I'm more English than ever'.[11]

On 28 June Kiderlen-Wächter travelled to Kiel during regatta week to obtain the Kaiser's approval for the Moroccan venture. Germany would use the presence of warships to obtain colonial concessions from the French, or at least to establish a foothold in southern Morocco. The German gunboat *Panther* arrived off Agadir on 1 July, and the German ambassadors accredited to countries which had signed the Algeciras agreement informed their governments of the German naval presence in southern Morocco. In the ensuing months of international crisis, Europe seemed closer to war than at any time for several decades. There was less excitement in Paris than in Berlin or London, especially as a change of government at the end of June had brought to power Joseph Caillaux, known to favour closer Franco-German collaboration. The German press hailed the venture at Agadir as proof that the empire was once again pursuing a vigorous foreign policy. Yet the Kaiser and Kiderlen-Wächter were surprised by the reaction from London. They had expected the British government to acquiesce; instead, it treated the matter as a grave threat to peace. Sir Edward Grey demanded an explanation from the German ambassador, whom Kiderlen-Wächter had left without any clear instructions. With rumours of Franco-German negotiation, the British government adopted a stern tone, and Grey welcomed the offer of David Lloyd George, chancellor of the exchequer, to deliver a strong warning in a speech at London on 21 July. While Lloyd George did not mention Agadir or Germany by name, he declared that Britain could not 'be treated, where her interests were vitally affected, as if she were of no account in the Cabinet of Nations' and he emphasized that 'peace at that price would be a humiliation, intolerable for a great country like ours to endure'.[12]

At the time the Kaiser was cruising on board *Hohenzollern*. He had doubts about Kiderlen-Wächter's performance, believing him to be making demands for territorial concessions in central Africa from France which no government could possibly make. To Bethmann-Hollweg he insisted that there must be no mobilization of German forces while he was on his cruise, and a representative in attendance reported back to Berlin that the Kaiser was unlikely to approve of any measures which could lead to war. Alarmed by the cancellation of a goodwill visit from England and the squadron of Vice-Admiral Jellicoe, at the end of his cruise he received a report from Kiderlen-Wächter and instructed him to moderate the demands he was making from the French. To his dismay the conservative press in Berlin were becoming more and aggressively patriotic, talking of 'national dishonour' and 'unspeakable shame' while they portrayed the Kaiser as a coward; the generals were likewise taking a tough line.

Admiral Georg von Müller, head of the naval secretariat, thought it essential to postpone any conflict with England until after the completion of the Kiel Canal so that Dreadnoughts could move freely between the North Sea and the Baltic. Tirpitz was also anxious to wait, convinced that with every passing year they would be in a more favourable position. The earliest possible date, he believed, would be spring 1914.

It was soon evident that only a minority in Germany were prepared to imperil the peace of Europe over Morocco, and the Kaiser agreed to a conference at Schloss Wilhelmshöhe on 17 August. After several weeks of negotiation, in November Germany recognized France's right to 'protect' Morocco, receiving in exchange a certain amount of the French Congo, which gave her river outlets for exports from the Cameroons. The Kaiser congratulated Bethmann-Hollweg on emerging successfully from a 'delicate crisis', and was disappointed when the *Reichstag* debated the Moroccan crisis a few days later, with conservative and liberal deputies attacking the inept foreign policy of the past five months and also the sovereign who had tolerated such alternations of bravado and retreat. The Crown Prince was present on one occasion, and noticed applauding the attack of a conservative deputy, Ernst von Heydebrand und der Lasa, as he nodded his approval. This show of support for one of the chancellor's arch-critics earned the Crown Prince a private rebuke from his father in the form of a stern lecture on the duties of the heir to the throne. In England and France there were disapproving comments on the future German Kaiser's lack of responsibility and his open support for such jingoistic speeches, particularly as he had often professed himself to be an ardent admirer of England and had been welcomed on his visits there with such friendliness. King George V told Count Metternich that he thought it a 'great act of insubordination' by the heir against his father.

The *Reichstag* elections of January 1912 made the Social Democrats the largest party in Germany, with 110 seats, against their 1907 total of 43. Though Bethmann-Hollweg could still muster support from parties of the right and centre to get legislation through the chamber, the result shocked the Kaiser. The Social Democrats were basically republican, and one of their leaders, Gustav Noske, had told a party meeting in 1910 that they would call for a republic at the forthcoming election. The possible consequences of the result were not lost on Wilhelm, who feared for the stability of his throne. There were lessons, he felt, to be learned from the Agadir crisis, as did Tirpitz, who decided that it had shown a need to reduce England's naval lead as soon as possible with a substantial shipbuilding programme to be embodied in a navy bill as part of the year's budget proposals. At the same time the general staff of the army, with a new chief of operations, Erich von Ludendorff, demanded an army bill. In 1910 Germany had spent exactly half as much on the navy as on the army, a proportion which the Prussian war ministry considered absurd as Germany was essentially a continental power; decisive events would be on land, they said, and her power rested on the strength of the army. The Kaiser had noticed deficiencies during the 1911 manoeuvres, and in a new year's address to the military commanders he promised that the army's needs would take precedence over those of the navy. An army league was founded in January, and in February he decided to ask the *Reichstag* for an army law as well as a navy law in the summer.

Like his ministers, the Kaiser thought he had been too well disposed towards Britain during the crisis. While remaining in touch with Tory friends in England who championed Anglo-German friendship and were critical of the radical Liberal government, he thought less of British military potential now than in earlier times and gave short shrift to a report from his ambassador in London favouring an Anglo-German understanding. British politicians, he told his entourage, were 'all sheep'.

At the end of January 1912 Sir Ernest Cassel, the German-born, English-resident banker, suggested a series of Anglo-German conversations. He hoped Germany might be persuaded to halt further shipbuilding programmes in return for colonial concessions and a pledge that neither country would join any coalition designed to attack the other. The Kaiser responded favourably to this proposal, presenting Cassel with a copy of the German naval programme, assuming that Grey and Churchill would be able to assess it calmly before the naval bill was publicly announced in Berlin. He also told Cassel that he would welcome a visit to Berlin from a senior member of the British government, preferably Grey or Churchill.

The only minister in London familiar with Germany was the war secretary Haldane. To allay suspicion in Paris and St Petersburg it was announced that he and his brother, a distinguished physicist, accompanied by Cassel, would travel to the German capital to study higher education for a committee considering the future of the University of London. On the day of their departure, the Kaiser opened a new session of the *Reichstag* and announced in his speech from the throne that the deputies would have to approve an army bill and a navy bill in the near future. Haldane had long conversations with the Kaiser and Tirpitz on 9 February. On the same day Churchill made a speech justifying Britain's case for naval supremacy on the grounds that for Britain it was a necessity, while for Germany it was a luxury. It went down badly with the Kaiser, who had previously met and liked Churchill but now complained of his arrogance. Haldane returned to Britain having achieved nothing. By the end of May, army and navy bills had been passed and approval given for a property tax to meet the expenditure.

Bethmann-Hollweg was increasingly alarmed at the whole thrust of German policy, knowing that his sovereign was only listening to two advisers. One was Tirpitz, who was obsessed with building up Germany's fleet until the English would not risk a naval encounter; the other was the increasingly anti-English Empress, who seemed to have more of a hold on her husband than ever before. In one of his bellicose moods, Wilhelm wrote to King George of the Hellenes (10 June) that he did not want war, 'but apparently England does and if they do we are quite ready'.[13]

A further threat to European stability came from the Balkans later that year. In October Russian agents encouraged an alliance binding the Balkan states of Serbia, Montenegro, Greece and Bulgaria to declare war on Turkey. Within three weeks the Balkan League had gained victories in Macedonia, Thrace and northern Albania, much to the delight of the Kaiser, who regarded their campaign against Turkey as a 'historical necessity'. The Turks, he declared, deserved to be 'flung out of Europe' as they had dethroned his friend the Sultan and 'repaid all the services we had rendered by going over to the English'.[14]

Reluctant at first to support a hard-line policy in Vienna that might lead to the outbreak of war on a wider scale, the Kaiser told Kiderlen-Wächter that he saw no threat to Austria's prestige, let alone existence, in a Serbian harbour on the Adriatic. To his chancellor he was more forthright when warned of a possible rupture of the alliance. War, he said, might mean the downfall of Germany; there was 'nothing whatever in the Treaty of Alliance to say that the German Army and the German people are to be pressed into the service of another State's political caprices, and be, so to speak, at her disposal for any and every purpose'.[15] Within a few days Bethmann-Hollweg and Admiral Müller persuaded him to change his mind. If Serbia persisted in threats to annex Albania or try and secure a harbour on the Adriatic, Austria would feel provoked into defensive or aggressive measures. Even so, they believed the German people would only support a war if Russia put herself in the wrong and threatened to attack Austria. Could Austrian ministers mediate on the matter? Within the week, after meeting Tirpitz and other naval officers at Kiel, the Kaiser's mood swayed more in favour of Austria, whom he felt to be the injured party. He thought he could detect a shift in the European and English press in Austria's favour.

In November 1912, soon after his return from Kiel, the Kaiser and Moltke met Franz Ferdinand at Berlin to discuss the Balkan power structure, assuring the latter that Austria-Hungary could count on German support whatever the circumstances. Next the Kaiser, noting that 'a European war is possible and for us perhaps a war for our very existence against 3 Great Powers',[16] sought from his ambassadors in Paris and London information on likely French and British reaction to worsening relations between the great powers. In particular Wilhelm wished to know whether Britain would take sides if the Balkan troubles could not be contained, as any Austrian move against Serbia would undoubtedly provoke Russia. On 3 December he approved a plan designed to ensure that if war broke out with France and Russia, any German fleet activity against France should be limited in a way that would probably allow Britain to stay neutral. Even so, regarding the word of his diplomats as suspect, he sent his brother Henry to England for a meeting with King George V.

On 6 December Henry asked whether, if Germany and Austria went to war with Russia and France, England would come to the assistance of both latter powers. The King answered, 'undoubtedly, Yes – under certain circumstances'. Telling Sir Edward Grey that the Prince was 'horrified' by the statement that Britain would not allow France or Russia to be crushed, the King went on to ask his cousin, 'Do you believe that we have less sense of honour than you? You possess signed Alliances: we unsigned Ententes. We cannot allow either France or Russia to be overthrown.' (On the previous Tuesday the German ambassador had reported a statement from Haldane that Britain would not let Germany defeat France if a Russo-Austrian conflict in the Balkans spread to western Europe). On his return to Germany, Henry told his brother that Britain was 'peace-loving' and that if war broke out Germany would have to reckon 'perhaps on English neutrality, certainly not on her taking the part of Germany, and probably on her throwing her weight on the weaker side'. Despite the verdict of those who have criticized Henry for being vague and muddle-headed, it is only fair to accept that he spoke the truth and that his brother chose to misinterpret him. In the margin of Henry's report, the Kaiser scribbled, 'Well that settles it, we can now go ahead with France.'[17]

This coincided with what has in retrospect been called a secret 'military-political conference', or less than a fortnight later by the angry chancellor, who was not present, a *Kriegsrat* or 'war council'.[18] On the morning of 8 December the Kaiser summoned a meeting at the Neues Palais, Potsdam. Present were Tirpitz, Moltke, Vice-Admiral von Heeringen of the naval staff and Admiral Müller of the Kaiser's naval secretariat. As well as the chancellor, the state secretary for foreign affairs and the minister of war were also absent. They were deliberately excluded because, as mere civilians, the Kaiser considered them responsible only for purely political questions and issues and not military or naval matters.

The Kaiser was alarmed by a report from Lichnowsky, ambassador in London, who had been warned by Haldane that in the event of a general European war England would side with France, as it could not tolerate Germany (or any other power) becoming dominant on the continent and uniting it under her leadership. Wilhelm said angrily that the telegram showed how little faith could be placed in England's friendship; that the English principle of the 'balance of power' was an 'idiocy' which would make the British a permanent enemy of Germany, as it was nothing more than an attempt to prevent other powers from defending their interests with the sword. If the Austrians did not face up to the Serbian menace, they would have trouble from Slav minorities within the Austro-Hungarian monarchy, and from now on the fleet must regard England as an enemy. Moltke thought war unavoidable, and said that the sooner it came the better. On behalf of the navy Tirpitz wanted to wait another eighteen months, specifically until completion of the widening of the Kiel Canal in the summer of 1914. Moltke said that the navy would still not be ready even then, and delay would place the army in an increasingly unfavourable position, as their enemies were arming more strongly, and the German army was very short of finance. According to Admiral Müller the meeting achieved almost nothing. Moltke later told representatives of the Saxon and Bavarian armies in Berlin that he wanted an early war against France, and that the Kaiser wanted naval and military staffs to 'prepare an invasion of England on a grand scale'.

With hindsight it has been suggested that the Kaiser was in one of his brief passing flamboyant phases. It has also been taken as proof that, without the influence of Eulenburg and the more pacifist Liebenberg circle – who had helped restrain him in the past – the Kaiser was increasingly open to manipulation by the generals and his military entourage. Equally plausible is a theory that he was deliberately surrounding himself with hawks who, he knew, were prepared for if not actually relishing the thought of a war in which the German empire would prove itself victorious once more. It was significant that the doves, notably Bethmann-Hollweg, who had urged acceptance of Haldane's proposals to slow down if not cease battleship construction, and not to attack Russia or France and been overruled, were pointedly excluded. This being the case, it is hard to absolve Kaiser Wilhelm II from a major element of responsibility for the outbreak of war eighteen months later. One may find it hard to dispute the contention that he neither wanted war in 1914 nor started it; it is equally hard to deny that he was largely to blame, by wilfully letting himself be manoeuvred into a position, or a frame of mind, in which he regarded an avoidable conflict as inevitable if not desirable.

Prince Henry's report of his talks with King George V reached Potsdam soon after the meeting, and gave his brother the impression that while England would not side with Germany, she might remain neutral although she might throw her weight on the weaker side. Taking British neutrality for granted, the Kaiser sought to collaborate with Grey to settle Balkan problems through a conference of ambassadors in London. The Prince wrote to King George V (14 December) to explain what he had told his brother; and to assure him that Germany had no intention 'of going to war with any one, and never had, this she has proved in more than one case, during 43 years! . . . I always have & always shall consider it my duty to avoid misunderstandings & try & smooth difficulties between both our countries.'[19] Herbert Asquith, the British prime minister, wondered whether the Prince was a fool or a knave; had he been made a fool of by Admiral Tirpitz and sent to England to allay suspicion, or did he know the true facts and was he merely posing as a candid friend to conceal his country's genuine warlike intentions? Asquith believed the latter, but Sir Frederick Ponsonby, who knew him and the German imperial family better, appreciated that Henry was a friend of Britain (and a more consistent one than his erratic brother). He recognized that Henry was trying his best to smooth matters between the Kaiser and King George V; he was a perfectly straightforward man who never gave the impression of having any Machiavellian cunning.

Meanwhile, Moltke, still keen for the early conflict which he thought would be to his country's advantage, secured the largest army bill yet imposed on the German people, almost four times as much as in the last year of Bismarck's chancellorship and more than double the French army estimates. Tirpitz it was who had his way, in the shape of a reprieve. In Berlin the view was that war was postponed; but among the officer corps the conviction hardened that a major war would soon begin. A week later Admiral Müller informed the Kaiser that large withdrawals of money had recently been made from bank accounts and that gold had been deposited in bank safety vaults, as well as bank deposits being sent abroad, as if the inevitability of conflict and major economic crisis were anticipated. The Kaiser remained inconsistent, writing excited comments on letters and memoranda and begging Tirpitz in his more sober moods not to 'hold me to my marginalia'. Uncomfortable with Austria's pretensions in south-eastern Europe, he told his ministers that his conscience would not permit him to go to war for a cause of no concern to his people.

Still Kaiser Wilhelm retained an exaggerated belief in the efficacy of dynastic diplomacy, believing that his cousins, King George V and Tsar Nicholas II, would somehow help between them to check the continent's desire for war. Yet those around him seemed to detect a deepening mood of resignation to the inevitability of a major war. In December 1912 he spoke of the approaching conflict as a 'fight to the finish between the Slavs and Germans'. A coalition, he said later, was forming against Germany. Among senior officers the general opinion, which reached the ears of the Kaiser, was that the Supreme War Lord of the empire had damaged German chances in any war by losing his nerve and failing to stand firm in 1905 and 1911, and this must not be allowed to happen again.[20]

In May 1913 royalties from all over Europe travelled to Berlin for the wedding of the Kaiser's daughter Victoria Louise to their cousin Ernst

August, Duke of Brunswick-Luneburg, grandson of Georg V, the last King of Hanover, on the 24th of the month. The banquets and gala operas, military parades and other trappings of imperial German splendour that preceded it were witnessed by the last great congregation of family and European royalty. Few realized that many of them would never see each other again.

However, there was much unease behind the splendour. Sir Frederick Ponsonby, who accompanied King George as he had so often attended King Edward abroad, was 'inclined to think that the visit helped towards establishing good feeling between the two countries', but it was difficult to disguise the fact that the states were practically rivals.[21] Not normally suspicious, King George thought the Kaiser seemed almost childish in his jealousy of the friendship between him and Tsar Nicholas, trying to ensure they were never left alone, imagining that they were plotting behind his back. Whenever they managed to hold a private conversation, the King thought he imagined that 'William's ear was glued to the keyhole'.[22] The Kaiser observed his ministers' requests and avoided talking politics with the King. Instead, he vented his feelings on the King's private secretary Lord Stamfordham at an officers' luncheon, taking him to task angrily for 'making alliances with a decadent nation like France and a semi-barbarous nation like Russia and opposing us, the true upholders of progress and liberty'.[23]

On the day after the wedding the Empress invited the Princess's former governess, Anne Topham, to dinner. Since her engagement, the Empress told her, 'the poor child did nothing but cry'. She was convinced that war would break out, her husband would go away to fight and they would never see each other again. The Court physician, Dr Zunker, tried to reassure her that even if there was war in the Balkans, it would all be over within six weeks.[24]

The month after his daughter's wedding, Kaiser Wilhelm II celebrated his silver jubilee. F.W. Wile, Berlin correspondent of the *Daily Mail* in London and the *New York Times*, paid him a fulsome tribute; twenty-five years, he wrote, had brought the Reich to the peak of its national greatness and 'under his active leadership the Fatherland has reached the pinnacle in its peaceful pursuit of commerce and industry and has become the mightiest military force in the world. . . . As Managing Director of Germany Ltd, Kaiser Wilhelm has had a difficult role to play yet has succeeded in fulfilling his duties with eminent success.'[25] On the weekend of 14–15 June Berlin was *en fête*, the streets decorated with jubilee arches bearing the imperial cypher and flags fluttering everywhere. Another cause for celebration was the centenary of the war of liberation and victory at Leipzig in October 1813, marked by the unveiling of a vast monument on the 'battlefield of the nations'. However, the Kaiser seemed unable to join in the festive mood. Friends and family thought he was suffering from depression as a result of his daughter's marriage.

On a visit to Germany in July King George V's eldest son Edward, Prince of Wales, gained a disturbing insight into relations between the imperial brothers, who were his second cousins. The nineteen-year-old Prince stayed first with Prince Henry and his family at Hemmelmark. Henry the sailor prince, who in the Prince's view had a 'more flexible and sympathetic approach to life', was more popular with others and evidently pro-British, both 'traits' that created differences between him and his brother who denied him the top naval posts, for which he was well qualified, purely out of jealousy. The Kaiser, his slightly awed guest decided, 'for all his striking uniforms and brusque manners . . . had undoubted charm'. When Prince Edward left, 'he expressed the hope that I had learned something of the German people from my stay, adding that, despite all the terrible things my country thought about them, he and they were really not so difficult to get along with'. Admitting that he was impressionable enough to believe the Kaiser, the Prince found him 'impatient, haughty, equally eager to please, to frighten, or to astonish; paradoxically stubborn-minded and weak-minded, and, above all, truly humourless. He did little in foreign affairs – or in anything else – that he did not shout from the housetops.'[26]

At fifty-four the Kaiser had mellowed a little with age, becoming less impulsive and less prone to making outrageous statements without thinking first. There were still no limits, however, to his knowledge of and eloquence on all important issues of the day, except for one – the suffragette movement. He found it incomprehensible that women should want the vote, and nobody could explain to him the difference between militant and non-militant suffragists, or why respectable married women with families should take suffrage just as seriously as 'disappointed spinsters'. To English and American women who visited Kiel for yachting in the last years of peace and told him their views, adding that they intended to bring the suffragette movement to Germany, he snorted that if they came to his empire to burn houses and horsewhip people the police certainly would not send them flowers and newspapers and let them go free two days afterwards.[27] The Empress and their daughter were forbidden to say one word on the subject, but Queen Mary, consort of the Kaiser's cousin King George V, would not be silenced. 'What could you possibly understand of politics?' he asked her patronizingly after one of his tirades against votes for women. 'Just as much as a man understands of furnishing a nursery and bringing up a family',[28] she replied calmly. As he had exasperated her by his recent visits to her children's nursery and proffered endless unsolicited suggestions to the nursemaids and governess, her riposte delighted everyone else present.

Issues of women's equality were not the Kaiser's only problem. At the same time he found it ironic that he, an older and hopefully wiser sovereign, was constantly confronted with the living spectre of a son and heir who enjoyed acting provocatively and associating with a group of fawning acolytes whose eyes were on the next reign. Those with long memories could be excused for drawing comparisons between 1913 and 1887. On his holidays abroad the presence of the Crown Princess did not stop her husband from flirting with other women, and he was quite unconcerned by his growing reputation as 'an international playboy'. Added to his eye for other ladies was his reputation for carrying on the family tradition by publicly irritating his father. It was probably through the influence of the Crown Prince's coterie that he became obsessed with the idea that his inheritance was under threat, and he telegraphed the chancellor to demand that his brother-in-law should not use the title of Duke of Brunswick till he had formally renounced the crown of Hanover for himself and his descendants. The Kaiser instructed the chancellor to tell his son firmly that the oath Brunswick had sworn on entering the German army was adequate.

As if this was not enough, war-hungry nationalists impatient with the Kaiser's restraint transferred their hopes to the Crown Prince, who resembled his father at a similar age – ambitious, impatient for glory if not to rule, over-sensitive to apparent slights and a prey to the influence of dubious favourites trying to promote their own interests. In Crown Prince Wilhelm's case, the man playing the role of the late Count Waldersee twenty-five years on was Baron Konstantin von Gebsattel, a retired general who bombarded the heir with calls for 'courage' in foreign policy, stricter controls on liberal and socialist newspapers, and the proclamation of a state of siege pending the introduction of repressive anti-Jewish laws. In November the Crown Prince forwarded the anti-Jewish bill to his father, who rejected Gebsattel's outburst as 'childish'; if Jews were forced to leave the German empire, he said, they would take their riches with them. While there was a case for controlling the scandalous, gossip-hungry papers under Jewish influence, mass expulsion of Jewry would force Germany to leave the ranks of the cultured nations. Perhaps he had at last seen the error of Stöcker's teachings, which had so influenced him as a young man. The tension between father and son was no secret, and Jules Cambon, the French ambassador, thought the Kaiser was jealous of his son's popularity with the Pan-Germans and the right. At a shoot the following March the foreign secretary, Theophilus von Jagow, begged

Prince Ratibor to pay close attention to his aim and not to kill the Kaiser, for the young one was 'much, much worse'.[29]

By the end of 1913 the German nation was bitterly divided. In November after civil unrest at Zabern, where the Alsatian population had been antagonized by insulting remarks from a young lieutenant of the local infantry regiment, the local commander ordered his troops to raid the offices of the local press. While the civilian commander of Alsace-Lorraine condemned their high-handed action, the Kaiser sided with the military authorities. When the affair was raised in the *Reichstag*, Bethmann-Hollweg loyally defended the army as servants of the Kaiser, though he told the latter in confidence that he thought the army commanders had seriously violated the law. While the Kaiser was determined to retain him in office, despite his unpopularity at Court, a motion of no confidence in the chancellor was passed by a majority of over 200 votes. Infuriated by calls for his resignation from a socialist deputy, who invoked the example of British constitutional custom, Bethmann-Hollweg rounded on the *Reichstag* and declared that the deputies wanted to infuse the army with revolutionary democracy, contrary to Prussian tradition where the army was an instrument of the imperial prerogative, dependent solely on the will of the supreme war lord.

Some feared a constitutional crisis in Germany similar to the army bills dispute that had brought Bismarck to power. Others gloomily anticipated revolution from the large, articulate and well-organized proletariat unsettled by rapid economic growth during the last thirty years. The chancellor was alarmed that a detachment of guards might descend on the *Reichstag* and send the deputies about their business, arrest dissidents and shut down the opposition newspapers. A coup in Berlin could unleash civil war and tempt the French across the border, using the plight of their people in Alsace as an excuse for a war of revenge. While the Kaiser was publicly contemptuous of what he called the parliamentary madhouse, he must have dreaded the latter possibility.

A group of staff officers had a more drastic solution. They believed that Germany's internal problems could be resolved by a victorious campaign against the French or the Russians; war would rally the population behind the Kaiser. While he shrank from risking the lives of his men for what he saw as a frivolous cause, he felt unable to argue with Moltke and his military secretariat. They pointed to the increasing strength of Russia's armies, France's decision to strengthen her army by introducing three years of military service and military 'intimacy' between France, Russia and England. Any continental war had to ensure the military participation of Germany's only ally, the multi-national Austro-Hungarian empire, at the right moment. Surrounded by those who demanded a 'preventive war', the Kaiser came to believe conflict in Europe was inevitable, if not desirable, and he was obsessed with taunts of cowardice, a charge levelled at him during the Transvaal crisis and again during the aftermath of Tangier and then Agadir.

Sometimes Wilhelm's outbursts astonished his guests. In November 1913 he entertained King Albert of the Belgians at Potsdam, and while showing him around Sans-Souci, suddenly remarked that 'the inevitable war' with France was close at hand. At dinner that evening the Kaiser and Moltke sought to find out how Belgium might react in the event of a Franco-German war. Refusing to commit himself, King Albert told him firmly that Belgium would remain neutral unless attacked. Nevertheless, he was so discomfited by what he had heard that afterwards he warned President Poincaré and the French government.

At the same time the Kaiser turned to Turkey searching for a counterbalance to what he saw as Russia's aggressive intentions on the Straits and in Asia Minor. A German military presence on the Bosphorus, he believed, would be welcomed by the British as a bulwark against Russian designs, as he suspected Russo-British tension over Persian affairs might dissolve the Anglo-Russian Entente and even coax Britain into the Triple Alliance. But he did not take into account that there was no such suspicion in Britain of Russia's intentions.

In March 1914 the Kaiser visited Vienna, meeting Emperor Franz Josef whom he found much aged, and Istvan Tisza, prime minister of Hungary. At Miramare he called on the Habsburg heir, Archduke Franz Ferdinand, and made the mistake of praising Tisza to him. Resenting Tisza's presence at Vienna, the Archduke maintained a stone-like taciturnity, saying so little that the Kaiser, a poor judge of such situations at the best of times, mistakenly thought both men were in agreement. The German embassy only discovered his *faux pas* later and had to arrange another hurried meeting between them to clear up misunderstandings.

Kaiser Wilhelm did not share his ministers' misgivings that the continued existence of the declining Austro-Hungarian empire was of vital importance to the German empire, as her only reliable ally. If Austria disintegrated, Germany would face a hostile Russia, France and possibly England. By 1914 the Habsburg empire was too weak to undertake military or diplomatic initiatives on her own, but the powers in Austria knew that German support could be taken for granted in any future war. For several months the Kaiser and Moltke, his chief of general staff, had encouraged Austria in any action she might wish to take against Serbia, having assured Count Berchtold, Austrian foreign minister, in September 1913, that a conflict in which the Germanic peoples would have to stave off a mighty impulse of Slavdom was inevitable. Moltke had no doubt that war was imminent, sensing that time was running out for the Triple Alliance, that the balance of power in Europe was moving and that Serbia and Russia should be dealt with before the Russian army was ready; and in May 1914 he told Hötzendorf of the Austrian general staff that every delay in war meant a lessening of their chances. When asked how long the coming joint campaign against Russia and France would last, Moltke said confidently that in six weeks of operations they would defeat France, or at least deal with her sufficiently to be able to turn their forces towards Russia in the east.

In the second week of June the Kaiser went to stay with Archduke Franz Ferdinand at Konopischt for what was intended as a private visit. Nevertheless, the subject of politics could not be avoided. When he ascended the throne, the Archduke told the Kaiser, he intended to make the dual monarchy of Austria-Hungary into a trialism, adding a southern-Slav bloc with its own parliament. What, he asked pointedly, would Germany's reaction be if the Austrian army was forced to discipline the Serbs and crush Slav terrorists? The Kaiser tried to evade the question, but the Archduke would not be brushed aside, and elicited from his reluctant guest a specific declaration that Germany never could nor should engage in a war for life and death on two fronts.[30]

Wilhelm left Austria on 16 June for a programme including visits to agricultural fairs, inspection of a wireless station, army manoeuvres and the annual Kiel regatta, where a courtesy squadron of British warships, including four battleships and three cruisers, was moored alongside the imperial high seas fleet. The British ambassador and many of his staff were there for four days of exchanges, yacht races, garden parties and dances. At Kiel Castle on 23 June Prince Henry and Princess Irene greeted the officers of the second battle squadron of the British fleet, under the command of Admiral Sir George Warrender. In the afternoon Prince Henry visited the British super-Dreadnought *King George V*, which he called 'the finest ship afloat'. On the following day Tirpitz arrived from Berlin in his battleship, hoisted his flag and invited the English officers to a champagne reception at which he described the development of the German navy to his guests. That afternoon the Kaiser sailed in the *Hohenzollern* through the Kiel Canal, now widened to take Dreadnought-class battleships, and formally declared it open. Airplanes and a zeppelin circled overhead, one airplane crashing into the sea, which rather upset the proceedings.

On 25 June the Kaiser was welcomed aboard *King George V*, wearing the uniform of an admiral of the British fleet, thus technically the senior Royal Navy officer present. Admiral Warrender served lunch in his private dining room, where they ate to the accompaniment of an orchestra playing works by German composers, and afterwards gave a speech hailing the spirit of good fellowship between British and German fleets. One disquieting incident disturbed proceedings. Sir Horace Rumbold, counsellor at the British embassy in Berlin, was invited aboard, and as he knew he would be meeting the Kaiser he wore a morning coat and top hat. The Kaiser decided Rumbold was wrongly dressed and pointed angrily at him, saying that one did not wear tall hats on board ship and if he saw it again he would personally 'smash it in'. Some observers were astonished at the Kaiser's display of temper; others took it as one of his jokes.

That same day the regatta began, and on the next day the Kaiser invited Warrender, the British ambassador Sir Edward Goschen, Prince Henry and Tirpitz to race with him aboard *Meteor*. Officers and sailors of the British squadron were fraternizing with the German officers and people of Kiel, with the German Admiralty offering hundreds of free railways passes for English sailors to visit Berlin and Hamburg every day. Yet there were disturbing undertones to the apparent goodwill on both sides. The Empress and her sons were not at Kiel, it was rumoured, because they hated England. Commander Müller, German naval attaché in England, was quietly warning German officers to be on their guard against the English, who were ready to strike; war was imminent, and the object of their visit was only to spy. Warrender offered Admiral Friedrich von Ingehol, commander-in-chief of the high seas fleet, and his officers complete freedom of all British ships except for the wireless room and the fire-control section of the conning towers. Ingehol tactfully declined, as he could not allow British officers reciprocal freedom of German ships.

On the afternoon of Sunday 28 June the Kaiser was racing in *Meteor* when Admiral Müller received an urgent telegram from the German consul in Sarajevo. He put to sea, caught up with the Kaiser's yacht and as the boats drew level he called out the grim news. On an official visit to the Bosnian capital that morning the Austrian heir, Archduke Franz Ferdinand, and his wife, Sophie, had been shot dead. Outwardly calm but inwardly horrified at the fate of two friends who had been his hosts only a fortnight earlier, as well as guests at Kiel the previous year, the Kaiser cancelled his race, returned to the *Hohenzollern* and to Potsdam the next morning, intending to go to the funeral at Vienna. He telegraphed his condolences to Emperor Franz Josef, but to his surprise he was asked not to attend. The German consul at Sarajevo reported a Serb plot to assassinate him as well, and Bethmann-Hollweg persuaded him to stay away. This was probably a ruse to keep him away from Vienna and thus prevent him from witnessing the inflexible Habsburg protocol which ensured that, even in death, the morganatically married heir could never be forgiven for having transgressed the dynastic code.

Meanwhile, events at Kiel were drawn to an orderly but swift conclusion. Flags were lowered to half-mast as functions were cancelled, and a final ceremony took place at which Warrender addressed sailors from both fleets on friendship between Britain and Germany, and finished by calling for three cheers for the German navy. A German admiral responded in kind, and they shook hands cordially. On the morning of 30 June the British squadron weighed anchor and sailed for home.

Kaiser Wilhelm never doubted who was responsible for the assassinations at Sarajevo. 'The Serbs must be disposed of, and very soon',[31] he wrote in the margin of a despatch from his ambassador in Vienna on 2 July. Not everybody in Berlin was united over how to deal with the crisis. While the foreign ministry wanted to restrain Austria-Hungary, to the general staff it was a perfect reason for war at a time when Germany was in better military shape for a lightning campaign than her potential adversaries. The navy was still unprepared, and nine weeks previously Tirpitz had told Admiral Müller that he needed at least another six to eight years. However, both men were disturbed by reports of a proposed Anglo-Russian convention for increased naval collaboration, and they favoured any policy to weaken Russia first.

The Kaiser sided with advocates of firm action against Serbia, even at the risk of a continental war. Count Szögyéni-Marich, Austro-Hungarian ambassador at Berlin, lunched with the Kaiser at Potsdam on 5 July, bringing a personal letter from Emperor Franz Josef which he handed him before the meal. It called the crime against his nephew a direct consequence of agitation carried out by Russian and Serbian Panslavists whose sole aim was to weaken the Triple Alliance and shatter the Austro-Hungarian empire. What, the letter asked, would be the Germany's policy if Austria decided to punish the 'centre of criminal agitation' in Belgrade?

While the Kaiser's instant reaction was one of sympathy with Emperor Franz Josef, because of the 'serious European complication', he could not answer before discussing the matter with Bethmann-Hollweg. Pressed after lunch by Szögyéni-Marich for an immediate answer, he said he was sure that Germany would give the utmost support to her ally Austria-Hungary. While prepared for hostile Russian reaction, he doubted the Tsar would fight to save Serbia. If war between Russia and Austria-Hungary was unavoidable, Germany would stand by Austria. Russia, he believed, was unprepared for conflict. Not all the central German figures were present, and there was no 'war council' as such. Tirpitz was on holiday, and the foreign secretary Jagow was on honeymoon. But after consulting several members of the foreign ministry and service departments, and General Falkenhayn, he was assured that the army was ready for any military emergency.

On 6 July the Kaiser told the industrialist Gustav Krupp von Bohlen that the Austrians intended to wipe out Serbia; Germany would support them even at the cost of war with Russia. That night he embarked on his annual three-week cruise on the *Hohenzollern*. His absence from Berlin saved his ministers from sudden switches of policy, which had often exasperated them in previous crises; Bethmann-Hollweg and Jagow could be selective in information they passed on to him, more so than if he was at Potsdam. Important messages were sent directly to him on board his yacht, and he did not see all the reports from Prince Lichnowsky, German ambassador in London. Wilhelm's comments during the cruise showed impatience with the Austrians for not bringing the crisis to a head sooner. Yet when he wondered whether to send the customary fraternal birthday message to King Peter of Serbia at such a time, Jagow advised him not to arouse suspicion by neglecting the normal courtesies and a telegram of greeting went to Belgrade on 11 July.

While the Kaiser was still at sea, the crisis gradually unfolded. By 18 July Bethmann-Hollweg and Jagow in Berlin were aware of Austria's intention to present Serbia with a 48-hour ultimatum on the evening of 23 July, and they knew the demands would be so draconian that the Serbs were unlikely to accept them. In his diary for 19 July, Admiral Müller wrote that the Kaiser, kept fully informed, was 'extremely excited' about the ultimatum. Diplomats in Berlin were confident that any war could be localized. The Kaiser doubted that Russia would back Serbia until reports of the reaction in St Petersburg, suggesting otherwise, reached him on the morning of 25 July. That evening the yacht set course for Kiel, 600 miles south, and within two days he was back at Potsdam. Müller noticed a certain coldness when Bethmann-Hollweg met him at the railway station at Wildpark. The chancellor, generals and ministers would have preferred the Kaiser to continue with his cruise.

On 25 July the passing of the first German warship and an order for the concentration of the German high seas fleet put Prince Louis of Battenberg in England on the alert. He cancelled all leave for his officers and ratings, kept his fleets concentrated and sent despatches to King George V and the foreign office in London to tell them what he had done. Prince Henry, who had been yachting at Cowes, visited King George, who advised him to return home as soon as possible as the news was bad. The King assured him that the English had no quarrel with any other European nations and hoped to remain neutral, but treaty obligations might still involve them in a European war. Not unduly alarmed, Henry and Irene went to Eastbourne where his sister Sophie, now Queen of the Hellenes, was staying before their return to Germany. On reaching Kiel two days later Henry wrote to the Kaiser, quoting King George's statement that he and his government would 'try all we can to keep out of this and shall remain neutral'. The Kaiser interpreted this as an official guarantee of English neutrality. When Tirpitz questioned its validity, the Kaiser told him sharply that he had the word of a King 'and that is enough for me'.[32] It was probably the most foolish miscalculation he ever made.

By now the drama was unfolding beyond their control. Already during the weekend, before the Kaiser's return, Moltke had drafted for the foreign ministry a message to be sent to Brussels, which justified a German march into Belgium in order to forestall an alleged invasion by the French. At the same time officials in the empire drew up emergency decrees providing for mobilization and internal security, which only needed the signatures of sovereign and chancellor to become effective. By the time the Kaiser was back, Austria had severed diplomatic relations with Serbia. Jagow warned the French ambassador that he could not support a British proposal to settle the dispute with Serbia at a conference in London as that would imply recognition of Austro-Hungarian, as well as Serbian, responsibility for tension in the Balkans. At the same hour, in the British Admiralty, the first sea lord was sending a signal to the commander-in-chief of the grand fleet ordering him to concentrate his battle squadrons at Scapa Flow. Jagow was still confident of British neutrality, but time was running out for those who shared the opinion of Kaiser and chancellor that Britain had to be kept out of a continental war if Germany was to emerge victorious from a short localized conflict.

Yet the Kaiser still seemed to be vacillating. Despite his words to Krupp a few weeks earlier, he seemed unconvinced that war was either necessary or inevitable. On the morning of 28 July he received a copy of the Serbian reply to the Austrian ultimatum. The Serbs had conceded almost everything, more than the Kaiser had expected, and he told Jagow that it was 'a great moral victory for Vienna'. There was now, he assumed, no reason for war; any remaining differences between the Serbs and Austrians should be settled by negotiations and military operations should be restricted to the temporary occupation of Belgrade. A telegram containing these proposals was not sent to the German ambassador for another twelve hours, and even then it was reworded in a way which seemed to be urging the Austrians on. That evening the Kaiser telegraphed Tsar Nicholas II, asking him for help 'in smoothing over difficulties that may still arise'. It crossed one from the Tsar asking the Kaiser to stop his allies from going too far. By the time it arrived, Austria-Hungary had already declared war on Serbia.

On the morning of 29 July Wilhelm's attitude seemed to be hardening towards war. His ambassador in St Petersburg was ordered to warn the Russian foreign minister that if Russia mobilized Germany would do likewise, and then it would be difficult to prevent the outbreak of conflict throughout Europe. For the next three days Kaiser and Tsar exchanged messages. Partial mobilization was also ordered in St Petersburg on 29 July, followed by general mobilization two days later. With this the Kaiser proclaimed a state of 'imminent war', and an ultimatum was drawn up requiring Russia to cease all military preparations. This was impossible, and on the evening of 1 August the German ambassador in St Petersburg delivered a declaration of war. Three hours later the Kaiser sent the Tsar a final message, stating that only immediate orders to begin demobilization and to prevent Russian troops from committing any act of trespass over German frontiers would 'avoid endless misery'. On this document the Tsar wrote 'Received after war declared'. At a family dinner on 30 July Wilhelm had tried to resist the advice of his brother Henry and most of his sons that should Russia mobilize on its German border he should issue a similar order to his own army. He still held a sentimental regard for his grandfather Kaiser Wilhelm I's deathbed words to maintain Germany's friendship with St Petersburg. On the following day the death blow was dealt to this sentiment with the news that Tsar Nicholas II had ordered Russian mobilization along the German border.

Now the Kaiser had to accept that war had broken out, he hoped it could be contained in extent and duration. It was essential that Britain should not fight, as British participation would spread the conflict to Africa and the Far East as well as impose a strain on Germany's maritime commerce. After the council Bethmann-Hollweg offered the British ambassador a neutrality agreement which guaranteed the territorial integrity of France and Belgium within Europe in any postwar territorial settlement, as long as Britain did not enter the conflict. This proposal reached the British foreign office on 30 July, and was taken as a sign that Germany was determined on war and intended to violate Belgian neutrality.

The Kaiser still believed that, like his chancellor, he 'understood the English'. His hopes were shattered on 30 July when he realized that Britain would probably enter the war on the side of Germany's enemies. Grey had informed Lichnowsky that London would not become involved unless the Austro-Hungarian-Russian-Serb war widened to include France and Germany, a declaration which the Kaiser called 'the worst and most scandalous piece of English pharisaism' he had ever seen.[33] King Edward VII, he remarked bitterly, was still stronger after his death than he, who was alive. However, the Kaiser was still eager to detect any faint sign of British neutrality. On 1 August, after signing the order for

obilization, he received a telegram from Lichnowsky holding
a hope, and also the possibility that Britain would guarantee
eutrality in a Russo-German war, as long as Germany did not
attack the West. Relieved, the Kaiser told Moltke that they now only
need wage war with Russia. When Moltke explained carefully that
military plans could not be improvised, the Kaiser snapped at Moltke
that his uncle would have answered him otherwise. German patrols were
already infiltrating Luxembourg, and the Kaiser ordered his principal
adjutant to send a signal halting all operations in the West, Moltke's
protests being to no avail. Shortly before midnight another telegram
from London came, affirming that there could be no pledge of
neutrality in the west.

By now the Kaiser had to admit that he could no longer influence
events. On Sunday 2 August an ultimatum was presented in Brussels
which sought free passage of German troops through Belgium. Germany
declared war on France on 3 August, and the first German units entered
Belgium in the small hours of the following day. The British ultimatum
was despatched to Germany that same afternoon. By midnight Britain
and Germany were at war.

Berliners swarmed excitedly to the palace and called for the Kaiser
who eventually appeared on the balcony. Dressed in uniform, looking
white and strained, he was cheered and saluted repeatedly. After a while
he raised his hands to call for silence, told them that he commended
them to God, and asked them to go into the churches and pray for help
for their soldiers. Henceforth, he added, 'I know no parties any more,
only Germans.'[34]

To his English colleague, the French ambassador Cambon commented
sadly that only three people in Berlin that night regretted the outbreak of
war – both of them, and the Kaiser. To the departing German
ambassador, King George V remarked ruefully that he did not believe the
Kaiser wanted war, but he was fearful of being thought a coward by his
people. Tsar Nicholas thought much the same, telling his sister Grand
Duchess Olga that Wilhelm 'was a bore and an exhibitionist, but he
would never start a war'.[35] More to the point, perhaps, had been the
words of King Edward VII in 1905 which predicted that the Kaiser would
unleash war not by his will but by his weakness, and five years later,
gloomily convinced that after his death his nephew would make war.
From her exile in Farnborough, Eugenie, former Empress of the French,
believed that the Kaiser was less responsible for the war than his generals
in spite of his sabre-rattling, but was powerless to check the course of
events throughout Europe; 'when the river reaches the waterfall no
earthly power can stop it'.[36]

'No German and, above all, no English pacifist, was filled with a profounder or more honest love of peace than was William II',[37] Bülow observed in retrospect. 'It was his own and our misfortune that his words and his gestures never coincided with his real attitude in the matter. When he boasted or even threatened people in words, it was often because he wanted to allay his own timidity.'

Charles Lowe, a former correspondent of *The Times* and an often fiercely critical observer of events around him, had little to say in defence of the Kaiser. While he admired the Germans as a race and, unlike many other Englishmen, felt that certain chauvinistic elements in the London press had much to answer for in the build-up to hostilities in 1914, he unequivocally condemned the man who was 'the chief creator of the war-spirit which he found it impossible to exorcise or resist, and was thus, so to say, devoured by his own offspring. For, at the last moment, when shrinking from the results of his own creative handiwork, he allowed the sword, in his own phrase, to be "thrust into his hand" – which was just as much as if he had drawn it of his own accord – thus proving himself to be a weak-willed and criminal ruler, the most nefarious of his kind who ever sat upon a throne.'[38]

Those who exonerated Kaiser Wilhelm II from responsibility for actually starting the war were on balance correct. Yet none of them claimed – or could ever claim with conviction – that few if any individual persons in Europe bore a greater responsibility for the ensuing four years of carnage.

## CHAPTER SEVEN

# The Kaiser at War

During the first months of the First World War Kaiser Wilhelm displayed great confidence in front of his troops, assuring them they would be home before the leaves had fallen from the trees. Like most of his statesmen and commanders he thought the war would be brief. The only countries that had made progress and become great, he said, were warring nations; 'those which have not been ambitious and gone to war have amounted to nothing'.[1] One week after the declaration of hostilities he was anticipating victory on the Western Front, after which he said he would travel to eastern Prussia or Silesia for the final phases of the Russian campaign. The naval leaders had not prepared any strategic plan, and they would be required to repel a British attack, or help to impose a settlement on England if she was to continue the war after Germany gained decisive land victories in the west and east.

According to Prussian tradition the sovereign normally left his capital in time of war so he could establish his field headquarters close to the front of battle. This had been the practice of Kaiser Wilhelm I, and the army assumed that his grandson would do likewise. However, the situation in 1914 was very different from that in Bismarck's day. The sovereign now had to retain responsible authorities in the capital, oversee political and diplomatic problems, maintain links with their ally Austria, and keep in touch with spokesmen of neutral governments. It was in contrast to the role of his brother Henry, commander-in-chief of the Baltic station in the German navy. Admittedly, his was largely a nominal post with fighting at sea left to other commanders and officers, yet at least he was closer to the centre of action, though as the most Anglophile of the Hohenzollerns he was the one who most dreaded taking up arms against his relatives and in-laws in England.

All the Kaiser's sons saw active service in the war, four of them on the Western Front. Crown Prince Wilhelm commanded the fifth army, Eitel Friedrich the 1st foot guards regiment, August Wilhelm was a front-line staff officer and Oskar commanded the Liegnitz King's grenadiers. The youngest, Joachim, a cavalry officer, was wounded while fighting in the battle in the Masurian Lake District of East Prussia. Adalbert had followed his uncle Henry and joined the navy, serving on board ship.

During the first week of August, two of the princes had married, Oskar (morganatically) to Countess Ina Bassewitz, who was created Countess of Ruppin, and Adalbert to Princess Adelaide of Saxe-Meiningen. Their cousins had also rallied to the cause of the fatherland, and within two months war claimed the first family casualty when Prince Max of Hesse, son of the Kaiser's youngest sister Margrethe, died of wounds sustained in action with the Prussian 1st life hussars.

On 17 August the Kaiser set up his headquarters at Coblenz, installed in the official residence of the Lord-Lieutenant of the Rhineland. Meanwhile, Bethmann-Hollweg, Tirpitz, members of the civil, military and naval administrations and general staff were accommodated within the city. Within a week good news came from the west – a French thrust into Lorraine was repulsed, Nancy was threatened and the German line was advancing systematically towards Brussels, Namur and Charleroi, within sight of Mons where the army planned to trap the British expeditionary force. Such apparent successes were in marked contrast to news from the east, where the sheer number of Russian troops was forcing General Prittwitz's army to contemplate withdrawal, thus abandoning large sections of East Prussia to the Russians.

Those closest to the Kaiser, family and personal suite alike, were alarmed by his sudden changes in mood. The Empress believed that events leading up to the outbreak of war had suddenly aged him, and insisted that he should be allowed plenty of rest, with his sleep uninterrupted unless there was urgent news. She and his adjutant, General Hans von Plessen, told his suite that their first duty was to keep him in good spirits, protected from bad news and hardship as much as possible. Defeats and reverses were not mentioned to him, and he was only shown positive battle reports or given news of victories.

A few days after establishing himself at Coblenz he went for a walk in the grounds with two senior officers. Stopping to rest, he sat on a bench which had room for two people but not three. When the officers promptly fetched another one, he turned to them and asked crossly if he was already such a figure of contempt that nobody wanted to sit next to him.[2] Next day he was elated by reports of action from Lorraine, and the following week he told recruits at Coblenz that final victory in the West was within their grasp.

Wilhelm would have been flattered to know that he had at least one fervent admirer. Within three weeks of the outbreak of war a Prussian officer, thought to be Count Hans von Pfeil, on a propaganda mission in Brazil wrote in ringing terms to a friend that he had misunderstood his sovereign and thought him a waverer. Now, he realized, he was 'a Jupiter, standing on the Olympus of his iron-studded might, the lightning bolts in his grasp. At this moment he is God and master of the world.'[3] This fanatical endorsement was not widely shared. For all his posturing and grasp of duties on military manoeuvres Germany's imperial warlord made an unimpressive commander. Unable to apply his mind to detail, his personality was hopelessly mercurial, he lacked his father's understanding of strategic operations and worst of all he was a poor judge of character. It was fortunate that he had the more experienced Moltke to make crucial decisions for him. On 22 August Moltke summoned General Ludendorff, who had worked with him on the general staff from 1908 to 1912 and recently captured the citadel of Liège, to take over as chief of staff in the eighth army on the Eastern Front. Meanwhile, General Paul von Hindenburg, aged sixty-six, a veteran of Bismarck's wars, was appointed to succeed Prittwitz. Within four days of his arrival in East Prussia a Russian army led by General Samsonov was soundly defeated; 110,000 Russian soldiers were killed and 90,000 taken prisoner.

The Kaiser's erratic temperament amazed his high command, who soon came to share the doubts concerning his sanity expressed by previous chancellors. In the first flush of victory he proposed that Russian prisoners of war should be driven on to a barren section of land in the Baltic and kept there to die of thirst and hunger, until the generals pointed out that this would be genocide.[4] He seemed to take pleasure in repeating stories of 6-foot high piles of dead bodies on the battlefield, and of one of his sergeant-majors who killed twenty-seven Frenchmen with forty-five shots. The next time they saw him, he might be walking round the battlefield with tears in his eyes as he covered the faces of those who had fallen. Although victory was partly due to the work of the senior staff officer under Prittwitz, Colonel Max Hoffmann, the main credit was accorded to the generals appointed by Moltke at a crucial time. At Hindenburg's request the battle was named Tannenberg, after the village in which he had established his headquarters and also in order to avenge a Polish victory over Germany on the same battlefield in 1422.

Soon afterwards the Kaiser left Coblenz and took up residence in the German legation, Luxembourg. Everyone was waiting for good news from the west, anticipating the defeat of France, until Moltke prudently reminded them that the French had merely been driven back. As his name was a byword for caution, nobody took him too seriously. Carried away on a tide of euphoria, the Kaiser seemed all but convinced that the lightning campaign would soon be over; if it was not to be a repetition of 1866 and another six weeks' war, it would surely not last much longer. Sharing his optimism, Bethmann-Hollweg began work on a memorandum of Germany's war aims, and a proclamation for the Kaiser to deliver to his subjects once Joffre, French Commander-in-Chief, had sued for an armistice. It would explain that victory had decided the issues between France and Germany, but it would still be necessary for Germany's armies to occupy northern France as long as her allies, particularly England, continued the war. This rather premature document was ready for the imperial signature on Sunday 6 September.

On 6 September the Kaiser was visiting Metz, where he watched artillery firing on an enemy position. In the evening he ordered preparations for a visit the next day to Châlons-sur-Marne, over a hundred miles away, where he would cross the Marne and visit the guards whom he had last seen four weeks earlier in action. Early the following morning he and his escort made their way in a convoy of several cars. Approaching Châlons they heard enemy fire, and a colonel was sent ahead to reconnoitre. He returned ninety minutes later with the unwelcome news that they wanted His Majesty to withdraw, otherwise they ran the risk of a cavalry patrol breaking through a quiet sector of the line and capturing him. Grimly they returned to Luxembourg.

That same day the seeds of disintegration of the Schlieffen Plan were sowed. Named after General Count Alfred von Schlieffen, chief of the general staff from 1891 to 1905, this had envisaged a war for Germany on two fronts: a lightning blow against France, culminating in a pincer movement engulfing Paris by one army attacking it from the north and another from the east, thus precipitating French collapse, and then advancing eastwards to inflict similar defeat on Russia. The invading armies had been advancing on France for three weeks under a fierce late summer sun in blistering heat, and found their task tougher than expected. Meanwhile, Moltke was giving way under the strain; a combination of panic, conscience, kidney disease and heart problems reduced him to a bundle of nerves. He instructed Lieutenant-Colonel Hentsch, his head of intelligence, to take over the responsibility of visiting each army headquarters in France. If disaster or defeat appeared imminent, he must order a general retreat to defensive positions along the River Aisne. Such a move would be a tacit admission that Germany ruled out any prospect of an early peace, and the supreme war lord himself was not consulted. On 9 September Hentsch realized that the Second Army was pulling back, and ordered the others to retreat.

Alarmed by this setback, and concerned at the state of Moltke's health, the Kaiser ordered him to hand over the functions of chief of the general staff to Falkenhayn, minister of war. The appointment was kept secret for another seven weeks as it was agreed that the people of Germany, as well as her enemies, should not know anything of the demoralized mood at headquarters. The Kaiser chose Falkenhayn personally against the advice of some of his circle, hoping his appointment would allow him more influence over the course of events. The new chief moved his headquarters to Mézières at the end of September, and the Kaiser and his suite followed him. A local industrialist's home at Charleville was commandeered for his use and he stayed there regularly over the next thirteen months, until he was persuaded that his presence made the building too obvious a target for enemy planes and requested to leave.

Falkenhayn soon made it clear that he did not intend to encourage the Kaiser to come south of the river and see for himself day-to-day conduct of battles in Flanders and northern France. By early November the Kaiser was complaining peevishly to Max of Baden that if people in Germany thought he was the supreme commander, they were mistaken. 'The General Staff tells me nothing and never asks my advice. I drink tea, saw wood, go for walks, which pleases the gentlemen.'[5] They found his capricious behaviour difficult to cope with, and it was more convenient for them if he absented himself from Charleville, concentrating his energy on visits to past battlefields like nearby Sedan, or sitting at his dinner table talking endlessly and playing cards. He saw little actual fighting, but his entourage found that the best cure for his restlessness was to keep him moving around. Discouraged from doing any work at headquarters, he soon sank into bored and nervous isolation, sometimes depressed, sometimes stridently over-confident. In one such mood, in December 1914, he insisted he would make peace with France and Russia, but not with Britain until she was brought to her knees; 'only amidst the ruins of London will I forgive Georgy'.[6] His hatred of Britain was encouraged by the Empress. In October 1915 King Alfonso of Spain, a neutral nation, appealed to her to intervene on behalf of Edith Cavell, an English nurse sentenced to death by German court-martial for helping enemy soldiers to escape. Dona refused on the grounds that women who behaved like men must be punished like men.

By the spring of 1915 it was evident that there would be no rapid victory. The Kaiser, chancellor and representatives of the foreign ministry had to decide whether to continue war on both eastern and Western Fronts, or to seek separate peace with Russia. A reluctant *Reichstag* had been asked to vote generous funds for a 'twentieth-century Trafalgar'. Should they risk everything on letting the fleet take on the British? How much German naval support should there be for Austria-Hungary and their new ally Turkey, whose warships under German command had been bombarding Russian bases in the Black Sea at the end of October?

The Kaiser hoped that his armies in the west would advance back to the Marne and beyond. Irrespective of Austrian and Turkish opinion, he favoured an early separate peace with Russia. Clinging persistently to the authority of Tsar Nicholas II as the arbiter of the Russian empire at war and peace, he asked his cousin Ernest, Grand Duke of Hesse, to establish contact with his sister Alexandra, Empress of Russia, and try to persuade the Tsar to discuss an end to hostilities. He also attempted to exploit the dynastic links of the Bavarian and Belgian royal houses in order to seek peace with King Albert of the Belgians, whose consort, Queen Elizabeth, was a Wittelsbach.

At the same time the Kaiser firmly opposed any Anglo-German engagement at sea, partly through uncertainty of military and naval superiority against the English and Russians, partly as sentimental and dynastic considerations still prevailed. While he still regarded the republican French as a race beneath him, fellow empires and happier days in a more peaceful age with cousins 'Georgie' and 'Nicky' still counted for much. Moreover, he wanted the war ended on acceptable terms without delay. Heavy casualty lists and sustained blockades directed against the people of the German empire were to be avoided at all costs; and weighty matters such as war and peace were still to be determined by Emperors and Kings. Wilhelm had no time for offers of mediation from Woodrow Wilson, President of the United States, and insisted to Colonel House, a special adviser who came on two missions to Europe in order to halt the war, that he and his cousins George and Nicholas would make peace when the time had come. 'Mere democracies' such as France and the United States could never participate in a peace conference, because war was 'a royal sport, to be indulged in by hereditary monarchs and concluded at their will'.[7] He could not appreciate that they no longer lived in the nineteenth century, when peace was kept or restored merely by a few friendly words between the cousins who reigned over and (in theory if not in practice) ruled much of Europe. 'He really believes in a tacit understanding between the monarchs to spare one another,' said Tirpitz, 'a quaint sort of notion!'[8] Years later his nephew Prince Sigismund, the last surviving son of Henry and Irene, admitted with hindsight that the Kaiser was out of touch. Family relationships and friendship between European monarchs proved useless in the search for peace. 'The secret groups who pulled the strings of global politics were so powerful that familial influences were quite incapable of stopping them, however hard they tried.'[9]

While no other contemporary sovereign shared his outdated and superficial view, other constitutional monarchs were prepared to make positive efforts in the cause of peace. Shortly before Christmas 1914 the Kaiser's friend Albert Ballin, managing director of the Hamburg-American steamship company, had privately informed him of an offer from King Christian X of Denmark, a neutral power sympathetic to Britain and her allies, who wanted to send the Danish shipping magnate Hans Niels Andersen on a mission to England and Russia as a preliminary to a mediated peace. If the Kaiser and his chancellor were in no mood to contact London, the Kaiser was willing to respond to peace overtures from Petrograd, as St Petersburg had been renamed early in September as a sop to anti-German feelings. When Andersen visited the Russian capital in March 1915 he found Tsar Nicholas cautious but interested in peace talks. On visiting Berlin two weeks later, Andersen first met the chancellor and then reported to the Kaiser. The latter, still setting much store by his old friendship with Tsar Nicholas, appreciated King Christian's intentions. In April the King suggested that a Russian emissary should come to Denmark to negotiate with a German representative, but this coincided with action at Gallipoli, which the British and Russians believed made victory more likely and the prospect of securing Constantinople virtually guaranteed that Russia would stay in the war. Not until August did the Tsar break a long period of silence by rejecting the offer.

As the war dragged on, the Kaiser was faced with a mounting threat to his authority. In peacetime he had seen himself as the central and supreme commander of the German navy, the arbiter of ship construction, of training schedules, of cadet admissions and of officer promotion. In war time he assumed that such responsibilities would remain in his hands. Tirpitz had nurtured this illusion, partly to keep out rivals and partly as he assumed that in war the Kaiser would gladly leave naval matters to him. Now Wilhelm listened less to Tirpitz than to his brother Henry and to his third son Adalbert, a lieutenant-commander serving aboard one of the newer battleships, believing that Tirpitz was increasingly deskbound and out of touch with naval matters.

Yet differences between both men went deeper. The Kaiser shrank from risking the main body of the German fleet in a premature naval battle; sovereign and chancellor disagreed with the principle of U-boat attacks on merchant vessels; and both wanted to restrain Zeppelin naval attacks on English cities, especially London. As ever the Kaiser's inconsistency was the despair of those around him. One moment he permitted cruiser raids on the English coast, then changed his mind, then authorized naval Zeppelins to raid English coastal towns in January 1915, then forbade attacks on London for another two months. At least he was consistent in his order that raids should be limited to the docks and industrial targets, opposed as he was to 'terror' bombing. In frustration Tirpitz offered his resignation as state secretary of the navy office in June 1915 and again eleven weeks later. Each time it was rejected by the Kaiser, who still asserted that he himself had created and trained the fleet, and how he intended to use it was exclusively the supreme commander's business. Everybody else, he said, would 'have to remain silent on this matter and obey'.[10]

Inevitably, there was mutual suspicion between the Kaiser and some of his senior advisers. To Tirpitz, Falkenhayn and Bethmann-Hollweg were 'the Hydra', and he was more an admirer of Hindenburg. In the spring of 1915 Tirpitz seriously considered trying to persuade the Kaiser to dismiss Falkenhayn and Bethmann-Hollweg, appoint Hindenburg to the joint responsibilities of chancellor and chief of the general staff, and to temporarily withdraw himself or retire on 'sick leave' for a couple of months, with the Crown Prince as Regent. Such a plan would need the support of the medical officers at Charleville, as well as the active support of the Crown Prince and Empress. The latter was increasingly concerned about her husband's volatile temperament and favoured his return to Germany from field headquarters in the interests of his health. She was more in tune with the general mood in Germany, where people looked for leadership more to Tirpitz and Hindenburg than to Falkenhayn and Bethmann-Hollweg.

While the Crown Prince had the utmost respect for Hindenburg and Ludendorff, and agreed that his father needed some measure of relief from the front, he kept his distance from Tirpitz. The latter was favourably impressed by the Crown Prince and had confidence in him; 'he has never learned how to work, but he has good judgment, lets people work, is not vain and will not carry on a rule of the cabinet. I also believe that he has a knowledge of human nature. But the Kaiser does not give him a chance.'[11] Another idea Tirpitz briefly canvassed, in league with Colonel Max Bauer, a chief of operations at supreme command, was to have the Kaiser declared incompetent by his doctors, but this drastic act of disloyalty found little support. The doctors refused to have anything to do with it, while the Kaiser suspected something of the kind, and from this time relations between the men cooled considerably. Nevertheless, Tirpitz soon realized that a gradual process of undermining the Kaiser's authority and simply not consulting him would be just as effective.

The Crown Prince would probably have been glad to assume the regency if asked. Father and son had been as one in the first weeks of war, and in August the Kaiser had conferred the Iron Cross II and I Class on him for leading his men to victory at the Battle of Longwy, but within a few months this harmony had disappeared. Wilhelm was jealous of his son's popularity, while the Crown Prince openly criticized the clique surrounding his father, calling them 'all weaklings without backbone, always striving to save the Kaiser from everything unpleasant and from difficult decisions. Believe me, I know my father very well. He shies away from every serious argument.'[12] He, the Crown Prince, only wanted to talk with people who told him the truth. 'But my father doesn't ever do that, but cuts off every discussion. A conversation with him consists of his doing all the talking while the other person listens.'[13]

In December 1915 Tirpitz formally requested the Kaiser to appoint him supreme commander of the fleet, but was turned down. For the next two months Tirpitz repeatedly asked him to allow unrestricted submarine warfare in order to bring England to submission. Mindful of the effect on American opinion that U-boat activity would surely have, Bethmann-Hollweg counselled caution. The Kaiser seemed indecisive, telling his admirals that if he was the captain of a U-boat he would never torpedo a ship if he knew women and children were aboard. Within a week he had been persuaded to let the attacks begin. One week later he allowed his chancellor to persuade him to change his mind in deference to American opinion, ordering that only 'armed merchantmen' could be attacked. At this Tirpitz submitted his resignation a third time, and it was accepted. While the Crown Prince called his departure from office 'a national disaster', the appointment of Admiral von Capelle promised a smoother working relationship between the Kaiser and chancellor.

Throughout most of 1915 Germany was on the defensive in the west, standing against British and French attacks, but making little progress in any sector compared with the steady advance in the east. For part of the year the Kaiser made his headquarters at the castle of Pless, Upper Silesia, near the Austrian frontier. Falkenhayn believed that the road to victory lay in defeating France and depriving England of her hold on the continent. Shortly before Christmas he visited the Kaiser at Potsdam and suggested that a concentrated assault on Verdun would 'bleed the forces of France to death', as reasons of national sentiment would lead the French general staff to deploy all their forces rather than lose a historic citadel on the road to Paris. The Kaiser accepted his reasoning and on 21 February 1916 the German fifth army, nominally commanded by the Crown Prince, began bombarding French positions on the hills north-east of Verdun. Three days later the Kaiser moved his headquarters back to Charleville, to await news of a German breakthrough at Verdun, 50 miles away. No such news arrived; the battle lasted some forty-three weeks, with heavy casualties on both sides. In the end, Germany lost one-third of a million soldiers. Long before the end the Kaiser had almost conceded defeat, complained that Falkenhayn told him nothing, and ruefully said that if he was of so little use he might as well go back and live in Germany.[14]

In naval affairs too, his word counted for little. Admiral Capelle consulted him, but generally only as a formality. The naval staff and commander-in-chief of the High Seas Fleet, Admiral Scheer, evolved a strategy that turned an intended raid on the English coast into the naval action off Jutland, known by Germans as the Battle of the Skagerrak. The Kaiser was informed of this, the first and last action between rival Dreadnoughts, as he was returning from the Eastern Front. At breakfast on 2 June 1916 he was told that his admirals were claiming a tactical victory in the North Sea, and that his fleet was anchored safely in the harbour at Wilhelmshaven. In fact the forty-four Dreadnoughts were only in action against each other for twenty minutes on the evening of 31 May, and instead of hurrying to see his fleet, the Kaiser went to his farm at Cadinen in East Prussia. Admiral Müller concluded that his thoughts were 'no longer with this war'.

Not until the following week did he go to the coast to inspect the damaged ships in pouring rain and assure the flagship crew that the spell of Trafalgar was broken. The battle had been indecisive, with both sides claiming victory. Müller knew that the German fleet was not powerful enough to inflict decisive losses on the British Royal Navy, and there was no chance of any naval action forcing England to make peace. The Kaiser had little choice but to accept his decision. With reluctance he held out against the more warlike members of his circle who still argued that the only way to humble the British was by giving the U-boat captains a free hand. Unrestricted submarine action, he feared, would precipitate the entry of the United States into war against Germany. Even if it did not, it might prevent grain from being shipped to neutral ports in Europe on which Germany relied for her food supply.

By the summer of 1916 there was discontent in Berlin over rising food prices, the fleet had yet to win the decisive victory so eagerly predicted, and worst of all growing casualty lists from Verdun proved that the mighty German army was invincible no longer. Twentieth-century warfare was a very different animal from the short decisive campaigns of Bismarck's day. Though depressed by the course of events, the Kaiser was kept shielded from the full force of public opinion, and given selected digests from censored newspapers to read. He spent little time in Berlin, and underestimated the strength of feeling against Bethmann-Hollweg, who shared his opposition to an unrestricted U-boat campaign. At the same time he was unaware of the popularity of Hindenburg and Ludendorff, neither of whom had his unqualified approval. He thought the elderly Hindenburg lacked initiative, distrusted his imperturbability and mistook his phlegmatic iron nerve for limited comprehension. Ludendorff he considered a dubious character, fired by personal ambition, and he resented the general's brusque, ungracious manner, which contrasted sharply with that of the sycophantic, fawning aristocrats at Court. The Kaiser's favourite was August von Mackensen, a commander on the Eastern Front, and he still had confidence in Falkenhayn. Hindenburg and Ludendorff opposed his general strategy, Bethmann-Hollweg resented his attempts to tighten censorship, and Austrian representatives blamed his concentration on Verdun for encouraging Russia to launch powerful attacks in the East.

In July 1916 an Anglo-French offensive on the Somme led Falkenhayn to divert men and supplies from the Verdun sector, thus discrediting his strategy further. The final factor in his fall was when Russian victories in Galicia tempted Roumania to enter the war on the side of the Entente powers, on 27 August. For a while the risk of Roumanian and Russian troops coming through the Carpathian passes and reaching Hungary seemed apparent, and for the first time the Kaiser was heard to remark pessimistically to himself that the war was lost. There were still odd flashes of his old bombast, and one day he remarked with a mood of resignation tinged with defiance: 'Here I am nearly sixty years of age, and must rebuild the whole of Europe!'[15]

The Kaiser's military secretariat proposed he should dismiss Falkenhayn and appoint Hindenburg instead, similar advice to that which Bethmann-Hollweg had recently suggested. The Empress agreed with them, the Kaiser gave way and a phone call to Brest-Litovsk on the afternoon of 28 August asked Hindenburg and Ludendorff to set out for Pless at once. Hearing that his rivals were being asked for their advice, Falkenhayn immediately offered his resignation. The next day Hindenburg and Ludendorff were told they would be chief and deputy chief of the general staff respectively. Not prepared to be a humble deputy, Ludendorff secured for himself the imposing new title of first quartermaster general. Four years earlier he had told his then superior, Moltke, that the easiest way to deal with the Kaiser in case of war was to ask him nothing – an accurate indication of the policy he intended to follow.

With their inferior artillery and munitions the Roumanians, no match for Germany troops, were soon driven back; in December 1916 Mackensen entered Bucharest, and by Christmas the country was under German occupation. But from the Western Front there was no good news. Hindenburg and Ludendorff were horrified by the desolation around Verdun and the Somme, and saw that such battles exhausted the troops. Ludendorff proposed a defensive policy in the west until shortages of men and equipment were made good, after which a decisive thrust could be made towards Paris.

By now the military command made it plain that they merely tolerated the imperial warlord's presence, seeing him as little more than a figurehead. Not consulted over the general strategic plan, Wilhelm spent much of the autumn and winter of 1916 at Pless, making journeys to Potsdam and also to Vienna to pay respects to the memory of his venerable ally, Emperor Franz Josef, who passed away on 21 November 1916, aged eighty-six. Kaiser Wilhelm joined his successor, the 29-year-old Emperor Karl, in prayer at the funeral bier, but did not stay for the obsequies two days later 'for security reasons'.

While the Kaiser took little part in purely military discussions he remained the final political authority. One matter on which he was consulted was the chancellor's desire to discuss peace once Bucharest had fallen to Mackensen's army. The Kaiser was interested in any chance of a general settlement, as long as the German proposal came from a position of strength and not weakness. On 12 December the chancellor told the *Reichstag* that Germany was prepared to discuss an end to hostilities in one of the neutral countries. Without giving detailed terms, Bethmann-Hollweg's speech mentioned reparation and a need for military and economic guarantees; he claimed the German front line was indestructible, and warned that Germany had it in her power to use submarines in order to starve a persistent enemy into surrender. A bellicose speech by the Kaiser to troops parading at Mulhouse a few days later was given wide publicity, and there was no favourable response by the Entente powers. The Germans rejected President Wilson's subsequent offer of soundings towards a mediated peace; the Kaiser told his suite that he was amazed at the Entente's lack of enthusiasm towards his chancellor's speech, and Germany would thus have to extend her war aims against France and Belgium. Early in January 1917 he told them that the coast of Flanders must belong to Germany, and King Albert could not be allowed to return to Belgium.

The Entente's lukewarm reaction led to calls in Germany for an intensification of the U-boat campaign. While the Kaiser had said privately that if he was the captain of a submarine he would never torpedo a ship if he knew that women and children were on board, his opposition to unrestricted submarine warfare gradually became less resolute and nobody else backed his chancellor, who still counselled restraint. Naval and military leaders appealed again to the Kaiser, and at a Crown Council at Pless on 9 January 1917 the supreme command assured him that submarine warfare would force the enemy to sue for peace before American aid could have any impact in Europe. When the chancellor told him he could not ask his sovereign to reject the unanimous recommendations of his military advisers, the issue was decided. Still fearing the consequences, the Kaiser reluctantly gave his assent. It was announced that unrestricted submarine warfare would begin on 1 February, and two days later the United States broke off diplomatic relations. On 6 April, after American merchant vessels had been sunk by German submarines, Congress in Washington passed a joint resolution declaring war on Germany, and within three months the Kaiser was told that the first American troops had landed in France.

Also in the first week of April the Kaiser and Empress met Emperor Karl and Empress Zita of Austria-Hungary at Homburg. The first time that all four had come face to face, they gathered at the request of Karl who intended to discuss his and his wife's contacts with the Entente through an intermediary (Empress Zita's brother Prince Sixtus of Bourbon-Parma, whose name had to be kept secret for the time being). If they had a friend in Germany, Zita later recalled, it was the German Emperor, but he was 'completely under the thumb of his generals', a dreamer who still believed in final victory, and because of that 'he handed over everything to Hindenburg and Ludendorff'. She found him a charming and attentive host, and when she feared she was taking up too much of his time as he must have more important things to do, he replied resignedly that he had plenty of time because of the war. There were no civil problems any longer and, 'as for the military side, my generals look after that and report to me every night what has happened!'.[16]

The Kaiser's suite believed that Bethmann-Hollweg would soon resign or be dismissed. As yet there was no obvious successor. Hindenburg said he did not yet feel able to face the *Reichstag*, and the Kaiser received coldly any suggestion that Tirpitz might be appointed, or even the long-disgraced Bülow be recalled, even though he was the choice of the supreme command and the Empress. Not yet ready to resign, the chancellor told a colleague that he still hoped to act as a brake on some of the more irresponsible policies the military command wished to impose on their sovereign. As the third winter of war was having a serious effect on the nation's morale, with soaring prices and food rationing, people should be promised a share in government of the German empire as some recompense for the hardship they had suffered when peace came. The Kaiser reluctantly agreed to a proposal made by Friedrich von Löbell, Prussian minister of the interior, that at some unspecified time after the war a more democratic regime would be introduced in Prussia. He did not want any sudden alteration of the constitution, fearing it might lead to democratization in the Prussian officer corps and he believed that an army without aristocratic officers had been the ruin of France.[17]

It was also his profound conviction that a parliamentary regime had proved 'bankrupt' in Britain and would be impracticable for Germany because of the large number of parties in the *Reichstag*. Nevertheless, a sense of urgency was added by news of the Russian Revolution and its effect on public opinion; the chancellor persuaded his sovereign to give a specific assurance that all Prussians would be granted equal franchise rights in elections to the lower house, and that the composition of the upper chamber would be reformed in a more democratic fashion when war was over. On Easter Sunday 1917 a decree was published in his name promising postwar franchise reform to bring democracy to Prussia and complete revision of the empire's constitutional structure. From Hesse the Kaiser's cousin Grand Duke Ernest telephoned him personally to assure him of the joy throughout Darmstadt at this message. Yet the sovereign's suite were distinctly hostile, as were Hindenburg and Ludendorff, who thought that such talk during a critical juncture of the war would demoralize the troops.

By summer they were openly hostile to the chancellor, especially when they were convinced that he favoured a negotiated and, to them, 'weak' peace. At the end of June the chancellor discussed an end to hostilities with the papal nuncio, Monsignor Eugenio Pacelli, later Pope Pius XII. The Kaiser received the nuncio after the chancellor had reported to him on the Church's attitude towards a general peace settlement. At the same time both commanders disapproved of the way the chancellor was handling a peace initiative in the *Reichstag*, and encouraged by the support of the increasingly bellicose Crown Prince and the English-hating Empress, they presented the Kaiser with an ultimatum; he could choose between Bethmann-Hollweg or them. To strengthen their position, Ludendorff advised his supporters in the *Reichstag* beforehand. The Kaiser privately complained that never before had Prussian generals resorted to such blackmail, but he was powerless to resist.

The chancellor resigned on 13 July, and the Kaiser showed little interest in selecting a successor. It was symptomatic of his low regard for civilian authorities; 'politicians hold their tongues in war-time, until strategists permit them to speak!'.[18] Initially, the Bavarian prime minister Count Georg von Hertling was proposed, but he declined on grounds of age, seventy-three. The choice eventually fell on Georg Michaelis, controller of food supplies for Prussia. The generals approved of him, sure that he would prove less contrary than his predecessor. Unambitious and easy-going, he lasted barely four months. Soon after he took office, in the first week of August, a political demonstration by the crew of the battleship *Prinzregent Luitpold* at Wilhelmshaven was regarded by the authorities as an act of mutiny and he failed to take firm measures against the socialist agitators responsible. A poor debater in the *Reichstag*, he soon lost heart and resigned with relief on 1 November, to be replaced by Hertling.

The Kaiser was now spending less and less time on German soil. As if to distract him from taking too much interest in any differences between civil and military authority, Hindenburg and Ludendorff encouraged him to travel around Europe, boosting the morale of his troops as well as of Germany's allies, inspecting regiments and visiting other rulers, including King Ferdinand of Bulgaria, and the Sultan. In the late autumn of 1917 a successful joint Austro-German offensive on the River Isonzo, leading to Italian disaster at Caporetto, brought the Kaiser hurrying to the Southern Front. In November he travelled to Trieste to meet Emperor Karl and Empress Zita again. Both were increasingly anxious for an early end to the war, but Kaiser Wilhelm's mood of elation made their hopes of a speedy negotiated peace appear defeatist and Charles thought better than to raise such a contentious matter.

By this time the Kaiser had recovered his spirits, having sunk into a mood of depression after the resignation of Bethmann-Hollweg. For the rest of the year, those around him thought, he seemed only to remember victories and successes. Such reverses as the loss of five Zeppelins in a single raid on England, defeat on the River Aisne and declining morale in a fleet that hardly ever put to sea apparently failed to trouble him. In conference he often seemed more ready to talk with moderation than most of the generals, though his table talk was as bombastic as ever. At one stage he told the party leaders of the *Reichstag* that when the war ended they would enter into a 'far-reaching agreement' with France; 'and ultimately all Europe, under my leadership, will begin the real war with England – the Second Punic War'.[19]

While still believing in eventual German victory, the Kaiser was sorely troubled by the fate of one of his cousins. In March 1917 revolution broke out in Russia and Tsar Nicholas abdicated. While the Kaiser tacitly accepted the inevitable end of a kindly but weak autocrat, he was concerned at the implications for himself and his empire. Even so he was not above using the situation for his own advantage. In April he learnt that in conjunction with the supreme command the chancellor had begun assisting Russian revolutionaries to return home, as they would disrupt the war effort of the provisional government and bring about a general collapse on the Eastern Front. The Kaiser insisted that some conditions should be imposed on the returning radicals, but by then Lenin and his friends had returned to the Baltic. His interest in the matter faded until December 1917, when he received a report on Germany's success in financing *Pravda* and other Bolshevik sources of propaganda. Wilhelm was increasingly worried by the plight of the former Tsar and his family; during the eight months of the provisional government's precarious hold on power they had been maintained in moderately comfortable captivity, but the rise of Lenin and the Bolsheviks posed a more sinister threat. The Kaiser sent a message to Petrograd through Copenhagen that the provisional government was responsible for the Romanovs' welfare and if the family decided to seek refuge in the west, German vessels would not attack any warship carrying them through the Baltic, where the former Empress's brother-in-law was commander-in-chief of the naval forces. This was ruled out in August when the Romanovs were removed to the inner heart of Russia, as Kerensky, leader of the provisional government, told the former Tsar, to protect them from the mounting fury of Bolshevik mobs in Petrograd.

On 26 November, after the Bolshevik revolution, Leon Trotsky formally requested an armistice. Ludendorff told the Kaiser that he needed a quick settlement in the East to release troops for a major spring offensive to take Paris and end war in the west. While he agreed with this policy, he knew little of the character of the new government in Russia, as he proposed to state secretary Richard von Kühlmann that if peace negotiations made good progress Germany should enter into an alliance or relationship of friendship with Russia. Kühlmann explained that it would be prudent to wait and see whether the congress of Soviets in Petrograd was one of the 'new political combinations' agreeable to them.

Peace talks opened at Brest-Litovsk on 22 December, Kühlmann heading the civil delegation and Hoffmann the military. The Kaiser backed the former to the hilt, especially when Ludendorff seemed anxious to rush through a settlement. A clash occurred between Wilhelm and Ludendorff when the former proposed a frontier line in Poland which he had decided after talks with Hoffman. Ludendorff angrily demanded to know what gave the Kaiser the right to seek the opinion of a subordinate general without reference to the supreme command. In earlier years, at the height of his self-confidence, the Kaiser would have demanded immediate resignation as the price of such impertinence. Instead, he remarked coldly that he would await a report from the supreme command on the issue. Ludendorff knew how to get his way, and told the press that he was about to resign after differences with His Majesty. Soon telegrams began arriving at the palace begging the sovereign to retain the services of Ludendorff, and he yielded.

In January 1918 Hindenburg demanded that the Kaiser should dismiss Rudolf von Valentini, who had been head of his civil secretariat for the last ten years, on the grounds that he had been over-sympathetic to Bethmann-Hollweg's plans for postwar reform. Wilhelm was furious with Hindenburg's impertinence, but knew he could not risk the loss of either him or Ludendorff at such a critical stage in the war. Should the Brest-

Litovsk talks fail, the eastern armies would have to march on Petrograd. In any case Ludendorff's staff had already been preparing for a spring offensive on the Western Front to begin in about two months. To lose one man would probably mean the loss of both, and culminate in a palace revolution ending in the Kaiser's abdication in favour of his eldest son. Valentini loyally eased the situation by voluntarily resigning.

The Kaiser was now increasingly despondent, weary and well aware that President Wilson was trying to assume for himself the mantle of leadership of the Entente and impose peace, after removing the Hohenzollern dynasty from Germany. He complained that the President was backing the Bolsheviks, and that there was a conspiracy of 'international Jewry' against him. If Trotsky continued to procrastinate at Brest-Litovsk, the German army would have to go to Petrograd and wipe out Bolshevism before it brought revolution to Germany. Only a week earlier a German-language broadcast from, ironically, Tsarskoe-Selo, the ex-Tsar's palace, had called on German troops to rise in revolt, murder the Kaiser and his chief military advisers and conclude a fraternal peace with their Russian comrades.

The Kaiser absented himself from afternoon sessions of the war council. The supreme command had been told what he wanted, and he left matters in their hands. German troops resumed their advance eastwards early on 18 February, pushing the line forward at 30 miles a day. After a week it halted at Narva, a hundred miles west of Petrograd. Five days later Russian delegates at Brest-Litovsk signed a treaty depriving Russia of a third of her prewar population, a third of her arable land and nine-tenths of her coalfields. The Kaiser celebrated with champagne at Homburg, ordered flags to be flown in every city throughout Germany and throughout the empire allowed all schoolchildren a day's holiday. He felt there now seemed no need to bury Bolshevism.

Leaving Homburg on 11 March, the Kaiser spent three days in Berlin and then went to Spa in Belgium, where headquarters were established for the offensive on the Western Front. As there was no accommodation ready for him he lived in the imperial train for over a month. The first wave of the German offensive broke on 21 March, with sixty-two divisions attacking along a 70-mile front on either side of St Quentin. In the following week the Germans advanced 40 miles, and he was sure they had won the battle, with the English utterly defeated. The allied armies suffered heavy losses, but so did the Germans. At the end of May a renewed assault took Soissons from the French, reached Marne again and brought German forces within 40 miles of the centre of Paris. In June and July the fourth and fifth waves resulted in a further advance, until Marshal Foch launched an allied counter-attack.

At last the imperial warlord was facing up to the inevitability of defeat. Up to the second week of June he had still appeared confident of eventual victory, ecstatic at every triumph of his armies. He still insisted on having wounded English prisoners-of-war, whom he encountered in southern Flanders, properly bandaged and taken to safety by German medical orderlies, despite orders to his troops to crush the enemy. Aware of Emperor Karl's increasing desire for peace, the Kaiser refused to consider such negotiations as long as his commanders were optimistic. As late as 18 June Ludendorff maintained that a French collapse would come soon, but by the beginning of July they too were resigning themselves to the tide turning the other way. One week later Kühlmann told the *Reichstag* deputies not to expect any end to the war as a result of a military decision alone; it was increasingly likely that peace would need to be negotiated, not fought for. The Kaiser disassociated himself from such defeatist talk, and Kühlmann was asked to resign. On 15 July Ludendorff began a third offensive in the West as a final desperate effort at German victory, but a combination of English, French, American and imperial forces proved more than a match for him, and within a week Hindenburg admitted to the Kaiser that they had failed.

Wilhelm was then in a mood of black depression over first reports of the murder of ex-Tsar Nicholas and his family at Ekaterinburg. Through the Swedish embassy, he had offered several times to give Grand Duchess Serge refuge in Prussia, but she always sent word back that she would never leave her convent where she worked as a nursing sister, or Russia, of her own free will. She paid the ultimate price, and was thrown down a mineshaft by her Bolshevik captors. The Kaiser's doctors feared a repeat of the collapse of nearly ten years earlier when he had taken to his bed and threatened to abdicate.

An allied counter-offensive freed Amiens on 8 August, in Ludendorff's words 'Germany's darkest day'. He and Hindenburg now conceded that the war was lost and accordingly informed the visibly shaken Kaiser. At a council in Spa on 14 August he proposed that an approach for peace should be made at a point of German recovery, rather than weakness. Defeat was not imminent, and he hoped the allied counter-offensive would lose momentum. He then travelled to Wilhelmshöhe to be with the Empress, who was recovering from a mild heart attack, staying from 19 August to 9 September. Wilhelm's distress at the news of successful offensives by British, French and American forces on a supposedly impregnable section of the Western Front, which finally convinced him that the war was irretrievably lost, coincided with an attack of neuralgia; declaring he was on the verge of collapse, he took to his bed for twenty-four hours, refusing to see anyone. The rest refreshed him, and when he got up he said that he had had 'a little nervous breakdown', but was now as good as new.[20]

That same day, 5 September, Albert Ballin asked him to approach President Wilson for peace talks before feeling hardened against the Hohenzollern dynasty. Ballin had been kept away from the Kaiser for much of the war as his alleged Anglophile opinions made him unwelcome to major figures at Court, especially the Empress. Now he came at the request of an emissary from Ludendorff, who hoped that a personal friend of the Kaiser could achieve more with him than the military commanders whom he apparently did not trust. Wilhelm told Ballin he had every confidence that Hindenburg would stabilize the front; then, but not before, would be the time for peace talks. Hindenburg believed that as German troops were still on French soil they could force peace on their own terms from a position of strength. Queen Wilhelmina of the Netherlands had offered to mediate with a peace conference in The Hague, and he had every intention of accepting, as did the Kaiser, assuring Ballin that he would accept such a proposal at the right moment. Ballin came away feeling that the Empress and Berg between them were trying to shield the Kaiser from reality.

Ironically, far from losing a throne, it appeared briefly that the Hohenzollerns or their family might gain one. In August the government of Finland, formerly a Grand Duchy under the Tsar of Russia which had recently declared independence, voted in favour of establishing a monarchy. Initially, ministers proposed to invite either Grand Duke Friedrich Franz of Mecklenburg-Schwerin, Kaiser Wilhelm's fifth son Oskar or his brother-in-law Friedrich Karl of Hesse to assume the role. A German prince was favoured as some guarantee of Germany's military support against Russia, and on 9 October Friedrich Karl was elected King of Finland by the legislature. Prudently, he declared that he could not give any answer regarding acceptance for two months as he did not wish to place any obstacles in the way of peace. Two months later, events all around them sealed the fate of the embryonic Finnish monarchy.

On 10 September the Kaiser visited the Krupp factories and delivered a speech to the workmen which they found contrived, unconvincing and above all condescending. Parties, he told them, had failed their empire in the war, and there was no time for party politics; what Germany needed was cohesion and unity. 'To every single one of us his task is given – to you with your hammer, to you at your lathe, to me upon my throne!' They were engaged in 'a long long fight for life', a devastating admission of failure to those who recalled his assurance in 1914 that the armies would be home by Christmas.[21] The Kaiser's words were greeted with furtive laughter and sullen silence at the end. A fortnight later at Kiel he addressed the crew of a minelayer and summoned 400 U-boat officers to hear a fiery 'traitors to the wall' speech – a last attempt to fan the flame of patriotic resistance.

News came that the Balkan Front was collapsing; in the last week of September British troops entered Bulgaria, red flags were flown in several Bulgarian towns and King Ferdinand, the prudent 'Foxy Ferdy', was suing for an armistice.* As the Kaiser had feared, Bulgaria's defection was followed swiftly by that of Turkey, and disintegration of Austria-Hungary would not be long in coming. In another mood of black despair he returned to Wilhelmshöhe to spend three days being cosseted by the Empress. On 28 September he returned to Spa, where the next morning he held a conference with Hindenburg, Ludendorff, Chancellor Hertling and Admiral Paul von Hintze, who had succeeded Kühlmann as foreign secretary. Ludendorff told them bluntly that with the imminent collapse of their allies the German army's position was desperate, the war was lost and there was no alternative but to seek peace urgently.

The Kaiser's entourage thought he had aged years in one day. Distressed by the situation facing him as a sovereign, he was also worried about the effect this news would have on his wife, still very weak and in no state for sudden shocks. Trying to prepare her gently for impending catastrophe, he warned her that they were 'approaching grave days and important measures will have to be sought to find internal rest and unity as well as external peace'.[22] On 2 October he returned to Berlin. Hertling had asked to be relieved of the chancellorship, and while discussing his successor with the Kaiser, an excited Ludendorff burst into their room unannounced to ask if the new government had been formed yet. The Kaiser told him angrily that he was not a conjurer, and when Ludendorff insisted that a new administration had to be formed at once because the peace offer needed to be despatched that same day, Wilhelm retorted that he should have been informed fourteen days ago.

The new chancellor, the Kaiser's second cousin Prince Max of Baden, was the one prominent loyalist liberal left, and perhaps the only man equally acceptable to the high command and the socialist deputies in the *Reichstag*. Aged fifty-one, he was the only chancellor of the reign younger than his sovereign. He accepted office reluctantly, as 'the only person who was suitable for carrying out the great liquidation with some

---

* Ferdinand of Bulgaria was the only crowned head of a defeated nation in 1918 who succeeded in saving the throne for his dynasty. He was succeeded by his son Boris, who reigned until 1943.

dignity',[23] and formed a government including representatives of the four largest political parties excluding the extreme right and extreme left, informed deputies in the *Reichstag* that they would approve and confirm the election of future chancellors and that Prussian electoral reform would be implemented soon. Having thus introduced constitutional measures that would have formed part of Bethmann-Hollweg's postwar programme, he felt confident enough to deal with the most urgent task of all – conclusion of the war. He accordingly authorized a formal approach to President Wilson for an armistice and peace terms based upon his Fourteen Points speech of 8 January 1918.

Time was running out, and it was apparent that the Entente powers were reluctant to conclude peace terms that did not acknowledge their full victory. The secretary of state sought to clarify Wilson's views through Swiss intermediaries, and a message received by Prince Max on 15 October reiterated the theme of a speech delivered at Mount Vernon on 4 July stating unequivocally that the destruction of arbitrary power was a vital condition of peace. The Kaiser declared angrily that the sole object of this was to bring down the Hohenzollerns and sweep the German monarchy away. It was, he assumed, a specifically American, republican reaction. At the same time he prepared a detailed memorandum outlining arguments favouring close union between Germany and Austria after the declaration of peace. He had assumed that the old Austro-Hungarian monarchy would have no place in the modern world, but imagined the Habsburgs would still rule the new states in central Europe and he would remain on the German throne. Though he had not told his sovereign, Prince Max hoped the Kaiser would have sufficient foresight to try and save the monarchy by abdicating of his own volition, as he had almost done ten years earlier. When the matter was broached by one of his chancellor's intermediaries, the Kaiser retorted that he could not shirk his duty; a successor of Frederick the Great did not abdicate.

Soon disillusioned with his new chancellor, Kaiser Wilhelm could not see that the latter intended to show that responsibility for ending the war now rested with the government, not with supreme command. On 26 October he agreed to the chancellor's request that Ludendorff should resign his post, to be succeeded as first quartermaster general by Wilhelm Gröner. Such little determination as the Kaiser had was reinforced by the Empress and Berg, both of whom tried to get him to stand up to those around him. The Empress begged him not to accept any more demands from Prince Max or the government. As the Prince was suffering from influenza, the Kaiser had a perfect excuse for not seeing him; he did not wish to catch the infection. The Empress and Berg urged him to get away from the politicians in Berlin and seek support from his loyal field army. The Kaiser was further dismayed by news from Vienna that Emperor Karl intended to seek a separate peace. Now, he declared, Germany stood alone against the entire world; they 'had to endure this war in order not to leave Austria in the lurch, and she has done so to us!'.[24]

On 29 October Hindenburg suggested the Kaiser should visit the front-line troops on a morale-boosting tour of duty. He left Potsdam that night in the imperial train, never to return. While his family thought it ominous that he should leave his capital at such a crucial stage, some members of his entourage knew it was only a matter of time before the question of abdication would be put directly to him, and the sooner he went the better. Even so, as events would prove, it was no more than a temporary flight from the inevitable. The Duchess of Brunswick was convinced that before he stepped on the train he had come to terms with abdication. Mindful of the fact that he ruled by the Grace of God over a nation entrusted to him, and that to renounce his throne would be a form of desertion, Wilhelm now saw that he had to offer himself as a sacrifice for the German people and his armed forces. Their enemies were ready to pay 'the price of an equitable and honourable peace' for it.[25]

As if attempting to mask his true feelings behind the public face, on his arrival at Spa the next morning he told Hindenburg bluntly that his chancellor and government were attempting to throw him out. On 1 November Dr Wilhelm Drews, minister of the interior, arrived at headquarters with a formal plea from the chancellor for him to abdicate.[26] The Kaiser turned on him angrily, asking him how, as a Prussian official and a subject who had taken the oath of allegiance, he had the insolence and effrontery to appear before him with such a request.

Meanwhile, in Berlin Albert Ballin, now seriously ill and with only a few weeks to live, admitted that Germany had caused the war. Ever loyal to his sovereign and friend, he laid all blame on the high command and ministers, noting with bitterness that if they wanted to give 'a convincing proof of the completeness of the success they have achieved, they can do no better than demand condign punishment for the man who has been held responsible for the war, and inflict it upon him. I do not believe that the Kaiser would grieve very much if he were given a chance now of retiring into private life without much loss of dignity.' More in hope than expectation, he suggested the sovereign, without losing his position, could be invested with the rights and duties similar to those of King George V of England who 'enjoys all the advantages of his dignity without having to take upon himself responsibilities which he is unable to bear. I quite believe that the Kaiser never derived much pleasure from his sovereign powers; at any rate, if he did, he has ceased to do so since this unfortunate war has been forced upon him.'[27]

The chancellor told his cabinet that His Majesty's abdication had to be voluntary 'and must be done in such a way as to protect both the Kingdom and the forces from harm and retain the honour of Germany'.[28] Prince Max endeavoured to enlist the help of other German Princes who were going to the Kaiser, so they could try and persuade him without being seen to put him under pressure. At his request Ernest, Grand Duke of Hesse, and the Kaiser's brother-in-law Prince Friedrich Karl of Hesse, came to see him. Ernest declined the task of speaking to Wilhelm, largely as they had never been on particularly good terms, and Friedrich Karl asked for time to think it over before agreeing. As a close relation, and as one who had been wounded while fighting at the front and also lost two sons in action, his credentials as an intermediary were unimpeachable. Friedrich Karl was at the chancellery to get a final briefing, with a draft proclamation for the Kaiser announcing his duty to renounce the crown of Prussia, when news came from the high command and the foreign office of a slight improvement in the situation at the front.

Later that week Gröner visited Berlin, spoke to the chancellor and other ministers, and agreed there could be no question of abdication while the army was still fighting, or discipline would break down as it had in Russia and chaos would follow. Next day he met Friedrich Ebert, the moderate socialist leader, who proposed that the Kaiser should abdicate at once and entrust the regency to one of his sons, but not the Crown Prince, who was hated by the German people. A loyal servant of his master and reluctant to accept such drastic measures, Gröner now had little room for manoeuvre. On 4 November a naval mutiny broke out at Kiel. With formerly loyal sailors waving red flags and threatening to take over the government, nobody could answer for the consequences if resistance was offered. The Kaiser was bitterly distressed. 'The fact that it was in my navy, my proud creation, that there was first open rebellion, cut me most deeply to the heart.'[29] Grand Admiral Prince Henry was not taking any chances; putting a red armband over the sleeve of his greatcoat and a red banner on his car, he drove his wife and son at high speed through a sailors' picket line to safety.

Returning to Spa, Gröner found the Kaiser reluctant to compromise. Fearing that Bolshevism at home was now a greater threat than the Entente forces, he talked of placing himself at the head of his field army, leading the men back into Germany, and putting down mutiny and revolution wherever it reared its head. One of his commanders, Count Schulenburg, advised him to stage a military showdown and effect a hero's death fighting either the allies or Bolsheviks at home.[30] Gröner agreed, as if the Kaiser was wounded he would win a hero's laurels and retain his throne, while if he was killed the dynasty would be saved for his heirs.[31] The Kaiser had no intention of sacrificing himself; suicide would be an admission of failure, as well as contrary to his religious convictions. Nevertheless, in his wildest moments he hoped that some of the Entente – especially the English, for whom he had reserved his most bitter invective for the last four years – might come to his aid and help restore law and order in Germany, thus preventing a repetition of the previous year's events in Russia. Armistice talks were beginning at Compiègne, and there was doubt as to the loyalty of many units in the army. Some of the Kaiser's suite felt he was living in a world of his own.

By the morning of 9 November, after consulting some of the commanders, Gröner knew there was no alternative. For his own safety the Kaiser would have to abdicate and go into exile. The less he prevaricated, the greater the chance of saving his dynasty and the monarchy. While accepting the logic of such arguments, Hindenburg's loyalty to his master was so deeply engrained that he hesitated to advise such a step. The Kaiser's aides still believed that their master should only hear what it was good for him to hear, while the general staff were realists, knowing that the situation was desperate. To Gröner fell the unenviable task of telling his sovereign that 'the army will march back home under its leaders and commanding generals in quiet and order, but not under the command of Your Majesty, for it no longer supports Your Majesty'.[32]

Wilhelm's reaction was one of bewilderment. Dismissing his attendants, he went into the gardens of the château, pacing up and down, talking to Hindenburg and some of the other generals. Early in the afternoon the Crown Prince arrived in an effort to strengthen his father's resolve. A staff-colonel was sent to consult regimental commanders, but returned to say that 'Bolshevik notions' were spreading rapidly throughout the troops. Schulenburg deplored defeatist talk, declaring that all good soldiers would stand by their oath to the colours. Gröner told him that oaths of loyalty no longer had any substance: 'In times of revolutionary upheaval, one should not have any illusions about the importance of the concepts of oaths of allegiance and commander-in-chief, for these concepts would in the end be only mere ideas.'[33]

The Kaiser and his eldest son lunched privately, their meal interrupted by a telephone message from Berlin. Faced with the threat of imminent revolution, Prince Max had taken the initiative and announced His Majesty's abdication and renunciation of the succession by his eldest son. Barefaced treason, raged the Kaiser, turning to Schulenburg for advice. The latter told him he must not yield to such an act of violence. Later that day, as Wilhelm was frantically sending ineffectual messages out to

Berlin by telegraph form, Hindenburg returned to advise that he could not guarantee the Kaiser's safety; he would have to abdicate and proceed immediately to Holland. He was followed by Admiral Scheer, who warned him he could no longer count on the loyalty of the fleet.

By 5.00 p.m. Wilhelm had decided to abdicate as German Kaiser, but not as King of Prussia, and to cross into Holland. One day, he imagined, he would return to his kingdom. He left his villa to dine on the royal train, where he was given a message from his son Eitel Friedrich to say that the Empress was still well and in good heart. This momentarily stiffened his resolve; turning to his suite, he said that as his wife was staying where she was, for him to go to Holland would be like a captain leaving a sinking ship. Later that evening Gröner rang to report that the situation was deteriorating rapidly. Mutinous troops were said to be marching on Spa, and the only road still open was the way to Holland – but it might not remain open for much longer. In a mood of resignation the Kaiser agreed to leave, but not until morning, and retired to bed.

At 2 a.m. the Kaiser's chauffeur at Spa was woken and asked to prepare His Majesty's car, stripped of insignia, for a long journey. Some five hours later a party containing Wilhelm Hohenzollern, several officers and a modest suite, arrived at the Dutch town of Eysden. The years of exile were just beginning.

CHAPTER EIGHT

# The Squire of Doorn

Nobody in Holland had been expecting the former monarch and his suite. Though each member of his entourage carried identity documents, none could produce a passport when they were asked by a Dutch sergeant. He telephoned his officer who arrived quickly and, with some embarrassment, received the Kaiser's request for asylum and his sword, and gave orders for the Eysden frontier station to be sealed pending official instructions from The Hague. The German cars remained at the frontier all morning. It was bitterly cold and the Kaiser paced up and down to keep warm, till he was allowed to accompany the officer to a railway station and sit in a waiting room. Soon afterwards the imperial train arrived; he lunched and dined in his restaurant car, still unaware of his eventual destination. Just before midnight word came from the German minister at The Hague that Queen Wilhelmina had agreed to give him sanctuary.

They still had nowhere to stay, so as they were having lunch Count Godard Bentinck was asked on the telephone if he could accommodate the former sovereign and his suite of fourteen officers, plus a large number of functionaries and servants, for three days in his seventeenth-century house at Amerongen. The men had never met, though the Kaiser had stayed briefly with the Count's brother on a visit to the Netherlands in 1909. Two years older than the former sovereign, the Count was a widower with three sons and a daughter. Though he had no particular sympathy with the Hohenzollern dynasty he took his obligations seriously as a Knight of St John of Jerusalem, an order of which the Kaiser was a titular commander.

The train left Eysden at 9.20 on the morning of 11 November and arrived at Maarn, 25 miles from Arnhem, six hours later. As Wilhelm stepped down from his saloon coach for the last time, he was met by the provincial governor of Utrecht and Count Bentinck, and taken by car on the thirty-minute journey to Amerongen. Tired and confused, he said barely a word until they crossed the moat, when he turned to the Count and asked for 'a cup of real good English tea'.[1] Amerongen had advantages as a place of refuge, as the region was little known and the house isolated behind double moats, a deterrent to zealous journalists and other intruders. These were not the worst of their fears, as it was rumoured that a Communist revolution was about to dethrone Queen Wilhelmina, and any such development would undoubtedly result in the Kaiser's capture or arrest as well.

That evening the full German party was treated to dinner, with several courses and the best wine. Soon the Kaiser was writing to the Empress, who remained in Potsdam, to tell her of the excellent hospitality. She was still weak after her recent stroke and heart trouble, and despite warnings about the threat she faced from revolutionaries, and an invitation from her second son Eitel Friedrich to take refuge with him at Villa Ingenheim, she refused to leave the Neue Palais, saying it would be cowardly to do so. Even so she longed to be reunited with her husband, and though he was undoubtedly safer than she was, she never ceased to worry about him, 'so alone in his misfortune'. Escorted by soldiers from Eitel Friedrich's regiment dressed in civilian clothes, the Empress joined her husband at Amerongen on 28 November, the day on which he formally signed a document of abdication as German Emperor and King of Prussia.

The *enfant terrible* who personified the public face of an empire that had paid the ultimate penalty of war, and the most terrible European war within living memory, was verbally castigated on all sides. Friedrich Ebert said at the time though the German people recognized Ludendorff as 'the guilty one', all the hate was directed against his sovereign. His fellow socialist party member Philipp Scheidemann admitted that had the war ended in German victory the monarch 'would have been rapturously acclaimed, or even raised to the status of demi-god. 'As things turned out they wanted a scapegoat and they found the Kaiser right in front.'[2]

Meanwhile, in England his cousin King George, not vindictive by nature, could be allowed a moment of triumphalism at the news of Wilhelm's abdication – ironically, as he noted in his diary, on 9 November, the birthday of his late father King Edward VII, 'the encircler'. 'How are the mighty fallen,' wrote the King. 'He has been Emperor for just over 30 years, he did great things for his country but his ambition was so great that he wished to dominate the world & created his military machine for that object. No man can dominate the world, it has been tried before, & now he has utterly ruined his Country & himself.'[3] King George lived for another seventeen years but never saw or corresponded with his cousin again.

A general election was about to take place in Britain. Within days of the Kaiser's departure from Germany, British authorities were discussing how he should be held to account. King George V's private secretary, Lord Stamfordham, told him (5 December) that most people had 'lost their balance' about the former warlord. 'The cooler heads advocate the Falkland Islands and no trial. But sending Napoleon to St Helena did not prevent his nephew becoming Emperor and the Kaiser's sons cannot all be hanged!'[4] The Northcliffe Press, publishers of the *Daily Mail,* led a campaign calling for 'the Huns to be brought to their knees', and for 'the arch-villain of Europe' to stand trial as well as his henchmen. Prime Minister David Lloyd George tried to ignore such hysterical outbursts and warned his fellow party members to do likewise, but after a campaign speech in which he was heckled by an audience out for retribution, followed by reaction from constituencies and letters all over the country, he and his war cabinet reluctantly agreed to take note of popular opinion. In another address a few days later he asked if there was to be one law for the poor wretched criminal and another for kings and emperors. Jurists had been consulted by the attorney-general and concluded unanimously that the Kaiser was guilty of an indictable offence for which he should be held responsible. A statement released to the press a week later confirmed his decision that the former monarch should be prosecuted: 'The men responsible for this outrage on the human race must not be let off because their heads were crowned when they perpetrated the deed.'[5]

Wiser counsels prevailed, notably those of Churchill, the foreign secretary Arthur Balfour and most of the diplomatic service. Any notion of retributive justice, or to put it bluntly, a demand to 'Hang the Kaiser!' smacked more of appeasing mob calls for vengeance or lynch law rather than of serious postwar European reconstruction. Their view was shared by leading statesmen from the British Empire and the United States. Nevertheless, provision for the former Kaiser's trial was included in the terms of the Treaty of Versailles, in which one specific Article arraigned him 'for a supreme offence against international morality and the sanctity of treaties' to be tried by a commission of five judges, one each from France, the United Kingdom, the United States, Italy and Japan. In June 1919 the supreme council of the conference agreed he should be held to account.

Most delegates to the peace conference knew that such a sop to popular indignation would never be pursued. The Kaiser's family suggested he should flee rather than fall into the hands of the Entente, but he refused to consider such an indignity. He contemplated giving himself up; if there was any prospect of improving the situation in Germany through such a step, 'then there would be no possibility of doubt regarding my surrender'. But he knew he could hardly expect a fair verdict from a court drawn from his antagonists, who would be his accusers and his judges,[6] and the Dutch government remained obdurate to all demands from the Entente. Almost as soon as he had arrived on their soil they made it clear that there was no intention of handing over a ruler who had sought asylum. On 8 December 1918 Count Lynden von Sandenburg, governor of the province of Utrecht, had formally asked the Kaiser to leave the country. The Dutch Socialist party wanted him out so that they would not be asked by the allies to hand him over, or be confronted by force. He declared that he was willing to go in order to avoid embarrassing the government, neutral Sweden or Switzerland being the obvious destinations. Sweden was nearer, and as a monarchy thought more suitable, but to travel there he would need to pass through Germany, and obtain permission from the republican government in order to do so. He still hoped that he might be permitted residential rights in Germany on condition that he renounced any political activity, but this came to nothing. However, the Dutch government insisted that their law prohibited handing over aliens who had sought refuge within their borders for political reasons, and as the Dutch were not signatories to the Treaty of Versailles they had every right to refuse requests for extradition. Their only condition was that the Kaiser should abstain from active politics as long as he remained in the Netherlands, a pledge he gave gladly.

While anxious to prevent him from being put on trial, Queen Wilhelmina kept her distance from him, partly for political and diplomatic reasons, partly because of protocol. It was unusual for a reigning Queen to have a deposed monarch within her borders. In fact they never met, though over the years the Kaiser received other members of the Dutch royal family, including Queen Mother Emma, the Queen's husband Hendrik, their daughter and heir Juliana and her husband Bernhard.

A petition was sent to King George V signed by three other deposed German princes, Friedrich August III, former King of Saxony, Wilhelm II, former King of Württemberg, and the last imperial chancellor, Max of Baden. It stated that the Kaiser 'acted to the best of his knowledge and with the highest intentions, in full consciousness of his kingly responsibility'. If His Majesty tolerated the trial 'of a great and at one time friendly and related Ruler, then every official authority, every throne (including the English throne) will be threatened'.[7] A reply drafted by the foreign office in London noted that indictment of the Kaiser figured in the text of the treaty and was thus the responsibility of all signatory powers, but by this time the delegates had all but decided against pursuing the matter further.

King George V firmly opposed calls for retribution. He was not consulted by Lloyd George about moves to extradite the Kaiser from Holland. When he read of them in the newspapers he warned his unrepentant prime minister that to parade him through the streets of London would provoke civil disorder, to be told that the illustrious prisoner would be lodged at

Syon, the Duke of Northumberland's house on the Thames, and brought down the river every day to stand trial in Westminster Hall. If this was unsuitable, proceedings could take place at Hampton Court, whereupon the King pointed out that they might have to evict all the courtiers' widows and others from their grace and favour apartments.[8]

The Kaiser himself was unperturbed by such talk; it was not far removed from some of his utterances, such as his wish to see all members of the *Reichstag* strung up after visiting a colonial exhibition and seeing an array of vanquished enemies' skulls on display. The Empress was far more anxious. Increasingly inclined to trust no race but her own, she was sure her husband's life was in danger. Sooner or later, she feared, somebody would carry him off to England or France, and he would share the fate of Tsar Nicholas II. She thought his extradition was imminent, and at Christmas 1918 she wrote a farewell letter to their children in case they never saw each other again. There were two clumsy kidnap attempts early in 1920, one when two American officers arrived at Amerongen, claiming they had orders to escort the Kaiser to Paris, but were sent away without reaching his apartments. The other was when an American stoker turned up and asked to speak to him in person or on the telephone. Family and local police ensured that the Kaiser was adequately protected from adventurers, cranks and journalists, and unlike his wife he felt secure.

No longer the autocrat, he soon slipped into the guise of the English country gentleman he had sometimes said he wanted to be. With no court barber to wax or colour his moustache, it reverted to natural shape and went grey, while a beard softened his features. He and Count Bentinck had common ancestors, William the Silent (where the Kaiser was concerned, somewhat ironic) and his third wife, Charlotte of Bourbon, and on the Kaiser's sixtieth birthday in January 1919 the Count presented him with a portrait of King William.

Meanwhile, three of the Kaiser's four sisters were still in Germany. Charlotte, Duchess of Saxe-Meiningen, died in October 1919, aged fifty-nine. The mischievous 'Charly', whom he had never trusted after her part in the letters and diary scandal early in his reign, had been a very sick woman for some years. Her life had also been embittered by estrangement from her daughter and son-in-law, Prince and Princess Henry of Reuss, with public insults and mutual vilification between them reaching such a pitch, even by the standards of gossip-ridden Berlin, that astonished observers were inclined to question the mental and emotional health of mother and daughter.[9] Porphyria, inherited from King Friedrich Wilhelm I of Prussia on her father's side, and from King George III of England on that of her mother, had made her life purgatory with recurring stomach pains, rashes and urinary problems, though in the end she succumbed to cancer.

Victoria's marriage to Adolf of Schaumburg-Lippe had been followed by one brief pregnancy which ended in miscarriage; he died of pneumonia in July 1916. She had stayed in the Schaumburg Palace, helping to nurse war wounded and support her charities. Apart from one night when mutinous sailors and revolutionaries threatened to storm the palace until pacified with the gift of cigarettes and temporary loan of her car to take convicts from the local prisons, Victoria was left alone till after the armistice, when Canadian troops occupied Bonn and military staff commandeered a wing of the palace until 1926. Among soldiers billeted there was her second cousin Edward, Prince of Wales. He was angry at finding photographs of 'his' family on display throughout the rooms, and even more so when she addressed him as 'dear', telling him that the Germans would have continued fighting for several more years but for the revolution. Grudgingly, he thought her 'a nice enough woman for a Hun'.[10] At the same time she met his brother Albert (later King George VI), who was amazed to find she knew nothing of war atrocities or treatment of allied prisoners, all of which had been kept a secret from her. She asked after the family and told him she hoped they could all be friends again before long, to which he replied tactfully that he thought it would not be possible for a good many years.[11]

Though Count Bentinck was a patient host, he could not expect to have the Kaiser as his guest indefinitely. In August 1919, with the consent of the Dutch government, the Kaiser bought a moated country house at Doorn, 5 miles west of Amerongen. Originally a fourteenth-century castle built by the bishops of Utrecht, Huis Doorn was demilitarized and rebuilt in 1780, and after nine months of renovation the Kaiser and Empress moved there in May 1920. Soon after moving to Doorn the Kaiser established a routine which he was to adhere to for the rest of his life until the last few weeks. He rose at 7 a.m. for a brisk walk, which ended with feeding ducks in the moat. Then his household gathered in the entrance hall for morning prayers. After breakfast he went gardening, accompanied by his duty adjutants and any guests present, either sawing trees for firewood – partly for burning at Doorn, partly to distribute to the local poor and needy – or planting young trees and tending to the rosarium. A light lunch at midday was followed by a rest, then tea served on a tray, a session for working at his desk, and light dinner at 8 p.m., after which the party sat in the drawing room to talk or listen to him reading, with bed at 10.30 p.m. or later. He remained very particular about his diet, and almost as sparing with food as he had been as a young man; he enjoyed fruit but disliked oysters, caviare and seasoned foods, would not touch meat which had been transported over a great distance and only ate vegetables that he was assured had not been grown in earth containing sewage. When invited to dinner parties he had, or pretended to take, a little of every course set before him so as not to disappoint his hosts.[12] He usually drank orangeade or lemonade, or *Assmannshäuser*, a red sparkling Burgundy, mixed with water, on special occasions.

All the time he took a natural interest in events in the infant German republic. His bitterness was directed at Jews above all others for conniving at his abdication, despatching a vitriolic anti-Semite tirade to Field Marshal August von Mackensen (2 December 1919) in which he blamed his former subjects for being 'egged on and misled by the tribe of Juda whom they hate'. No German should be allowed to forget, 'nor rest until these parasites have been wiped out from German soil and been exterminated! This poisonous mushroom on the German oak-tree!'[13] As Kaiser he had often told confidantes, when asked why he befriended Jews such as Albert Ballin and the statesman Walter Rathenau, that he did not regard them thus. 'Ballin a Jew?' he had retorted. 'No such thing! Ballin is a Christian!'[14] Ballin had died on 9 November 1918, probably by his own hand, though he had long been in failing health. Rathenau survived to become a well-respected politician in republican Germany, appointed minister of reconstruction and then of foreign affairs. A few years after Rathenau's murder in June 1922 by anti-Semitic thugs, the Kaiser wrote to an American friend, George Sylvester Viereck, that Rathenau had been 'a mean, deceiving, rascally traitor', and his fate had 'served him right'.[15] Later his racial prejudices became bizarrely selective. Jesus of Nazareth, he insisted, had never been a Jew. On the other hand, after attending an anthropological lecture he was suddenly convinced that the French and British were negroes. How appalling, he wrote to Viereck, that the English allowed 'Niggerboys' to join the boy scouts; it was the 'beginning of treason to their Race formerly only executed by the French Negroids!'.[16]

At first he still hoped for a restoration of the monarchy. In March 1920 Count Bentinck told him of a right-wing coup in Berlin led by Wolfgang Kapp and General Lüttwitz. Grasping the hand of his aide Captain Sigurd von Ilsemann, the Kaiser told him triumphantly that they would have champagne that night, just as they did during the war when brought news of a victory. Some days later they heard that the coup had come to nothing. Very few members of the officer corps had given their support, and when President Ebert's government fled to Stuttgart and called a general strike, the right-wing movement collapsed and Kapp fled to Sweden. His suite counselled patience, and he made it clear he would not take part in any half-baked conspiracy. A restoration could only take place with the wholehearted consent of the Berlin government.

According to his brother-in-law Bernhard, former Duke of Saxe-Meiningen, 'not even the most blue-blooded conservative' would have him back, and 'he would like to play Mussolini, but he's overlooked the fact that his people are not Italians.'[17] For two misguided attempts by the former Emperor Karl of Austria-Hungary to regain his Hungarian throne Wilhelm could express little approval.

Six days after moving to Doorn Wilhelm and Dona were visited by the Crown Prince, who had fled to the Netherlands at the time of the armistice and was interned on an island in the Zuyder Zee as an officer serving in a belligerent army. He stayed over Whitsun and his youngest brother, Prince Joachim, joined them. It was not a happy family reunion; the patriarch was irritated by his sons' behaviour, and disapproved of Joachim's heavy gambling. Disillusioned by the war and its aftermath, and estranged from his wife, Joachim returned to Germany and three weeks later he shot himself at a hunting lodge near Potsdam.

It was a grave blow to the Empress. Knowing she would take it badly, her husband and other children decided to tell her he had been killed in an accident. Though she took the news with outward calmness she seemed to know the truth, and she was never the same again. At Amerongen she had been unable to walk unaided across a room. Now she became increasingly weak and apathetic, confined to a wheelchair. By night she was restless, sleeping fitfully and talking to her absent children much of the time, sometimes the Crown Prince but most often to Joachim. One night when August Wilhelm was keeping watch, she bade all the children goodbye in her sleep. Deeply distressed, he warned them that her end could not be far away.

To their surprise she survived Christmas and the new year, but by the time of their fortieth wedding anniversary in February 1921 she was clearly dying. Her husband and son Adalbert were at her bedside on the morning of 11 April, when she slipped into unconsciousness and then death, having left a final request that she should be laid to rest 'in the homeland'. The republican government agreed she could be interred in the royal mausoleum at the Neue Palais, Potsdam. 'I must send my wife away like a parcel',[18] he said tearfully, as the coffin was taken from Doorn to the village station, decorated with flowers, placed in an ordinary freight car and driven to Germany. Her widower was not allowed to accompany her coffin further than the station at Maarn, some way from the Dutch–German frontier

Though her ill-health over the last few years had prepared him for the worst, he was grief-stricken by her death, and wept like a child. For three weeks he was seriously ill, his misery exacerbated by bronchitis, and a nurse was called to care for him. When the Duchess of Brunswick arrived to help, she found his expression 'painfully blank'. He looked 'timid and embarrassed, and I believe he did not wish the world to see the dreadful despair which had overcome him'.[19] Of all the British royal family, only his Aunt Beatrice, the widowed Princess Henry of Battenberg, wrote a letter of condolence. He was bitter at this meagre response from his cousins, and also that Queen Wilhelmina only wrote him a brief message without making any gesture such as sending a hearse or court car to remove the coffin.

With regular visits from his brother Henry and children, and other friends, the Kaiser's spirits gradually recovered. Soon he had so many guests that additional accommodation had to be built for their benefit. Another visitor, Baron de Radowitz, was a Prussian officer who had attended Bonn University with the Kaiser's sons and served on his staff during the war. Germany was awash with conflicting rumours about the former ruler's health and well-being, so he came to Doorn to see for himself. He was struck by the change in the sovereign with untidy hair and full beard, sharp steel-coloured eyes which almost bulged from their sockets and yellowing skin. His physical bearing otherwise seemed good, the Baron noted, 'but due to his unkempt appearance he did not seem at all to me like the old Wilhelm I had known in the days of his pomp and glory'. It also astonished him that while in Germany Wilhelm's castles had been filled with his photographs and paintings, there were none to be seen inside Doorn. It seemed as if he was so bowed in humility that he wanted to forget all about the days of pomp and grandeur, with nothing to remind him of such times.[20]

Even with or without guests, the Kaiser was not to be alone for long. It was rumoured that he might marry his childhood friend Frau Gabriele von Rochow, or Baroness Lili von Heemstra, whose family had once owned Doorn. Nothing came of these, but among the letters he received on his sixty-third birthday in January 1922 was one from the small son of Prince Schönaich-Carolath, who had been killed in the war. Wilhelm knew the family, and he invited the boy to come and stay, bringing his mother. Princess Hermine, daughter of Prince Henry XXII of Reuss, twenty-eight years his junior, had been one of the Empress's godchildren. A dark, vivacious, strong-willed young woman left with a young family of five children aged between fifteen and three years, she came to visit Doorn (without her son) in June 1922.

It had been one of the Empress's last wishes that her husband should marry again after she was gone, and in July the couple became engaged. The Kaiser's children, who had all adored their mother, expected him to take another wife – but not so soon. His three eldest sons, while not exactly welcoming their future stepmother, respected their father's decision and uttered no word of complaint. The others were utterly dismayed; their mother's place, they thought, could only be taken by someone with exceptional qualities which, in their view, Princess Hermine did not possess. August Wilhelm impulsively begged him not to remarry, while Oskar and the Duchess of Brunswick wrote and jointly signed a letter asking him to reconsider. Wilhelm replied that he understood and respected their feelings and did not take them amiss as he still loved them too much, but it would be 'yet another pain for me if you were to turn your back on your lonely father, so there can be no question of your departure or even of shaking the dust of Doorn from your feet'.[21]

A deputation representing monarchist supporters in Germany came to ask him not to contract a second marriage so soon after the Empress's death as it would be a further blow to the dynasty. Some suspected Hermine of opportunism, for in widowhood she had fallen deeply into debt through the mismanagement of her estates in eastern Germany, and a generous pre-nuptial agreement had been signed by both, ensuring that he would maintain her as well as make regular grants to her sons and daughters. To those who objected Wilhelm answered that he was now a private citizen and free to do as he wished.

Wilhelm and Hermine were married on 5 November 1922, and he created her Her Royal Prussian Highness the Princess Liegnitz, the title which his great-grandfather King Friedrich Wilhelm III had given his second wife. At the wedding breakfast Prince Henry proposed a toast 'To Her Majesty the Empress and Queen'. Two of the Kaiser's surviving sisters Victoria, the widowed Princess Adolf of Schaumburg-Lippe, and Margrethe, also attended. Hermine was the niece of Victoria by marriage, and it amused the latter to think that her eldest brother was now becoming her nephew.[22]

Despite his personal misgivings the Crown Prince was also there. Afterwards he wrote to his old friend Admiral von Karpf that Princess Hermine was a clever and capable woman who intended to make his father's life easier. 'You will be able to imagine how difficult this whole second marriage has become for me, but I try to think kindly in such questions, and I cannot concede either that the second marriage, as one so often hears, has hurt the idea of the monarchy, which today, in my opinion, is not yet at all on the programme.'[23] Less generous were the Kaiser's three youngest surviving children, who refused to attend the wedding, as did the Crown Princess, now estranged from her husband.

Princess Hermine, or 'Hermo' as her husband called her, was very different in character from Dona. She was less placid, yet less prone to violent prejudices. The Duchess of Brunswick found it hard to accept her stepmother, who 'lacked my mother's goodness and her quiet ways. She was lively and industrious, liked to argue and was ambitious.'[24] Yet at length she admitted that Hermine did well in encouraging her husband to take up old interests again, particularly his archaeological studies and his writing. Only thirty-four at the time of their marriage, she helped to keep him young in spirit, and made him take a pride in his appearance again so he no longer looked the untidy, down-at-heel individual Radowitz had found earlier that year. She shared his enthusiasm for gardening, and together they created a rosarium and pinetum at Doorn. She handled her husband's children with tact and had a portrait of the late Empress hung in her boudoir next to one of her husband. However much the Crown Prince tried to like her he never succeeded, agreeing with the Crown Princess who resented her regal pretensions and always referred to her coldly as 'the new wife'.

The Kaiser's retinue at Doorn disliked her grasping ways and bogus dignity, and considered her to be a disruptive presence. They were required to address and refer to Hermine as Empress, and she was annoyed when the German government persistently described her as 'wife of the former German Kaiser' in her passport. She certainly brought happiness into his later years by filling the house with company, and loved entertaining their friends and relatives. Yet before long husband and wife were peevishly complaining about the other. He resented her nagging, domineering manner, while she found him childish, impetuous and difficult to live with.

A programme of explaining and justifying his years of rule was soon begun by the Kaiser. With assistance from a visiting specialist he prepared a highly selective book of 'comparative tables' summarizing the history of Europe between 1878 and 1914. Though he composed the body of the manuscript, it was largely rewritten prior to publication by Eugen Zimmermann, editor of the Scherl publishing house in Berlin, and appeared in book form in 1921. Also with help he wrote a book on Corfu, including an account of archaeological discoveries on the island during the latter years of his reign. A first volume of reminiscences, published in Germany and in England as *My Memoirs 1878–1918* in 1922, was little more than a very one-sided account of relations with his chancellors, ghost-written with the aid of a journalist. In the words of Winston Churchill, 'No more disarming revelation of inherent triviality, lack of understanding and sense of proportion, and, incidentally, of literary capacity, can be imagined.'[25] It was followed by a second book, published in German as *Aus Meinem Leben* and in English as *My Early Life* in 1926, detailing his life from birth to accession.

During these first years of exile the Kaiser still hoped for a restoration, although this was never more than a remote possibility. His actions did not give the impression of a man determined to regain his throne. The self-serving memoirs in which he blamed everyone but himself, his rudeness to former friends and associates and above all his remarriage to an 'unsuitable' woman regarded as a conniver all counted against him. Even Hermine herself, returning from a visit to Germany in 1923, had to admit sadly that there was no enthusiasm for him, let alone for a restoration.

With the Kaiser's second marriage the interior of Doorn and its furnishings reflected its owner's personality and his past. A study was fitted out with a high desk at which he wrote while seated on a full-size riding saddle mounted on stilts. Just as his widowed mother had found consolation in her last years by surrounding herself with her cherished *objets d'art*, so did he, with possessions from Potsdam and Berlin – paintings, photographs and statues of himself and his family, collections of snuff boxes and Wedgwood, tapestries and silver, passed down from the collections of Kings of Prussia back to Frederick the Great.

The Kaiser's personal wealth in exile was limited. All the royal palaces and other estates, as well as their contents, had been seized by the republican government on the fall of the monarchy, and he was almost penniless when he arrived in Holland. At the end of November 1918 his personal belongings were freed, and his goods and cash were gradually transferred to Holland, including over 1,500 pieces of table silver, paintings, furniture and Oriental rugs. When he asserted that he was not only entitled to his personal fortune but also to an inheritance established by his ancestors consisting of real estate in Berlin, the claim was eventually acknowledged and resulted in a settlement of about 70,000,000 marks. From this he was expected to support himself, his family and entourage, as well as the purchase, maintenance and upkeep of Doorn. During the hyper-inflation of 1923 his finances suffered so severely that he was reduced to selling some of his first wife's pearls. The Dutch government required him to restrict his staff severely, but with his financial constraints such an order was hardly necessary. At Doorn he had only two adjutants on duty at any one time, a physician, and his servants, all housed in a large gatehouse at the entrance to the estate. They found their master extremely demanding, received no pay other than their rail fares to and from Holland and after a few years most of them returned to Germany with relief.

The Kaiser's travelling days were over, and he was satisfied with Doorn and the immediate surrounding area. He did not wish to embarrass the authorities by seeking permission to drive into other provinces, where his presence would create additional security problems, and the risk of hostile demonstrations should tourists recognize him. Short excursions with Hermine in his large Mercedes satisfied him, with observers much amused by his love of being driven fast; 'he is gone almost before one realizes he is there!'.[26]

Throughout the 1920s several collections of diplomatic documents, histories of imperial Germany and the war and memoirs of statesmen were published, often written with a sense of self-justification and frequently at the expense of their contemporaries' reputations. The Kaiser read many of them, annotating them in the margins with a mixture of amusement and irritation. Harold Nicolson's biography of his father, the diplomat Lord Carnock, published in 1930, wrote grandly of the Kaiser that it was 'only possible to interpret the impulses of this wayward and intelligent monarch by referring them to the strange psychic abscess produced by his love-hate for England'. In the margin of his own copy he wrote, 'Hand the gentleman a glass of water!'[27]

He also provided some writers with reminiscences and photographs for their work. Among them was Karl Friedrich Nowak, whose *Das Dritte Deutsche Kaiserreich* was published in Germany in 1929, and in England as *Kaiser and Chancellor* the following year. The Kaiser read the manuscript before publication, telling the author wryly that nobody could charge him with obsequiousness. Another regular visitor to Doorn was Bülow's nephew Herr Reichel. Released from prison after serving a sentence for deception, he changed his name to Joachim von Kürenburg and tried to convince Eulenburg's biographer, Johann Haller, of his uncle's homosexuality, but Haller cold-shouldered him after learning of his past. On the former Kaiser von Kürenburg made a better impression, and later wrote a biography based partly on personal conversations with his subject. In one of their talks he stressed that, for anybody to understand his nature, they must not forget that he was half English. 'I have never been able to think purely like a Continental and that is why I have so often been misunderstood or misjudged. Undoubtedly, my mother had a great influence on my nature; it was due to her education that I could get along so easily with the English.'[28]

Much as the Kaiser tried to take the writings of others with good humour, he never ceased to chafe at their criticisms. To a few select friends he poured out his bitterness at what he saw as an endless campaign of vituperation against him, particularly by English writers, his anger exacerbated by the love-hate feelings he had always had for England and his lifelong desire to be accepted and admired by his mother's country. His *bêtes noires* were still his uncle, King Edward VII, 'the encircler', and Sir Edward Grey, whom he never ceased to believe had engineered the war. The German edition of Kürenburg's book, published in 1951, took its title, *War Alles Falsch* ('Did I then never do anything right?'), from the words the Kaiser wrote across a photograph he gave the author in November 1935 after his first visit to Doorn. He looked to Kürenburg to portray him sympathetically and carry out his undertaking to 'deal justly' with his case and, since no other procedure was possible in defence, to present to what he saw as the 'court of world opinion' a reasoned plea in mitigation for his actions.[29]

In 1928 his mother's godson Sir Frederick Ponsonby disturbed his equilibrium by editing and publishing *Letters of the Empress Frederick*. Ponsonby had never doubted that, by passing him her correspondence at Friedrichshof in February 1901, she intended them to be published in due course. Increasingly angered by the distorted portrait of her which emerged from book after book, his hand was forced by Emil Ludwig's biography of the Kaiser, based on official German state documents and published in 1926. Its destructive remarks about the Empress were a travesty of the truth. When he consulted King George V and Queen Victoria's surviving children as to the desirability of publishing the correspondence, their reactions differed from wholehearted approval to deep misgivings. Informed out of courtesy before publication, Wilhelm maintained that his mother's correspondence belonged to the house of Hohenzollern and should be placed in the family archives. The clandestine removal of such letters was 'next to theft', and if necessary he would place the matter in the hands of a lawyer versed in international publication law.[30] After lengthy wrangles and legal consultation, Ponsonby and his publisher Sir Frederick Macmillan argued that the Empress had conferred on him the deed of gift, and the onus was on the Kaiser to prove that in so doing she had not transferred the copyright at the same time. Unable to prevent the book from appearing – though in theory he could have sued as a British subject under the Act of Settlement – he purchased German publication rights on condition that he could write the preface. He thus presented a creditable if less than fully understanding insight into her character which, in the eyes of more indulgent biographers, justified his unfilial behaviour to some extent. Wilhelm's two youngest sisters, the former Queen of the Hellenes and the Landgravine of Hesse, both believed that their mother had given Ponsonby the letters to publish, and wrote to thank him for carrying out her wishes so faithfully.

On those who had served or worked with him Wilhelm had mixed views. In 1927 he wrote to Prince Fritz Eulenburg, son of 'poor Phili', that he was always convinced of his father's innocence of the charges brought against him. The trials of 1907 and 1908, the Kaiser maintained, were the 'first blow' against the monarchy, the shock of which was absorbed by his father as the 'sacrificial martyr'. It was scant consolation to Fritz, whose disgraced, ailing father had died in 1921. His opinion of Bismarck mellowed with time, though not of Bülow and Holstein. Bülow died in 1929 and the Kaiser sent a wreath to his funeral, inscribed with neat irony 'To my Unforgettable Chancellor'. Bülow's four volumes of memoirs had long been ready for publication, and after his death there was no reason to withhold them any longer. The Kaiser faithfully read them right through, saying afterwards that it was the first case he knew of a man committing suicide after he was dead. The faithful but not uncritical Ilsemann was less condemnatory. After finishing the second volume he noted that the Kaiser had changed little since those days. Almost everything he did then still happened, the only difference being that 'his actions, which then had grave significance and practical consequences, now do no damage'.[31]

Three of the Kaiser's other four siblings died in the next ten years. Prince Henry had given a solemn undertaking to the German ministers 'not to interfere with the government'. He and Irene continued to live peacefully at Hemmelmark. When hyper-inflation wrought havoc on the nation's finances he put the bookbinding skills acquired during childhood to good use by binding school books for the children of his dependants on his estate. Always a welcome visitor at Doorn, he brought copies of new German books which his brother read with interest. In the spring of 1929 he fell ill with bronchitis and pneumonia, and he died on 20 April, aged sixty-six. Among messages of condolence sent to his widow was one from King George V. In London *The Times* paid tribute to his 'certain English attributes of moderation, good humour, and plain sense, while the Hohenzollern strain predominated in his elder brother'.[32] Readers of this obituary notice must have wondered how Germany (and Europe) might have fared with Henry on the throne instead.

Victoria, Henry and Wilhelm's sister, had had a life which almost rivalled in tragedy – albeit, in this case, partly self-inflicted – that of the mother, whose name she bore. Bored and lonely at Schaumburg Palace after her husband's death, she found diversion in singing lessons, riding, playing tennis, jazz and the cinema. Just as hyper-inflation and spiralling prices were taking their toll on her finances, her faithful gentleman-in-waiting and comptroller Herr von Salviati died. His successor Baron Solemacher helped to sort out her chaotic affairs by selling some of her jewellery, furniture, horses and car.

To help raise money she also wrote her memoirs, published in Britain by Eveleigh, Nash & Grayson. They reflected her generous, forgiving nature and betrayed little of the family unhappiness she had seen since adolescence. A few pages mentioned her ill-starred betrothal to 'Sandro', which ended after her father's death when 'the marriage was definitely broken off by other people, who claimed a right to act on my behalf'. Her own feelings, she added, 'I need not enter into now; but my mother never forgot the part Bismarck had played and never forgave him.'[33] Apart from the chancellor, everyone else escaped unscathed. Not a word was written against her eldest brother whom she praised for 'his kindness of heart, his conscientiousness and his sincere piety'; it was 'well-nigh unbearable to see the whole weight of the world's greatest misfortune put upon him, and to hear people trying to make him out a sort of blood-thirsty tyrant, which he is far from being. Impulsive and self-willed he may be, but he is not a tyrant'.[34] This passage may have made her the toast of Doorn, but others who remembered the events of forty years earlier would have been excused for querying part of the statement.

While selling cherished family treasures, Victoria was introduced by her antique dealer Bielskov, a Russian refugee familiar with her gullible nature, who had assumed the more socially acceptable name of Count Ich-Bielskov, to a young man whom he called his cousin, Alexander Zubkov. Like him, he said, Zubkov had lost everything in the Russian Revolution. Thirty-four years younger than her, Zubkov was an accomplished confidence trickster who had tried almost every vice and indulgence possible in his short life. Kindly, naïve and far too trusting for her own good, Victoria believed his hard luck stories, showered gifts and money she could ill afford on him, and he went away to spend it on prostitutes, gambling and cocaine. Coming back for more, he proposed to Victoria and in 1927 they were engaged. Her horrified brothers and sisters begged her to reconsider, but she would not listen.

They were married at Bonn registry office on 19 November, the thirty-seventh anniversary of her first wedding. The church in Bonn would not conduct a wedding as the bride was a Protestant and her husband a member of the Russian Orthodox Church, so they found a Russian bishop to hold a ceremony at the Schaumburg Palace two days later in the old Russian tradition. Witnesses included the bride's godson Baron Solemacher, a former gentleman of the bedchamber to Kaiser Wilhelm, and Count von Merenberg, a son-in-law of Tsar Alexander II, but none of her family were present.

Naturally, the disastrous *mésalliance* was doomed. Intrigued by the marriage of a Hohenzollern princess to a vagrant less than half her age, the press reported their every move in public, shadowing them and constantly approaching the palace to ask her for interviews. The Schaumburg-Lippe treasury stopped a monthly allowance of 3,000 marks, which she had received since the death of her first husband. At Doorn her brother, resenting the publicity almost as much as she did, told his entourage that his sister had forfeited all right to belong to his family. The first serious row between husband and wife came after he argued with and assaulted a waiter at a Berlin coffee house. He continued to spend her money freely on his private vices, making surreptitious trips to Paris and Monte Carlo, gradually returning to Schaumburg Palace less and less. The last straw was when he came to her with an offer he said he had had from an American film company to make a picture of their life story if they would travel to the United States and play their own roles in person. A fee of $150,000 dollars plus expenses was proposed, he told her – 'more than all the money we owe'.[35]

Horrified by his unashamed admission of 'their' debts, at last Victoria had to face the truth about her husband. After another bitter quarrel he absconded with most of her dwindling funds. Shattered by his betrayal and desperately worried by her precarious financial position, she suffered a complete nervous collapse and took to her bed with acute depression and heart trouble. She had to call in the receivers and move out of Schaumburg Palace. Her maid Clara Franz found her a single furnished room in Mehlem, a suburb of Bonn, where she spent most of her time lying in bed, sobbing by day and crying herself to a disturbed sleep at night. As her condition deteriorated Clara wrote to Kaiser Wilhelm begging him for assistance, but received no reply. Meanwhile, Zubkov had found temporary employment as a waiter at a restaurant in Luxembourg, which displayed a poster outside its premises announcing that patrons would be served by 'the Kaiser's brother-in-law'. Wilhelm tried to take the restaurant to court in order to have the notice removed, but in vain. He too received several letters from Zubkov, asking for funds to help his sister. As Zubkov pointed out, Wilhelm was not only his brother-in-law but also his nephew by his second marriage, which made their family ties close enough to discuss how 'poor Vicky' could be helped. Zubkov received no letters in reply, only a succession of formal printed acknowledgements from the court of the chamberlain at Doorn, all of which he sold.

Princess Victoria, languishing in her rented room in Bonn, and probably unaware of anything that went on beyond her four walls, never received any money. By the autumn she had begun divorce proceedings against her husband, but she was losing all interest in life. A neglected cold turned to pneumonia, and in November she was admitted to hospital where she died ten days later. It was rumoured that she had committed suicide, or that her illness was the result of an attempt to throw herself in the river.

The other former crowned head of the family, Queen Sophie of the Hellenes, had seen her husband Constantine called upon to abdicate twice. After the first time, in 1917, their second son Alexander was created a puppet King. He contracted a morganatic marriage, only to die in agony from the effects of a badly treated monkey bite. King Constantine was recalled, but abdicated a second time two years later after a disastrous war between Greece and Turkey and died in January 1923, his spirit broken and his health ruined. The widowed Queen settled in a villa at Florence, and was invited to several royal weddings and christenings throughout Europe in the next few years. Relations saw how much she had aged after her experiences, while her letters betrayed a similar world-weariness. Writing to King George V (15 March 1928) about a stay in England after putting her youngest daughter Katherine into school, she said she had absolutely nothing to do with politics, 'so hope I can give no offence by living quietly – and out of the world in a small place if my means permit. I am too old and sad and tired to go out in society.'[36]

In January 1929 Sophie came to visit her brother at Doorn for his seventieth birthday. He greeted her politely yet distantly, and in their conversation he never once touched on her past sorrows, asked about her plans for the future, or showed any sympathy for what she had been through. Two years later she entered hospital at Frankfurt for an operation, cancer in its advanced stages was diagnosed, and she died peacefully in January 1932. Of the siblings only Margrethe, who had known the sadness of losing two of her six sons on active service in the war, was still alive and in good health.

Also in January 1932, a few days before his seventy-third birthday, the Kaiser had a minor heart attack, brought on by bronchitis and accompanied by swelling in the legs. Thanks to regular exercise and careful diet, he was very fit for a man of his age. He soon recovered, and despite his previous distaste for whisky, on medical advice he now took a small drop each evening after dinner in order to keep colds at bay.

Of all states that had raised the sword against Germany, Russia was the one on which the Kaiser looked most kindly. It had always been his regret that the treaty at Björkö was never allowed to stand, as he felt it would have allowed Germany to lead the continent as a guardian of peace with no wish for conquest. He took great interest in right-wing movements in other European countries; Benito Mussolini's leadership of Italy and General Miguel Primo de Rivera's regime in Spain under King Alfonso XIII were to him adequate proof of Europe's recognition that parliamentarianism was bankrupt and had nothing to offer. Perhaps Wilhelm watched the faltering career of Britain's would-be Fascist leader Oswald Mosley with curiosity.

While the Kaiser had become a voracious reader – and in the 1920s many books of memoirs and history vied for his attention – Hitler's *Mein Kampf* was not on his list. Wisely, he spared himself from wading through the two lengthy volumes, in historian Karl Dietrich Bracher's words 'a tedious compilation of turgid discourses on repetitious themes'.[37] Of the Nazi doctrine of patriotism and wholehearted belief that Germans were the highest species of humanity on earth, and its demands for more *Lebensraum* (living space) and a united political Europe under German leadership, the Kaiser could not but approve. In view of remarks expressed in his correspondence from Doorn it is hard to imagine that he had anything but sympathy for its racial, anti-Semite elements. Though he only showed perfunctory enthusiasm for Hitler as a person or for his party, he continued to hope that he would help him regain his throne, if not for him then for one of his sons or grandsons.

Such ambitions were about all the Kaiser and his heir still shared. The latter was leading an aimless life, unofficially separated from his wife and indulging in one short-lived affair after another, drinking and smoking more than was good for him. Three of his brothers, Eitel Friedrich, August Wilhelm and Oskar, joined the Stahlhelm, an ultra-right-wing organization for ex-servicemen committed to upholding and promoting order, discipline and national fellowship, though only August Wilhelm was enthusiastic about the Nazis. Two of the Crown Prince's sons served in the Wehrmacht. The Kaiser's other surviving son, Adalbert, had long since disassociated himself completely from his family and country, taken the name Count Lingen, and settled as a private citizen in La Tour de Peilz, on the shores of Lake Geneva.

If the Kaiser had actually read *Mein Kampf,* or spoken to somebody who did, he would have spared himself years of living in a fool's paradise. Hitler's manifesto laid bare not only his vision of Germany's future and his hatred of Jews, but also his contempt for the Hohenzollerns and Habsburgs, alongside liberal and Marxist ideals, middle-class values, bourgeois nationalism and capitalism and similar schools of thought. Nevertheless, at least three of the Kaiser's cousins were attracted by Nazi doctrines. Charles, Duke of Coburg until 1918, was a fervent supporter, while two daughters of Alfred, the previous Duke, Grand Duchess Cyril of Russia and Princess Ernest of Hohenlohe-Langenburg, both expressed interest either because they were attracted by the Nazis' anti-communism and anti-Semitism (many of the Bolsheviks had Jewish blood) or as they supported Hitler's vision of a regenerated Germany. Hermine and some members of the suite at Doorn were more sympathetic to the Nazi regime and undoubtedly influenced the Kaiser to some extent. As she was cultured and well-read it is hard to imagine that his second wife did not study the book herself, though in mitigation it has to be said that she and her husband found it prudent to maintain amicable business relations with the regime, particularly where negotiations concerning Hohenzollern properties in Germany were concerned. As Wilhelm was forbidden to enter the country, she had to act on his behalf and meet Nazi leaders from time to time.

Sometimes the Nazi hierarchy came to Doorn. Hermann Goering, Prussian Minister President and one of Hitler's closest associates, stayed with them in January 1931 and again in May 1932, and gave them the impression that he favoured a Hohenzollern restoration. Goering had been a loyal servant of the Second Reich, and received the honour of *Pour le Merité* during the war. Heinrich Brüning, chancellor from 1930 to 1932, also favoured re-establishing the German empire, with Hindenburg as regent for one of the Kaiser's grandsons. Yet the Kaiser and Crown Prince both believed their chances were better with Goering than with Brüning or Hindenburg. It was a grave error of judgment; the Nazis were not monarchist conservatives, but uncompromising republicans and radical revolutionaries of the right. To Hitler, Kaiser Wilhelm I had been a grand seigneur, but his grandson was 'a strutting puppet of no character'. While consolidating his position in the early days, Hitler had appreciated the propaganda value and respectability that some connection with the former reigning house would bring the Nazi party, but in his view monarchy was 'an absurdity'. In the summer of 1933 Goering and Friedrich von Berg, the Kaiser's comptroller, signed an agreement that would confer a substantial annual allowance on the Kaiser, the Crown Prince and remaining princes from the Prussian state. If any of them dared to criticize the Nazi regime, payments would cease forthwith.

Hermine was spending more and more time in Berlin, partly as husband and wife evidently got on each other's nerves and could only take so much of each other. She had an inordinate sense of her own importance, was susceptible to flattery and unlike Dona, showed a disconcerting independence of mind as well as readiness to force her unsolicited opinions on Wilhelm. She found life at Doorn frustrating and disliked the damp climate, and after a few years of marriage did not conceal her impatience with his friends who came to stay and talk endlessly about 'the old days'. Their retinue were always relieved to see her depart for Germany, and she was not encouraged to hurry home. With her lack of discretion, the Kaiser realized that he had to be careful what he said to her. 'Around my wife I must place every word on the scales',[38] he told his faithful Ilsemann, who like most of his retinue disliked her more with each passing year. By the 1930s she clung more steadfastly than her husband to the idea of a crown. Either through grim determination or sheer naivety, she sent word from Berlin that the monarchical cause was making steady progress under the Nazis, oblivious to Hitler's refusal to have anything to do with her 'petticoat politics'. The Kaiser was already disillusioned with the Nazi regime, and deplored his wife's apparent eagerness to run round after them vainly soliciting their support and goodwill on his behalf.

Hitler's ascendancy made the Entente powers look back on 'the old days' more fondly than they might have cared to admit. In 1933, eleven years after relinquishing office, Lloyd George admitted to Prince Louis Ferdinand, second son of the Crown Prince, that they had neither expected nor intended to overthrow the Hohenzollerns; if only they had remained in power in Germany, 'then we wouldn't need to give ourselves such headaches now about Herr Hitler'.[39] In the best tradition of selective political amnesia, he had conveniently forgotten that only fifteen years earlier he had let himself be swept along by demands of the popular press in his general election campaign partly on an empty promise to 'hang the Kaiser'.

In June 1934 Randolph Churchill, then pursuing a career as a political journalist prior to fighting a seat at Westminster, visited Doorn to interview the Kaiser. Though Wilhelm generally refrained from talking to the press, he was prepared to make an exception for the son of an English politician of whom he still cherished friendly memories, and invited him to lunch. But when pressed for his views on Hitler Wilhelm avoided the question and talked about matters in the Far East. Hermine was happier to oblige, telling Churchill with some asperity that he knew nothing of 'the new Germany'. She was shocked when Churchill told them that he regarded Hitler as a danger and an enemy.

Once he had seized power Hitler dropped all pretence of any sentimental attachment to the institution of monarchy. Hindenburg died in August 1934, allegedly with the words 'Mein Kaiser' on his lips. The Kaiser, who had sent the president a message as he lay dying, received this news with scorn, calling the dead man 'the traitor of Spa'. While monarchists in the officer corps considered restoring the crown, the Nazis acted quickly, Hitler proclaiming amalgamation of the presidency and chancellorship. Within twenty-four hours of Hindenburg's death, Hitler received oaths of allegiance from the commanding officers of the armed forces. The former Kaiser had expected to see the Hohenzollerns recalled; if not himself or his son, at least his grandson. He angrily told Ilsemann that blood would have to flow, that 'of the officers and the civil servants, above all of the nobility, of everyone who has deserted me'.[40] They were added to his mental list of those on whom he would take revenge when he returned to power, along with the Social Democrats, who had plotted revolution against him and cost the throne, and even the generous Dutch authorities, who had provided him with a safe haven, for failing to treat him with due respect while in exile.[41]

At length the Kaiser had to resign himself to the likelihood of dying an exile, and the probability that Germany would never again be a monarchy – or at least not in his lifetime. Now aged seventy-five, he had spent fifteen peaceful years in the Netherlands. Had he been recalled to the throne, he would have bowed to what he saw as a dynastic duty rather than embrace once again with any great enthusiasm the crown which he had worn for thirty often turbulent years. In any case, the omens for exiled monarchs summoned back to their thrones were not encouraging, as the fate of his brother-in-law King Constantine of the Hellenes had shown.

To the outside world Wilhelm and Hermine presented a tranquil picture. The villagers regarded their mildly eccentric squire amiably, a familiar sight strolling through the park on summer evenings, straw boater tilted gently to the right, an ebony cane in his hand. Many a souvenir hunter visited him and came away cheerfully with a small log cut by the imperial hand, signed with a large 'W' in indelible pencil. He was honorary president of the Doorn Study Circle, *Doorner Arbeitsgemeinschaft*, a group whose aim was to assemble a collection of writings and pictures dealing with the history of Mediterranean and Indian civilizations. He opened the annual meetings of the group and sometimes presented erudite papers on archaeology and other historical subjects, usually written for him by other members and interspersed with his own irrelevant interjections, denouncing socialism and bolshevism. For light reading the Kaiser enjoyed the novels of P.G. Wodehouse, Dorothy L. Sayers and Ellery Queen. He liked private film shows, particularly historical epics; Herbert Wilcox's *Victoria the Great* was a particular favourite, and he asked one of his suite to send a message of congratulation to the director on the convincing manner in which Anna Neagle had portrayed his grandmother.[42]

In England the descendants of his 'unparalleled grandmama' had latterly entertained sons of the Crown Prince and of the Duchess of Brunswick. Though he had resented King George V's silence on the death of Dona in 1921, when 'Georgy' died in January 1936 the Kaiser sent Queen Mary his condolences, and she sent him a gold box from the King's desk as a keepsake. Wilhelm also despatched an aide to Berlin to ask that he should be represented at the King's funeral. The new sovereign King Edward VIII suggested that the Crown Prince should do so, but the foreign office thought this choice too contentious and instead recommended the Crown Prince's fourth son Friedrich, who had been a guest at Cowes.

Two years later, the Kaiser feared that Europe was about to erupt in war again. He was so relieved by the outcome of the meeting of the British prime minister, Neville Chamberlain, with Hitler at Munich in September 1938 that he wrote to Queen Mary, expressing his delight. 'May I with a grateful heart relieved from a sickening anxiety by the intercession of Heaven unite my warmest sincerest thanks to the Lord with yours & those of the German & British People that He saved us from a most fearful catastrophe by helping the responsible statesmen to preserve peace!'[43] It was his first direct contact with his British cousins since before the war.

The Foreign Office in London kept an eye on the Kaiser's activities. In February 1938 senior officials in Whitehall had learnt from two sources of a plot thought to have been devised by Karl Goerdeler, the former mayor of Leipzig. There would be a naval coup at Kiel, and a warship would broadcast a recorded message from the Kaiser calling on royalists to support one of his grandsons in restoring sane government to Germany. Later that year Major Ewald von Kleist came secretly to England, met Churchill at Chartwell and told him that a group of generals were hoping to establish a new government in Berlin, probably of a monarchist character.

How much the Kaiser knew of these projects is debatable, but he and his sons were now increasingly disenchanted with if not hostile to the Nazi movement. The mindless violence of *Kristallnacht*, Hitler's night of anti-Jewish savagery, in November 1938, an episode which even disgusted some of the other Nazis, horrified him; it was 'pure bolshevism'[44] and 'an infamous blot' on Germany's reputation. For the first time in his life, Wilhelm said, he was ashamed to be a German;[45] he was shocked by anti-Jewish violence and attacks on synagogues throughout Germany. Such events 'at home', he told the Duchess of Brunswick, were a scandal, and it was high time the army intervened. 'All the old officers and upstanding Germans should have protested, but they witnessed murder and arson, and no one lifted a finger.'[46]

If his daughter's recollections were accurate, it is difficult to reconcile these condemnations with the Kaiser's letters to Poultney Bigelow a decade earlier. One (18 October 1927) advocated 'regular international all-worlds pogrom *à la Russe*' as the best cure for 'the Hebrew race'; another (15 August 1929) bracketed Jews and Mosquitoes together as 'a nuisance that humanity must get rid of in some way or other. . . . I believe the best would be gas!'[47] Such outpourings were disturbingly close to Hitler's musings in *Mein Kampf* that if during the First World War, 'twelve or fifteen thousand of these Hebrew defilers had been put under poison gas, as hundreds of thousands of our very best workers from all walks of life had to endure at the front, then the sacrifice of millions at the front would not have been in vain' and 'twelve thousand scoundrels eliminated in time might perhaps have saved the lives of a million decent, valuable Germans'.[48] Though the squire of Doorn might verbally deplore the Führer's campaign of murder and arson on the streets of Berlin to his daughter in 1938, it was scarcely more than the realization of certain solutions which he had not merely envisaged but suggested to Bigelow.

An alleged interview in an American magazine was reported in the *Daily Telegraph* on 8 December, in which the Kaiser damned the Nazi movement and the regime. Two days later a statement from Doorn called it a fabrication, saying he always observed a silence over current political questions. The foreign office in London therefore showed no enthusiasm for a proposal from John Boyd-Carpenter, whose family had known the Kaiser before the war, that he should visit Doorn to obtain a statement from him intended to ease the general situation in Europe.

On Wilhelm's eightieth birthday in January 1939 he received telegrams of congratulation from King George VI, Queen Elizabeth and Queen Mary. Hitler showed his hostility by forbidding all active and reserve officers to send good wishes to their former commander-in-chief. Even so Mackensen and another of the Kaiser's former marshals, Crown Prince Rupert of Bavaria, went to attend celebrations at Doorn, where the imperial standard and the flag of Prussia fluttered proudly from the tower. Many members of the Kaiser's family were there, as well as representatives of the imperial officer corps, and other royalties including Grand Duke Vladimir of Russia and Prince Friedrich Christian of Saxony. The Court chaplain preached at a thanksgiving service, followed by dinner, a showing of the film *The Life of Frederick the Great* and a ball.

In the third week of August 1939 the Kaiser gave an audience to two representatives of the Foreign Office in London, Robert Bruce Lockhart and John Wheeler-Bennett. To them he confided his conviction that they were unlikely to avoid another major war; Hitler was the slave rather than the master of events, and 'the machine [was] running away with *him* as it ran away with *me*'. They also realized that he and his wife had seen through the Führer's regime; by this time Hermine was equally disillusioned. The Kaiser complained that he was a prisoner in his own house, and the Nazis treated him far worse than the socialists ever did, while his wife warned their guests to beware of the *Umbegung*, her husband's entourage at Doorn. They were spies, she said, who reported everything to the Nazis. She admitted that they had done some good, 'but they are evil, and great harm will come from them'.[49]

Yet Wilhelm's feelings of disgust at Nazi excesses and their espionage methods did nothing to modify his uncompromising anti-Semitism. To the end of his days he declared Germany to be the land of monarchy and therefore of Christ, while the constitutional monarchy of Britain was the home of liberalism, Satan and the Antichrist. Several private letters to family and friends argued passionately that the enemy of Germany was not the British people but the English ruling classes. In 1914 and again in 1939, he maintained, Jews and Freemasons had unleashed war against Germany to establish an international Jewish empire held together by British and American gold, and it was Germany's duty with the help of God to liberate the British people from 'the Antichrist Juda'.[50] His entourage were shocked at the hatred which he still nursed for those who had opposed him in the past. While the public in Germany and Britain saw only a charming elderly country squire in serene retirement, the inner man was still a vindictive, embittered character who never ceased to hold others responsible for his defeat and abdication, and still hoped that they or their heirs would soon get their just desserts.

On 3 September Germany and Britain were at war for the second time in just over twenty-five years. Within forty-eight hours the Hohenzollerns suffered another casualty when the eldest child of the Kaiser's fifth son Oskar, another Oskar, was killed fighting on the Polish Front. Wilhelm's wartime loyalties were divided, for he was deeply indebted to the country which had afforded him and his Court sanctuary – even though it was at war with Germany. Through the German ambassador at The Hague he sent a message to Hitler expressing relief at his survival of an assassination plot in Munich on 8 November. Ten days later he sent a telegram of condolence to Queen Wilhelmina when the Dutch steamer *Simon Bolivar* was sunk in the North Sea. Between October 1939 and January 1940 he arranged for two-thirds of his personal funds to be transferred for safe keeping to Switzerland. In the second week of November 1939 the British embassy in The Hague was informed that if the Kaiser's future was to be questioned by the Dutch authorities, the Foreign Office in London would seek to have him transferred to Sweden or Denmark, and only in the last resort to the United Kingdom.

At 3.30 a.m. on 10 May 1940 gunfire was heard in Doorn, and at 7.00 the Dutch commandant sent orders that the Kaiser, his wife and their suite were to consider themselves interned. All but four of their German servants were required to leave, their radios were confiscated and their telephone wires cut. The grounds of the estate were patrolled, and there were orders to shoot anyone moving outside the house after 8 p.m. The Kaiser was asked to sign an undertaking that he would do nothing to harm the Dutch government or the country. That same day, in England, Chamberlain resigned as prime minister, and was succeeded by Winston Churchill. Within a few hours he recommended the Foreign Office to advise the former sovereign privately that he would be received with consideration and dignity in England if he wished to seek asylum there. The proposal was approved by Lord Halifax, the foreign secretary, and King George VI, and then telegraphed to the ambassador at The Hague on 11 May. Reaction in Whitehall was hostile, with Sir Robert Vansittart, principal diplomatic adviser to the foreign secretary, asking 'why the old architect of evil should be allowed to come here'.[51] Many people, he pointed out, would strongly object.

On receipt of the message the Kaiser asked for time to reflect. If he accepted, he and Hermine could fly out on a RAF plane which would reach Holland within a few hours. But he could not believe that the British regarded him as anything but an enemy. Twelve members of his family were serving with the German army, and he did not want to appear a traitor to them. He had never flown in an aeroplane, and at eighty-one he had little desire to start. On the evening of 12 May the Foreign Office received a reply from the ambassador that the offer of asylum was gratefully declined. The ambassador was being tactful, as the Kaiser told Ilsemann that he saw it as merely a ruse to involve him in a game of 'political chess' with Germany, and an anti-German propaganda move by Churchill. He would rather be shot in Holland, Wilhelm retorted, than be photographed with Churchill in England; the British offer was 'a temptation of Satan'.[52] Certainly he did not wish it to be known that he had been in contact with the British prime minister while he was watching the successful German advance in France with interest.

On 14 May the Wehrmacht entered Doorn, the Kaiser's servants were freed from internment, and a German patrol came to guard him. Suddenly he was no longer the gentle Dutch country squire, but a retired German warlord whose heart beat more strongly at every sign of German success. Even so he was pledged to help, or at the very least not to embarrass, the nation who had befriended him over more than two decades of exile. He was photographed bare-headed and in silent prayer beside the graves of fallen soldiers from both armies. Yet he could do no more than maintain a dignified silence in public as an observer of events.

Later that month the family sustained another wartime casualty. On 23 May the Crown Prince's eldest son Wilhelm was severely wounded in fighting near Valenciennes, and died three days later in a military hospital. At his funeral in Potsdam, a crowd of 50,000 sympathizers followed the cortège. Angered by this apparent pro-monarchist demonstration, Hitler ordered every remaining Hohenzollern on active service to be taken off the army list and accept civilian employment. There was, however, one moment of domestic happiness at Doorn that month when Hermine's daughter Henriette was married to the Kaiser's grandson Karl Franz Josef, only son of his unhappy son Joachim who had taken his own life in 1920.

Despite this petty gesture against his house – or, as some believed, as an attempt to placate the Führer – on 17 June, three days after German troops entered Paris, Wilhelm called for champagne and telegraphed his congratulations to Hitler whose victories, he declared proudly, were comparable only to those of Frederick the Great at Leuthen in 1757 and of his grandfather in France in 1870. It must have seemed like providence after their failure in the First World War. To the Duchess of Brunswick he wrote triumphantly that the German war flag flew over Versailles; 'Thus is the pernicious Entente Cordiale of Uncle Edward VII brought to nought.'[53]

The Crown Prince followed his father's example in telegraphing his support to the Führer. In the last two weeks of June he congratulated him on his 'genial leadership, the incomparable bravery of our troops and their first-class equipment', which had succeeded in only five weeks 'in forcing Holland and Belgium to capitulate, in driving the remnants of the English Expeditionary Corps into the sea, and in defeating decisively the bravely fighting French army in a series of magnificent encircling battles . . . the way is free for a final reckoning with Perfidious Albion'.[54] That the Crown Prince could express such ingratitude to Holland, the nation which had generously given his father sanctuary for over twenty years, and pour such damning criticism on England, the country which was nominally an enemy but for which he had often expressed his admiration, suggested that he still hoped to ingratiate himself with Hitler and, against the odds, persuade him to grant the Hohenzollern heir a military position.

Despite his public silence, in private the Kaiser was thrilled by every German success, which he felt was about to achieve what he had failed to do a quarter of a century earlier. To his sister Margrethe, the widowed Landgravine of Hesse, he wrote (3 November) that the hand of God was creating a new world and working miracles; 'We are becoming the *U.S. of Europe* under German leadership, a united European Continent, nobody ever hoped to see.'[55] Margrethe's husband had died in May, and while both had distanced themselves from Wilhelm for some years, their feelings towards him had mellowed in later life.

Almost to the end the Kaiser corresponded with his old friend Poulteney Bigelow. On the centenary of his mother's birthday (21 November 1940), it saddened him to think that no notice was taken of it 'at home'; there was no memorial service or committee to remember her efforts on behalf of welfare for the Germans. 'Nobody of the new generation knows anything about her.'[56] But at the height of Nazi

Germany's struggle with England and her allies, it was hardly the moment for Hitler to let his people celebrate the much misunderstood woman once derisively known by her detractors in Berlin as *'Die Engländerin'*.

The next generation of his family, and their safety in a continent racked by war for the second time in twenty-five years, caused Wilhelm some anxiety. Soon after Christmas he was concerned at the plight of his nephew King George II of the Hellenes and his family. Crown Princess Frederica, daughter of the Duchess of Brunswick and therefore the Kaiser's granddaughter, had been forced to seek sanctuary with her small children Sophie and Constantine, the latter a babe in arms, from German divisions threatening Athens. This, and his continuing disapproval of the Crown Prince, cast a shadow over his last months. The Kaiser's eldest son's infidelities and unsuccessful marriage saddened him as much as the aimless heir's strained relationship with his stepmother.

However, Kaiser Wilhelm was nearing the end of his life. In January 1941 he celebrated his eighty-second birthday quietly. Old age had brought heart trouble, though apart from a mild stroke in 1938 he had remained healthy. By March he could no longer do any work in the garden, and had to spend increasing amounts of time in bed or in a wheelchair. On 24 May an intestinal obstruction was diagnosed, and the doctors summoned the Duchess of Brunswick and her brothers August Wilhelm and Oskar. Though his presence had rarely been welcome at Doorn, the Crown Prince dutifully visited his father, now frail and bedridden but lucid and cheerful. When told that the British battleship *Hood* had been sunk by the German *Bismarck*, he told them that if they brought him more good news like that he would soon get well.[57] But on 3 June he had a heart attack and realized it was the end. He told Hermine that he was ready to die, fell into a coma and without regaining consciousness passed peacefully away at 11.30 the next morning. In Germany the news was announced with single column headlines on the front page.

Eight years earlier the former Kaiser had prepared elaborate instructions for his funeral. If allowed to return to Germany during his lifetime, he wanted to be buried in the mausoleum at Potsdam. Should he die in exile, it was his wish to be laid to rest on his estate at Doorn, without any display of swastika flags. He had anticipated that the Führer would endeavour to use his death for propaganda purposes, and indeed Hitler planned to arrange a state funeral for him in Berlin. Frustrated in his efforts, the Führer sent a swastika-decked wreath to the ceremony instead.

On 9 June detachments from the German army, navy and airforce, mounted a last parade for their former sovereign. His widow, surviving sons and daughter, several grandsons and dignitaries from all over Germany followed a slow-moving motor hearse from Doorn to a small chapel near the main entrance to the park. His body was laid to rest there to await the construction of a small mausoleum. At the simple ceremony there was no funeral oration, no tolling of cathedral bells, no sombre music, only a chorale and simple march as the guard of honour walked away, and a volley fired by marksmen as a final salute. It was a modest farewell to the man who had once been the most hated and vilified figure in Europe, if not the world.

# Genealogical Tables

## THE HOUSE OF HOHENZOLLERN

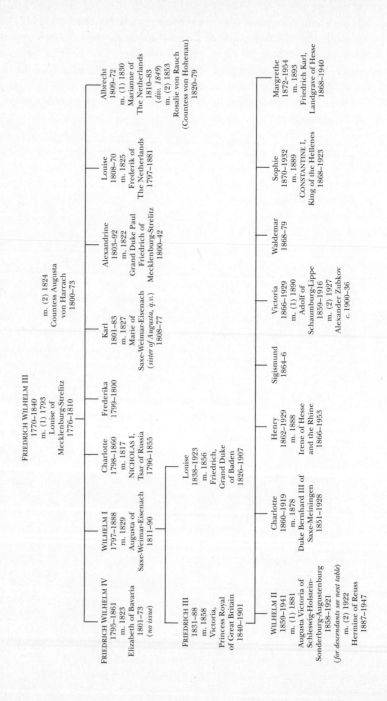

FRIEDRICH WILHELM III
1770–1840
m. (1) 1793
Louise of
Mecklenburg-Strelitz
1776–1810

m. (2) 1824
Countess Augusta
von Harrach
1800–73

FRIEDRICH WILHELM IV
1795–1861
m. 1823
Elizabeth of Bavaria
1801–73
(*no issue*)

WILHELM I
1797–1888
m. 1829
Augusta of
Saxe-Weimar-Eisenach
1811–90

Charlotte
1798–1860
m. 1817
NICHOLAS I,
Tsar of Russia
1796–1855

Frederika
1799–1800

Karl
1801–83
m. 1827
Marie of
Saxe-Weimar-Eisenach
(*sister of Augusta, q.v.*)
1808–77

Alexandrine
1803–92
m. 1822
Grand Duke Paul
Friedrich of
Mecklenburg-Strelitz
1800–42

Louise
1808–70
m. 1825
Frederik of
The Netherlands
1797–1881

Albrecht
1809–72
m. (1) 1830
Marianne of
The Netherlands
1810–83
(*div. 1849*)
m. (2) 1853
Rosalie von Rauch
(Countess von Hohenau)
1820–79

FRIEDRICH III
1831–88
m. 1858
Victoria,
Princess Royal
of Great Britain
1840–1901

Louise
1838–1923
m. 1856
Friedrich,
Grand Duke
of Baden
1826–1907

WILHELM II
1859–1941
m. (1) 1881
Augusta Victoria of
Schleswig-Holstein-
Sonderburg-Augustenburg
1858–1921
(*for descendants see next table*)
m. (2) 1922
Hermine of Reuss
1887–1947

Charlotte
1860–1919
m. 1878
Duke Bernhard III of
Saxe-Meiningen
1851–1928

Henry
1862–1929
m. 1888
Irene of Hesse
and the Rhine
1866–1953

Sigismund
1864–6

Victoria
1866–1929
m. (1) 1890
Adolf of
Schaumburg-Lippe
1859–1916
m. (2) 1927
Alexander Zubkov
c. 1900–36

Waldemar
1868–79

Sophie
1870–1932
m. 1889
CONSTANTINE I,
King of the Hellenes
1868–1923

Margrethe
1872–1954
m. 1893
Friedrich Karl,
Landgrave of Hesse
1868–1940

# The Family of Wilhelm II

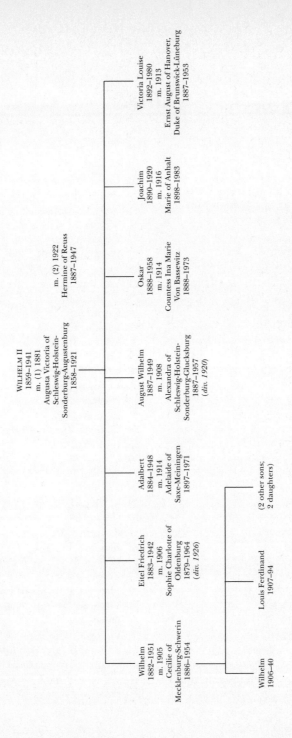

WILHELM II
1859–1941
m. (1) 1881
Augusta Victoria of
Schleswig-Holstein-
Sonderburg-Augustenburg
1858–1921

m. (2) 1922
Hermine of Reuss
1887–1947

Wilhelm
1882–1951
m. 1905
Cecilie of
Mecklenburg-Schwerin
1886–1954

Eitel Friedrich
1883–1942
m. 1906
Sophie Charlotte of
Oldenburg
1879–1964
(div. 1926)

Adalbert
1884–1948
m. 1914
Adelaide of
Saxe-Meiningen
1897–1971

August Wilhelm
1887–1949
m. 1908
Alexandra of
Schleswig-Holstein-
Sonderburg-Glucksburg
1887–1957
(div. 1920)

Oskar
1888–1958
m. 1914
Countess Ina Marie
Von Bassewitz
1888–1973

Joachim
1890–1920
m. 1916
Marie of Anhalt
1898–1983

Victoria Louise
1892–1980
m. 1913
Ernst August of Hanover,
Duke of Brunswick-Lüneburg
1887–1953

Wilhelm
1906–40

Louis Ferdinand
1907–94

(2 other sons;
2 daughters)

# *Notes*

## PREFACE

1. Winston Churchill, 19.
2. *Contemporary Review*, June 1941.
3. *The Times*, 5 June 1974.
4. Balfour, 433–4.
5. Röhl and Sombart, *New Interpretations*, 24 (hereafter Röhl, *NI*).
6. Ibid., 25.
7. Cecil, I, xi.
8. Röhl, *NI*, 1–2.
9. *This England*, Summer 1998.

## CHAPTER 1

1. Poschinger, 21.
2. Martin, III, 373.
3. Anon., *Empress Frederick: a Memoir*, 41–2.
4. Victoria, *Letters 1837–61*, III, 253.
5. Anon., *Empress Frederick: a Memoir*, 68.
6. Victoria, *Dearest Child*, 108.
7. Bennett, 84.
8. Pakula, 124.
9. Bennett, 84–6.
10. Pakula, 124.
11. Bennett, 85.
12. Röhl, *Kaiser and his Court*, 25 (hereafter Röhl, *KC*).
13. Sinclair, 45.
14. Pakula, 126–7.
15. Roberts, 115.
16. Röhl, *KC*, 25.
17. William II, *My Early Life*, 22.
18. Röhl, *KC*, 25–6; Palmer, *The Kaiser*, 4 (all Palmer references are to this title).
19. Cecil, I, 13.
20. Corti, *English Empress*, 53 (all Corti references are to this title unless specified otherwise).
21. Victoria, *Letters of the Empress Frederick*, 20.
22. Woodham-Smith, 396.
23. Victoria, *Dearest Mama*, 203.
24. Victoria, *Dearest Child*, 224.
25. Bennett, 87.
26. Corti, 5.
27. Pakula, 128.
28. William II, *My Early Life*, 1.
29. Frith, I, 351–3.
30. Corti, 89–90.
31. Victoria, *Dearest Mama*, 96.
32. Corti, 96.
33. Bennett, 125.
34. Victoria, *Dearest Mama*, 203–4.
35. Ibid., 216.
36. Corti, 139.
37. William II, *My Early Life*, 18.
38. Corti, 139.
39. Morier, II, 97.
40. Corti, 159.
41. Radowitz MS.
42. Bigelow, 48.
43. William II, *My Early Life*, 30.
44. Kohut, 43.
45. Victoria, Princess of Prussia, 4.
46. Victoria, *Letters of the Empress Frederick*, 131.
47. Victoria, *Darling Child*, 89.
48. William II, *My Early Life*, 73.
49. Victoria, *Darling Child*, 149.
50. William II, *My Early Life*, 108.
51. Pakula, 364.

52. Palmer, 16.
53. William II, *My Early Life*, 61.
54. Ibid., 146.
55. Röhl, *NI*, 73.
56. Pakula, 366.
57. William II, *My Early Life*, 147.
58. Victoria, *Letters of the Empress Frederick*, 177.
59. Ibid., 178.
60. Ibid., 179.
61. Dorpalen.

## CHAPTER 2

1. Victoria, *Beloved Mama*, 86.
2. Corti, 213.
3. Victoria, *Letters 1886–1901*, I, 485.
4. Balfour, 83.
5. William II, *My Early Life*, 184.
6. Victoria, *Letters of the Empress Frederick*, 183.
7. Victoria, *Beloved Mama*, 96.
8. Daisy, Princess of Pless, 195.
9. Marie, Queen of Roumania, I, 221.
10. Cecil, II, 4.
11. Cecil, I, 71.
12. William II, *My Early Life*, 246.
13. Cecil, I, 81.
14. Corti, 226.
15. Ludwig, 16.
16. Cecil, I, 77.
17. William II, *My Early Life*, 190.
18. Ibid., 201.
19. Holstein, II, 347.
20. Ludwig, 31.
21. Edmond Taylor, 202.
22. Palmer, 28.
23. Daisy, Princess of Pless, 203.
24. Ludwig, 32.
25. Hull, 20.
26. Ibid., 64.
27. Röhl, *NI*, 48.
28. Kollander, 163.
29. Arthur Ponsonby, 361.
30. Cecil, I, 265.
31. Holstein, II, 254.

32. Röhl, *NI*, 101.
33. Corti, *Alexander von Battenberg*, 129–31.
34. William II, *My Early Life*, 199.
35. Ludwig, 21.
36. William II, *My Early Life*, 5.
37. Röhl, *Purple Secret*, 119 (hereafter Röhl, *PS*).
38. Victoria, *Letters of the Empress Frederick*, 284.
39. Corti, 244.
40. Mackenzie, 65.
41. Rodd, *Social and Diplomatic Memories*, I, 123.
42. Balfour, 111.
43. Holstein, II, 348.
44. Victoria, *Letters of the Empress Frederick*, 256–7.
45. Ibid., 257.
46. William II, *My Early Life*, 279.
47. Royal Archives, RA Z 66/109.
48. Röhl, *NI*, 44.
49. William II, *My Early Life*, 229–30.
50. Röhl, *KC*, 199.
51. Cecil, I, 104.
52. Holstein, II, 363.
53. Arthur Ponsonby, 290–2.
54. Corti, 261.
55. Röhl, *KC*, 202.
56. Corti, 263.
57. William II, *My Early Life*, 286.
58. Schwering, 25–6.
59. The *Graphic*, 17.3.1888.
60. Bülow, I, 619.
61. Corti, 269.
62. Ibid., 270–1.
63. Ibid., 271.
64. Röhl, *KC*, 15.
65. Corti, 271–2.
66. Röhl, *KC*, 15.
67. Cecil, I, 118.
68. Mackenzie, 154–5.
69. Arthur Ponsonby, 296.
70. Victoria, *Letters 1886–1901*, I, 405.
71. Arthur Ponsonby, 297.
72. Victoria, *Letters 1886–1901*, I, 403.

73. Röhl, *KC*, 15.
74. Victoria, *Beloved and Darling Child*, 70.
75. Victoria, *Letters of the Empress Frederick*, 311.
76. Nowak, 21–3.
77. William II, *My Early Life*, 295.
78. Corti, 295.
79. Pakula, 487.
80. Princess Victoria to the Hon Mrs Talbot, 5.6.1888. MS letter from private collection by courtesy of Ian Shapiro.
81. Corti, 280.

CHAPTER 3

1. Sinclair, 220.
2. Reid, 101.
3. Nowak, 26.
4. William II, *My Early Life*, 298–9.
5. Victoria, *Letters 1886–1901*, I, 417.
6. Hough, 143.
7. Ibid., 144.
8. Ludwig, 57.
9. Cecil, II, 79.
10. Ludwig, 56–7.
11. Victoria, *Letters 1886–1901*, I, 410.
12. St Aubyn, 279.
13. Victoria, *Letters of the Empress Frederick*, 324.
14. Nowak, 29.
15. Palmer, 36.
16. Victoria, *Letters of the Empress Frederick*, 322.
17. Röhl, *KC*, 75–6.
18. Victoria, *Letters 1886–1901*, I, 424.
19. Ibid., 425.
20. Ibid., 429.
21. Victoria, *Letters of the Empress Frederick*, 349.
22. Cassels, 185.
23. Victoria, *Letters 1886–1901*, I, 440–1.
24. Magnus, 309.
25. Marie, Queen of Roumania, I, 285.
26. Victoria, *Letters of the Empress Frederick*, 348.
27. Marie, Queen of Roumania, I, 284.
28. Topham, 27.
29. Balfour, 139.
30. Topham, 54.
31. Heckstall-Smith, 53.
32. Topham, 25.
33. Hull, 33.
34. Cecil, II, 49.
35. Holstein, II, 382.
36. Pakula, 510.
37. Sinclair, 231.
38. Magnus, 213.
39. Röhl, *KC*, 21; Röhl, *PS*, 223.
40. Victoria, *Letters 1886–1901*, I, 504.
41. Victoria, *Letters of the Empress Frederick*, 363.
42. William II, *My Early Life*, 87.
43. A.J.P. Taylor, 246.
44. Corti, 331.
45. Pakula, 530.
46. Ibid., 531.
47. Nowak, 217–18.
48. Palmer, 50.
49. Nichols, 34.
50. Cecil, I, 191–2.
51. Corti, 339.
52. Victoria, *Empress Frederick Writes to Sophie*, 21.
53. Pakula, 544.
54. Palmer, 54.
55. Magnus, 228.
56. Anon., *The Kaiser, as he is* (article).
57. Röhl, *Germany without Bismarck*, 72.
58. Victoria, *Letters of the Empress Frederick*, 429.
59. Balfour, 158.
60. Whittle, 150.
61. Röhl, *Germany without Bismarck*, 86.
62. Hull, 204.
63. Röhl, *NI*, 35.
64. Röhl, *KC*, 21–2.
65. Henry Ponsonby, 297.
66. Topham, 12.
67. William, Crown Prince, *Memoirs*, 15.

68. Alice, 93.
69. Hull, 19.
70. Topham, 28.
71. Fischer, 289.
72. Röhl, *NI*, 35.
73. Röhl, *Germany without Bismarck*, 116.

## CHAPTER 4

1. Röhl, *Germany without Bismarck*, 121.
2. Arthur Ponsonby, 363.
3. Grant, 24.
4. Balfour, 180.
5. Massie, 164.
6. Cecil, I, 300.
7. Röhl, *Germany without Bismarck*, 128.
8. Eckardstein, 56–7.
9. Frederick Leopold, 115.
10. Victoria, *Empress Frederick Writes to Sophie*, 212.
11. Grant, 30.
12. Chamier, 103.
13. Lee, I, 725.
14. Röhl, *Germany without Bismarck*, 218.
15. Ibid., 229.
16. Röhl, *NI*, 38.
17. Fischer, 298.
18. Holstein, IV, 35.
19. Cecil, II, 77.
20. Bülow, II, 200.
21. Victoria, *Empress Frederick Writes to Sophie*, 73.
22. Bülow, II, 200.
23. Sinclair, 239.
24. Bing, 136.
25. Victoria, *Letters 1886–1901*, III, 360.
26. Zedlitz-Trutschler, 118.
27. Victoria, *Letters 1886–1901*, III, 375–8.
28. Ibid., 381.
29. Bülow, II, 305.
30. Palmer, 98.
31. Pearson, 195–6.
32. Bülow, II, 356–7.

33. Röhl, *KC*, 95.
34. Röhl, *NI*, 43.
35. Röhl, *KC*, 22–3.
36. Röhl, *NI*, 38.
37. Reid, 203.
38. Aston, 223.
39. Bülow, II, 499.
40. Eckardstein, 189.
41. Newton, 199.
42. Eckardstein, 192.
43. Magnus, 272.
44. Brook-Shepherd, *Uncle of Europe*, 101.
45. Lee, II, 11.
46. Pakula, 592.
47. Frederick Ponsonby, 110.
48. Reid, 196.
49. Wake, 348.
50. Eckardstein, 217.
51. Van der Kiste, *Crowns in a Changing World*, 7.
52. Bülow, II, 528.
53. Pakula, 597.
54. Daisy, Princess of Pless, 53.
55. Cecil, II, 84.
56. Newton, 207.
57. Van der Kiste, *Crowns in a Changing World*, 10.

## CHAPTER 5

1. Van der Kiste, *Crowns in a Changing World*, 12.
2. Daisy, Princess of Pless, 70.
3. Kaiser Wilhelm II to King Edward VII, 2 February 1903. MS letter from private collection.
4. Röhl, *NI*, 32.
5. Ibid., 31.
6. Palmer, 110.
7. Kürenberg, 125.
8. Brook-Shepherd, *Uncle of Europe*, 255.
9. Jonas, 35–6.
10. Ludwig, 230.
11. Brook-Shepherd, *Royal Sunset*, 103.
12. Bülow, II, 190–1.
13. *The Times*, 5.7.1906.

14. Randolph Churchill, 196.
15. Bülow, III, 303.
16. Cecil, II, 114.
17. Jonas, 43.
18. Ludwig, 330.
19. Magnus, 214.
20. Röhl, *KC*, 61.
21. Ibid., 62.
22. Heckstall-Smith, 53.
23. Bülow, III, 303.
24. Hull, 53.
25. Lee, II, 554.
26. Ibid., 557.
27. Ibid., 559.
28. Esher, II, 255.
29. Daisy, Princess of Pless, 175.
30. Clark, 116.
31. Balfour, 278.
32. Palmer, 130.
33. Ibid., 131.
34. Balfour, 276.
35. Palmer, 132.
36. Bülow, III, 312.
37. Lloyd George, I, 22.
38. Bülow, III, 313.
39. Christopher, 47.
40. Hull, 34–5.
41. Cecil, II, 52.
42. Ibid., 134.
43. Magnus, 400.
44. Hull, 149.
45. Bülow, III, 365.
46. Ibid., 368.
47. Ibid., 369.
48. William, Crown Prince, *Memoirs*, 87.
49. Jonas, 44.
50. Cecil, II, 139.
51. Röhl, *PS*, 224.
52. Lee, II, 623.
53. Cecil, II, 174.

## CHAPTER 6

1. Brook-Shepherd, *Uncle of Europe*, 345.
2. Röhl, *NI*, 107.

3. William II, *My Memoirs*, 127–8.
4. Röhl, *NI*, 42.
5. Topham, 237–9.
6. Ibid., 266.
7. Leslie, 337.
8. William II, *My Memoirs*, 124.
9. Esher, III, 4.
10. Davis 143.
11. Röhl, *PS*, 152.
12. Nicolson, 188.
13. Cecil, II, 173.
14. Röhl, *KC*, 167.
15. Ludwig, 378.
16. Röhl, *KC*, 171.
17. Nicolson, 206–7.
18. Röhl, *KC*, 165.
19. Van der Kiste, *Crowns in a Changing World*, 86.
20. Balfour, 339.
21. Frederick Ponsonby, 297–8.
22. Rose, 166.
23. Ibid., 167.
24. Topham, 275.
25. Victoria Louise, 76.
26. Duke of Windsor, 100.
27. Topham, 261–2.
28. Hull, 263.
29. Jonas, 82.
30. Kürenberg 227.
31. Palmer, 166.
32. Nicolson, 245.
33. Cecil, II, 204.
34. Chamier, 283.
35. Vorres, 131.
36. Alice, 151.
37. Bülow, II, 441.
38. Lowe, 248.

## CHAPTER 7

1. Davis, 144.
2. Müller, 23.
3. Röhl, *NI*, 23.
4. Röhl, *KC*, 207.
5. Müller, 42.
6. Hull, 266.

7. Röhl, *KC*, 207.
8. Ludwig, 409.
9. Victoria Louise, 82.
10. Palmer, 186.
11. Jonas, 97.
12. Ibid., 96.
13. Ibid., 97.
14. Cecil, II, 233.
15. Davis, 145.
16. Brook-Shepherd, *Last Habsburg*, 74.
17. Cecil, II, 245.
18. Ludwig, 413.
19. Ibid., 415.
20. Röhl, *NI*, 40.
21. Ludwig, 421.
22. Victoria Louise, 119.
23. Cecil, II, 279.
24. Ibid., 286.
25. Victoria Louise, 131.
26. Balfour, 402.
27. Huldermann, 285.
28. Victoria Louise, 132.
29. William II, *My Memoirs*, 283.
30. Hull, 290.
31. Cecil, II, 289.
32. Jonas, 119.
33. Ibid., 119.

CHAPTER 8

1. Balfour, 414.
2. Victoria Louise, 129.
3. Gore, 308.
4. Nicolson, 337.
5. Rowland, 468–9.
6. Victoria Louise, 145–6.
7. Nicolson, 337.
8. Rose, 231.
9. Röhl, *PS*, 157.
10. Ziegler, 85.
11. Wheeler-Bennett, 120–1.
12. Hermine, 256.
13. Röhl, *KC*, 14.
14. Ludwig, 419.
15. Röhl, *KC*, 194.

16. Ibid., 209.
17. Cecil, II, 310.
18. Radowitz MS.
19. Victoria Louise, 150.
20. Radowitz MS.
21. Victoria Louise, 160.
22. Victoria, Princess of Prussia, 208.
23. Jonas, 145.
24. Victoria Louise, 162.
25. Winston Churchill, 28.
26. Bentinck, 49.
27. Palmer, 220.
28. Kürenberg, 331.
29. Ibid., xi.
30. Waters, 154; Frederick Ponsonby, 113.
31. Röhl, *NI*, 29.
32. *The Times*, 22.4.1929.
33. Victoria, Princess of Prussia, 74.
34. Ibid., 182.
35. Lynx, 147.
36. Van der Kiste, *Kings of the Hellenes*, 150.
37. Bracher, 166.
38. Cecil, II, 345.
39. Victoria Louise, 127.
40. Röhl, *KC*, 15.
41. Röhl, *NI*, 32.
42. Neagle, 241.
43. Pope-Hennessy, 592.
44. Cecil, II, 345.
45. Balfour, 419.
46. Victoria Louise, 177.
47. Röhl, *KC*, 210.
48. Bracher, 525.
49. Lockhart, 38.
50. Röhl, *KC*, 211.
51. Palmer, 224–5.
52. Cecil, II, 351; The *Listener*, 5.7.1984.
53. Palmer, 226.
54. Jonas, 200–1.
55. Röhl, *KC*, 211.
56. Pakula, 602.
57. Cecil, II, 353.

# Bibliography

All titles are published in London unless otherwise stated.

## I MANUSCRIPT SOURCES

Royal Archives, Windsor

Ian Shapiro, Argyll Etkin Ltd (privately owned letters)

Dale Headington, Regal Reader (Baron de Radowitz journal extracts, 1922, privately owned)

Other correspondence in private possession

## II BOOKS

Alice, Princess, Countess of Athlone. *For my grandchildren*, Evans Bros, 1966

Anon. *The Empress Frederick: a Memoir*, James Nisbet, 1913

——. *Recollections of Three Kaisers*, Herbert Jenkins, 1929

Aronson, Theo. *The Kaisers*, Cassell, 1971

Aston, Sir George. *HRH The Duke of Connaught and Strathearn: a Life and Intimate Study*, Harrap, 1929

Balfour, Michael. *The Kaiser and his Times: with an Afterword*, Penguin, 1975

Barkeley, Richard. *The Empress Frederick, Daughter of Queen Victoria*, Macmillan, 1956

Bennett, Daphne. *Vicky, Princess Royal of England and German Empress*, Collins Harvill, 1971

Benson, E.F. *The Kaiser and English Relations*, Longmans, Green, 1936

Bentinck, Lady Norah. *The ex-Kaiser in Exile*, Hodder & Stoughton, 1921

Bigelow, Poultney. *Prussian Memories, 1864–1914*, Putnam, 1915

Bing, E.J. (ed.). *The Letters of Nicholas II to the Empress Marie Feodorovna*, Ivor Nicholson & Watson, 1937

Bracher, Karl Dietrich. *The German Dictatorship: the Origins, Structure, and Consequences of National Socialism*, Weidenfeld & Nicolson, 1971

Brook-Shepherd, Gordon. *The Last Habsburg* (Karl, Emperor of Austria-Hungary), Weidenfeld & Nicolson, 1968

——. *Royal Sunset: the Dynasties of Europe and the Great War*, Weidenfeld & Nicolson, 1987

——. *Uncle of Europe: the Social and Diplomatic Life of Edward VII*, Collins, 1975

Buchanan, Meriel. *Queen Victoria's Relations*, Cassell, 1954

Bülow, Prince Bernhard von. *Memoirs*, 4 vols, Putnam, 1931

Cassels, Lavender. *Clash of Generations: a Habsburg Family Drama in the Nineteenth Century*, John Murray, 1973

Cecil, Lamar. *Wilhelm II, Vol. I, Prince and Emperor, 1859–1900*, University of North Carolina, 1989

——. *Wilhelm II, Vol. II, Emperor and Exile, 1900–1941*, University of North Carolina, 1996

Chamier, J. Daniel. *Fabulous Monster* (Wilhelm II), Edward Arnold, 1934

Christopher of Greece, Prince. *Memoirs*, Right Book Club, 1938

Churchill, Randolph S. *Winston S. Churchill, Vol. II, Young Statesman, 1901–1914*, Heinemann, 1967

Churchill, Winston. *Great Contemporaries*, Odhams, 1947

Clark, Alan (ed.). *A Good Innings: the Private Papers of Viscount Lee of Fareham*, John Murray, 1974

Corti, Egon Caesar Conte. *Alexander von Battenberg*, Cassell, 1954

——. *The English Empress: a study in the relations between Queen Victoria and her Eldest Daughter, Empress Frederick of Germany*, Cassell, 1957

Cowles, Virginia. *The Kaiser*, Collins, 1963

Daisy, Princess of Pless. *The Private Diaries of Daisy, Princess of Pless, 1873–1914*, ed. Desmond Chapman-Huston, John Murray, 1950

Davis, Arthur N. *The Kaiser I Knew: My Fourteen Years with the Kaiser*, Hodder & Stoughton, 1918

Duff, David. *Hessian Tapestry*, Frederick Muller, 1967

Eckardstein, Baron von. *Ten Years at the Court of St James's, 1895–1905*, Thornton Butterworth, 1921

Esher, Viscount Reginald. *Journals and Letters*, ed. Oliver, Viscount Esher, 4 vols, Ivor Nicholson & Watson, 1934–8

Fischer, Henry W. *The Private Lives of William II & his Consort: a Secret History of the Court of Berlin*, Heinemann, 1904

Frederick Leopold of Prussia, Princess. *Behind the Scenes at the Prussian Court*, John Murray, 1939

Frith, William Powell. *My Autobiography and Reminiscences*, 2 vols, Bentley, 1887

Gore, John. *King George V: a Personal Memoir*, John Murray, 1941

Grant, N.F. (ed.). *The Kaiser's Letters to the Tsar*, Hodder & Stoughton, 1920

Heckstall-Smith, Anthony. *Sacred Cowes*, Anthony Blond, 1965

Hermine, Empress. *Days in Doorn*, Hutchinson, n.d., *c.* 1927

Holstein, Friedrich von. *The Holstein Papers: the Memoirs, Diaries and Correspondence of Friedrich von Holstein*, ed. Norman Rich and M.H. Fisher, 4 vols, Cambridge University Press, 1955–63

Hough, Richard. *Louis and Victoria: the First Mountbattens*, Hutchinson, 1974

Huldermann, Bernhard. *Albert Ballin*, Cassell, 1922

Hull, Isabel V. *The Entourage of Kaiser Wilhelm II 1888–1918*, Cambridge University Press, 1982

Jonas, Klaus W. *The Life of Crown Prince William*, Routledge & Kegan Paul, 1961

Kohut, Thomas. *Wilhelm II and the Germans*, Oxford University Press, 1991

Kollander, Patricia. *Frederick III: Germany's Liberal Emperor*, Westport, Connecticut, Greenwood, 1995

Kürenberg, Joachim von. *The Kaiser: a Life of Wilhelm II, Last Emperor of Germany*, Cassell, 1954

Lee, Sir Sidney. *King Edward VII*, 2 vols, Macmillan, 1925–7

Leslie, Anita. *Edwardians in Love*, Hutchinson, 1972

Lloyd George, David. *War Memoirs*, 6 vols, Ivor Nicholson & Watson, 1933–6

Lockhart, R.H. Bruce. *Comes the Reckoning*, Putnam, 1947

Lowe, Charles. *The Tale of a 'Times' Correspondent (Berlin 1878–1891)*, Hutchinson, 1927

Ludwig, Emil. *Kaiser Wilhelm II*, Putnam, 1926

Lynx, J.J. *The Great Hohenzollern Scandal: a Biography of Alexander Zubkov*, Oldbourne, 1965

Mackenzie, Sir Morell. *The Fatal Illness of Frederick the Noble*, Sampson Low, 1888

Magnus, Philip. *King Edward the Seventh*, John Murray, 1964

Marie, Queen of Roumania. *The Story of My Life*, 3 vols, Cassell, 1934–5

Martin, Theodore. *The Life of His Royal Highness the Prince Consort*, 5 vols, Smith, Elder, 1874–80

Massie, Robert K. *Dreadnought: Britain, Germany, and the Coming of the Great War*, Jonathan Cape, 1992

Morier, Sir Robert. *Memoirs and Letters*, 2 vols, Edward Arnold, 1911

Müller, Georg Alexander von. *The Kaiser and his Court: the Diaries, Note Books and Letters of Admiral Georg Alexander von Müller, Chief of the Naval Cabinet 1914–18*, ed. Walter Görlitz, Macdonald, 1961

Neagle, Dame Anna (Mrs Herbert Wilcox). *There's Always Tomorrow*, W.H. Allen, 1974

Newton, Lord. *Lord Lansdowne: a Biography*, Macmillan, 1929

Nichols, J. Alden. *Germany after Bismarck: the Caprivi Era 1890–1894*, Harvard University Press, 1958

Nicolson, Harold. *King George V, his Life and Reign*, Constable, 1952

Nowak, Karl Friedrich. *Kaiser & Chancellor: the Opening Years of the Reign of the Emperor William II*, Putnam, 1930

Pakula, Hannah. *An Uncommon Woman: the Empress Frederick*, Weidenfeld & Nicolson, 1996

Palmer, Alan. *The Kaiser: Warlord of the Second Reich*, Weidenfeld & Nicolson, 1978

——. *Twilight of the Habsburgs: the Life and Times of Emperor Francis Joseph*, Weidenfeld & Nicolson, 1994

Pearson, Hesketh. *Gilbert and Sullivan*, Hamish Hamilton, 1935

Ponsonby, Arthur. *Sir Henry Ponsonby, Queen Victoria's Private Secretary; his Life from his letters*, Macmillan, 1942

Ponsonby, Sir Frederick. *Recollections of Three Reigns*, Eyre & Spottiswoode, 1951

Poschinger, Margaretha von. *Life of the Emperor Frederick*, ed. Sidney Whitman, Harper, 1901

Reid, Michaela. *Ask Sir James: Sir James Reid, Personal Physician to Queen Victoria and Physician-in-ordinary to Three Monarchs*, Hodder & Stoughton, 1987

Rich, Norman. *Friedrich von Holstein: Politics and Diplomacy in the Era of Bismarck and Wilhelm II*, 2 vols, Cambridge University Press, 1965

Roberts, Dorothea. *Two Royal Lives: Gleanings from Berlin and from the Lives of Their Imperial Highnesses the Crown Prince and Princess of Germany*, T. Fisher Unwin, 1887

Rodd, James Rennell. *Frederick, Crown Prince and Emperor: a Biographical Sketch Dedicated to his Memory*, David Stott, 1888

——. *Social and Diplomatic Memories*, 3 vols, Edward Arnold, 1922–5

Röhl, John C.G. *Germany without Bismarck: The Crisis of Government in the Second Reich, 1890–1900*, Batsford, 1967

——. *The Kaiser and his Court: Wilhelm II and the Government of Germany*, Cambridge University Press, 1994

# Bibliography

Röhl, John C.G and Sombart, Nicolaus (eds). *Kaiser Wilhelm II: New Interpretations*, Cambridge University Press, 1982

Röhl, John C.G., Warren, Martin and Hunt, David. *Purple Secret: Genes, 'Madness' and the Royal Houses of Europe*, Bantam, 1998

Rose, Kenneth. *King George V*, Weidenfeld & Nicolson, 1983

Rowland, Peter. *Lloyd George*, Barrie & Jenkins, 1975

St Aubyn, Giles. *Edward VII, Prince and King*, Collins, 1979

Schwering, Count Axel von. *The Berlin Court under William II*, Cassell, 1915

Sinclair, Andrew. *The Other Victoria: the Princess Royal and the Great Game of Europe*, Weidenfeld & Nicolson, 1981

Stevenson, R. Scott. *Morell Mackenzie*, Heinemann, 1946

Taylor, A.J.P. *Bismarck: the Man and the Statesman*, Hamish Hamilton, 1955

Taylor, Edmond. *The Fossil Monarchies*, Penguin, 1967

Taylor, Lucy. *'Fritz' of Prussia: Germany's Second Emperor*, Nelson, 1891

Topham, Anne. *A Distant Thunder: Intimate Recollections of the Kaiser's Court*, New York, New Chapter Press, 1992

Tschudi, Clara. *Augusta, Empress of Germany*, Swan Sonnenschein, 1900

Van der Kiste, John. *Crowns in a Changing World: the British and European Monarchies*, Stroud, Sutton, 1993

——. *Frederick III: German Emperor 1888*, Gloucester, Sutton, 1981

——. *Kings of the Hellenes: the Kings of Modern Greece 1863–1974*, Stroud, Sutton, 1994

Victoria, Queen. *Dearest Child: Letters between Queen Victoria and the Princess Royal, 1858–1861*, ed. Roger Fulford, Evans Bros, 1964

——. *Dearest Mama: Letters between Queen Victoria and the Crown Princess of Prussia, 1862–1864*, ed. Roger Fulford, Evans Bros, 1968

——. *Your Dear Letter: Private Correspondence between Queen Victoria and the Crown Princess of Prussia, 1865–1871*, ed. Roger Fulford, Evans Bros, 1971

——. *Darling Child: Private Correspondence of Queen Victoria and the Crown Princess of Prussia, 1871–1878*, ed. Roger Fulford, Evans Bros, 1976

——. *Beloved Mama: Private Correspondence of Queen Victoria and the German Crown Princess, 1878–1885*, ed. Roger Fulford, Evans Bros, 1981

——. *Beloved and Darling Child: Last Letters between Queen Victoria and her Eldest Daughter, 1886–1901*, ed. Agatha Ramm, Stroud, Sutton, 1990

——. *The Letters of Queen Victoria: a Selection from Her Majesty's Correspondence between the Years 1837 and 1861*, ed. A.C. Benson and Viscount Esher, 3 vols, John Murray, 1907

——. *The Letters of Queen Victoria, Second Series: a Selection from Her Majesty's Correspondence and Journal between the Years 1862 and 1885*, ed. George Earle Buckle, 3 vols, John Murray, 1926–8

——. *The Letters of Queen Victoria, Third Series: a Selection from Her Majesty's Correspondence and Journal between the Years 1886 and 1901*, ed. George Earle Buckle, 3 vols, John Murray, 1930–2

Victoria, Consort of Frederick III, German Emperor. *The Empress Frederick Writes to Sophie, Her Daughter, Crown Princess and Later Queen of the Hellenes: Letters 1889–1901*, ed. Arthur Gould Lee, Faber, 1955

——. *Letters of the Empress Frederick*, ed. Sir Frederick Ponsonby, Macmillan, 1928

Victoria, Princess of Prussia. *My Memoirs*, Eveleigh, Nash, 1929

# Bibliography

Victoria Louise, Duchess of Brunswick. *The Kaiser's Daughter: Memoirs of H.R.H. Viktoria Luise, Duchess of Brunswick and Lüneburg*, ed. Robert Vacha, W.H. Allen, 1977

Vorres, Ian. *The Last Grand-Duchess: Her Imperial Highness Grand-Duchess Olga Alexandrovna*, Hutchinson, 1964

Wake, Jehanne. *Princess Louise, Queen Victoria's Unconventional Daughter*, Collins, 1988

Waters, W. H-H. *Potsdam and Doorn*, John Murray, 1925

Wheeler-Bennett, John W. *King George VI, his Life and Reign*, Macmillan, 1958

Whittle, Tyler. *The Last Kaiser: a Biography of William II, German Emperor and King of Prussia*, Heinemann, 1977

William II, ex-Emperor. *My Ancestors*, Heinemann, 1929

——. *My Early Life*, Methuen, 1926

——. *My Memoirs, 1878–1918*, Cassell, 1922

William, Crown Prince. *The Memoirs of the Crown Prince of Germany*, Thornton Butterworth, 1922

Windsor, Duke of, formerly King Edward VIII. *A King's Story: Memoirs of HRH the Duke of Windsor*, Cassell, 1951

Woodham-Smith, Cecil. *Queen Victoria, her Life and Times, Vol. 1, 1819–1861*, Hamish Hamilton, 1972

Zedlitz-Trutschler, Count Robert. *Twelve Years at the German Imperial Court*, Nisbet, 1924

Ziegler, Philip. *King Edward VIII: the Official Biography*, Collins, 1990

## III Journal Articles

Andrew, Christopher. 'Secrets of the Kaiser', The *Listener*, 7 June 1984, pp. 10–1

Anon. 'The Kaiser, as he is' (translation from the *Strand Magazine*), *Zürcher Wochen-Cronik* (Zurich Weekly Chronicle), 7 September 1912

Coupe, W.A. 'Kaiser Wilhelm II and the Cartoonists', *History Today*, November 1980, pp. 16–22

Cruyningen, Arnout J.P.H. van. 'Wilhelm II at Doorn', *Royalty Digest*, January 1994, pp. 204–6

Dorpalen, Andreas. 'Empress Augusta Victoria and the Fall of the German Monarchy', *American Historical Review*, LVIII, 2 (1952), pp. 17–38

Horbury, David. 'A Tragic Princess: Princess Victoria of Prussia', *Royalty Digest*, March 1997, pp. 258–62; April 1997, pp. 295–9; May 1997, pp. 338–42

Lalor, William Mead. 'Charlotte of Prussia – the Elegant Cousin Charly', *Royalty Digest*, March 1996, pp. 271–5

——. 'A Forgotten Empress' (Hermine, second wife of William), *Royalty Digest*, March 1995, pp. 270–3

Van der Kiste, John. 'Princess Margaret of Prussia: the Granddaughter who Saved Queen Victoria's Letters', *Royalty Digest*, June 1992, pp. 366–8

## IV Journals – General References

| | |
|---|---|
| *Daily Telegraph* | The *Listener* |
| The *Graphic* | *The Times* |
| The *Illustrated London News* | *This England* |
| The *Independent* | *Western Morning News* |

# *Index*

Abbreviations: F – Friedrich III; W – Wilhelm II

# Index

# Index